Building and Managing the Meta Data Repository: A Full Lifecycle Guide

Building and Managing the Meta Data Repository

A Full Lifecycle Guide

David Marco

Wiley Computer Publishing

John Wiley & Sons, Inc.

NEW YORK · CHICHESTER · WEINHEIM · BRISBANE · SINGAPORE · TORONTO

Publisher: Robert Ipsen

Editor: Robert M. Elliott

Managing Editor: John Atkins

Associate New Media Editor: Brian Snapp

Text Design & Composition: North Market Street Graphics

Designations used by companies to distinguish their products are often claimed as trademarks. In all instances where John Wiley & Sons, Inc., is aware of a claim, the product names appear in initial capital or ALL CAPITAL LETTERS. Readers, however, should contact the appropriate companies for more complete information regarding trademarks and registration.

This book is printed on acid-free paper.

This publication is designed to provide accurate and authoritative information in regard to the subject matter covered. It is sold with the understanding that the publisher is not engaged in professional services. If professional advice or other expert assistance is required, the services of a competent professional person should be sought.

Library of Congress Cataloging-in-Publication Data is available from publisher.

ISBN 0-471-35523-2

Printed in the United States of America.

10 9 8 7 6 5 4

Advance praise for David Marco's
Building and Managing the Meta Data Repository: A Full Lifecycle Guide

"If you believe that meta data is the glue that holds a data warehouse together, then this book is the key ingredient that data warehousing managers need to make their projects stick. Like good meta data, the information in this book is accurate, comprehensive, and understandable. It should be required reading for data warehousing developers."

Wayne Eckerson
Director of Education and Research
The Data Warehousing Institute

"Meta data is one of the critical success factors for a successful data warehouse. Its implementation has eluded most organizations because they have no clear direction of how to make it happen. David Marco's book sets that direction and is a blueprint for implementation."

Sid Adelman
President
Sid Adelman & Associates

"Meta data management is key to the future success of eBusiness. Marco's book is packed with practical experience. Everyone considering or implementing a meta data strategy for data warehousing, business intelligence, or eBusiness should have this book on their desk."

G. Allen Houpt
Business Manager, Knowledge Management
Computer Associates International, Inc.

"I thank God for blessing me in every way a person can be."

David Marco
February 8, 2000

Contents

Foreword

In the beginning were punch cards and paper tape. Then came disks and random access. Databases soon appeared, followed by online applications. Next we had spider web environments, which led to data warehouses. From warehouses came data marts, operational data stores, and exploration warehouses.

Each form of information processing led to another more sophisticated form. And eventually these forms of processing grew into a framework called the corporate information factory.

But cohesion across the different forms of processing was not so easily achieved. Each form of processing had its own objectives and techniques, most of which were peculiar to itself. Trying to create and maintain a sense of unity across the different forms of information processing was very difficult to do.

The only hope for enterprise-wide cohesion lies in meta data. But meta data is an illusive topic because it comes in so many forms. Each form of processing in the enterprise—in one way or another—has its own form of meta data. But meta data for magnetic tapes is quite different than meta data for near line storage, which in turn is different from meta data for data marts, and so forth. In addition, meta data that needs to connect a data warehouse with an ODS is different from meta data that is found in an ETL.

What we need is a little order and organization around here. If we are ever to achieve integration and harmony across the enterprise, the starting point surely is meta data.

But trying to come to grips with meta data is like trying to wrestle an octopus. Underwater. Holding your breath. There simply are so many facets that achieving progress becomes a very difficult thing to do. Drowning is a distinct possibility.

David Marco's book represents a milestone effort in attempting to confront the beast. From the conceptual to the mundane, David comes to terms with the many facets of meta data. The willingness to face first one aspect and then another sets David apart from unidimensional efforts to date that have addressed one or maybe two aspects of meta data, usually from the perspective of a given tool.

For a modern look at meta data, read what David Marco has to say.

—W.H. Inmon
Chief Technology Officer,
Pine Cone Systems

Acknowledgments

Several people deserve my gratitude for their hard work in making this book a reality. In particular, I would like to thank the following individuals for their help and support throughout this endeavor:

- Sid Adelman, Adelman & Associates
- Mark Cooper, Federal Express
- Jon Geiger, Intelligent Solutions
- Kiumarse Zamanian, Informatica

I was also fortunate to have an outstanding pair of "Mikes" working with me on this effort:

- Mike Jennings, Hewitt Associates
- Mike Needham, Enterprise Warehousing Solutions, Inc.

Mike Jennings is one of the brightest people in this industry, and he did an outstanding job working with me on the data quality and data delivery chapters. Mike is a fantastic writer, a great technologist, and an even better person. Second is Mike Needham, a truly exceptional technical architect and data modeler. His work on the chapters on meta data modeling and meta data tool evaluation is without peer.

I would also be remiss if I did not thank several people who have made a tremendous difference in my professional career. From the first person who thought that one of my articles was worth publishing, to the first person who thought I was qualified to go to a conference and speak to their membership about data warehousing, I thank them all for their support:

- Bill Inmon, Pine Cone Systems
- Frank McGuff, Informix
- Ron Powell, DM Review
- Jean Schauer, DM Review

Last I'd like to thank the entire team at John Wiley & Sons, and specifically I'd like to express my deepest gratitude to my editor, Bob Elliott, who from day one has always believed in this project and my ability to make it happen. He has contributed to making this book the very best that it can be. Bob is simply the best editor there is.

Introduction

When we first started building computer systems in the 1950s and 1960s, we realized that a "bunch of stuff" (knowledge) was needed to build, use, and maintain these systems. But we didn't know how to integrate this computer system's knowledge with "the other stuff" we needed to know about the markets and industries that we were competing in. Fortunately, over time we learned that what our information systems needed was data about the business data we were using. In other words, we needed *meta data*.

When we talk about meta data, we are really talking about *knowledge*. Knowledge of our systems, business, competition, customers, products, and markets. In our era such knowledge can provide the competitive edge that determines business success or failure. In this era, more than ever before, companies must be smarter than their competitors in order to survive and, hopefully, thrive. Meta data can provide a very real competitive edge, but only if we thoroughly understand it and know how to use it effectively.

How This Book Is Organized

When I purchase a book on information technology (or any other subject, for that matter) I look for several things, but mostly, I look for a book that I can personally connect with . . . one that both entertains and teaches. I also look for a book that gives me solid, practical advice along with its theoretical foundation. I particularly look for information that can be gained only through experience—if a book can teach me even one useful lesson or prevent a possible mistake on one of my projects, then it is worth its weight in gold. In writing this book, I've tried to keep my own preferences in mind, offering readers a solid foundation in meta data (without assuming pre-existing knowledge of the topic) and drawing on my years as a consultant to provide practical and useful information.

In addition to providing a foundation for understanding meta data, Part One of this book discusses the specific value that meta data can bring to an organization; that is, how meta data can help a company to increase revenue or decrease expenses. This information should be particularly useful for anyone trying to sell the concept of meta data to executive-level management. Part One also examines some of the major trends that are affecting the meta data industry, such as the ongoing standards battle and the emergence of Extensible Markup Language (XML). Meta data is inarguably one of the fastest-changing areas of information technology, and it is crucial to understand (as much as possible) the changes that are coming down the road so that we can build repositories that are flexible enough to adapt to these changes.

In Part Two, I focus on how to implement a meta data repository, providing the details on planning an appropriate architecture, staffing a repository team, building a meta data model, and choosing the necessary meta data tools. This section also includes detailed information on using meta data to ensure the quality of the data in your data warehouse and data marts and for generating useful information from the repository and decision support system (DSS).

We all know that truth can be stranger than fiction and that real life is often funnier than any fictional comedy. Some of the "war stories" that I've included in Parts One and Two of the book may convince you that decision support and meta data repository projects are often stranger and funnier than fiction too. Many of these stories provide some entertaining moments, but all of them are intended to teach what to do and at other times what not to do.

Who Should Read This Book

Meta data repositories can provide tremendous value to organizations if they are used appropriately and if everyone understands what they can, and can't, do. "Everyone," of course, is a broad term, but specifically, the following individuals are likely to benefit from reading all or at least parts of this book:

- **Business Users.**   A meta data repository can significantly increase the value of information residing in decision support and operational systems because it provides a semantic link between the information technology (IT) systems and business users. When business users understand how to use meta data effectively, they have more confidence in the accuracy and completeness of the decision support information and are more likely to rely on it for strategic business decisions.

- **IT Managers.**   IT managers can use a meta data repository to deliver significantly more value to the business units that they support and to ensure the quality of the information in the data warehouse, thereby helping business users and executive management make solid decisions based on accurate, timely information. In addition, a repository can make an IT development staff more productive and reduce development costs for the department.

- **Developers.**   Developers need to learn the key tasks for implementing a meta data repository project. These tasks include physical meta data modeling, project plan development, program design, meta data tool evaluation metrics, meta data access techniques, and advanced technical architecture design.

- **Project Sponsors.**   These individuals need to understand how meta data can benefit an organization so they can sell the concept to executive management. Underestimating the scope of a repository project is one of the primary reasons for the failure of such projects, and sponsors need a clear understanding of meta data and its potential return on investment (ROI) to ensure ongoing levels of funding and personnel as well as the initial project commitment. Without this understanding, sponsors cannot be effective advocates for meta data.

About the Web Site

This book will be accompanied by the Web site **www.wiley.com/compbooks/ marco.** This free Web site will have links from the various meta data integration and access tools vendors, plus other meta data related features. In addition, all readers of this book are encouraged to sign up for a free subscription to Real-World Decision Support (RWDS) at www.EWSolutions .com/newsletter.asp. RWDS is an electronic newsletter dedicated to providing informative, vendor-neutral, real-world solutions to the challenges of implementing decision support systems and meta data repositories.

Laying the Foundation

## CHAPTER 1

Introducing Meta Data and Its Return on Investment

Before deciding to build a meta data repository, you need to fully understand what meta data is and isn't, and what value a meta data repository can bring to your organization. In this chapter, we look briefly at the history of meta data and then move quickly to examine why it is needed and how it can provide competitive advantages to businesses that use it wisely.

In the Beginning

Information technology (IT) is still in its infancy and, like an infant, growing at an incredibly rapid pace. Worldwide spending for IT was forecasted to be $2.2 trillion in 1999, and is expected to climb to $3.3 trillion by 2002. The growth is even more apparent if we step back and look at the past. The first general purpose electronic computers were created in the late 1940s, and only a little more than 20 years ago we were still programming with punch cards. (Many of us still have nightmares about dropping our punch cards and having to put them back in order!)

Today, our industry is in the crawling stage of development. Computers have changed virtually every aspect of our lives, but we're still just learning to walk.

Information Technology Begins to Walk

Our existing IT systems are sophisticated enough to run our day-to-day business transactions for our companies. If our businesses were static entities, this would be enough. But we all know that business is anything but static. Businesses change continually in response to social, technical, political, and industrial forces. Because our companies are controlled by our IT systems, these systems must change accordingly, or our companies will not be able to respond to the many and varied market forces.

Unfortunately, our computer systems are anything but changeable. In fact, we have built systems that are nothing more than islands of data and are about as easy to change as it is to move an island. This is true of even our most sophisticated systems. It's easy to understand how this happened. Think back to the late 1970s and early 1980s. Data storage was very expensive, and IT developers were relatively cheap, so we, the "brilliant" programmers, decided to save storage space wherever we could, even if we knew that doing so made the IT system more cumbersome to maintain or could cause problems in the future. The most obvious example of attempting to conserve storage space was using two digits for the year/date field. When we did this we never expected to be using these same IT systems in the new millennium. We firmly believed that "in 20 years we'll have replaced this old system with a shiny new one." Boy, were we wrong! The task of building new and better systems was more difficult than we ever anticipated.

The problem I just mentioned is obviously the infamous Year 2000 (Y2K) issue that we have heard and read so much about. Y2K clearly illustrated that our systems do not easily adapt to change. It also helped us to realize that we don't understand the data in our systems or our business processes. But we do know that in order for our systems to support our business needs, we must have a better understanding of our data, and better control of our systems so as to be able to adapt them for our ever-changing business requirements. Fortunately, as our industry grows older, it also grows wiser. We now see that meta data offers an answer to these needs, and it is now garnering the industry attention that it so richly deserves.

Defining Meta Data

The most simplistic definition of meta data is *data about data*. I have always had problems with this definition because it does not truly encapsulate the full scope of meta data. In Chapter 2, Meta Data Fundamentals, I will provide a detailed definition of meta data, but for now let's start with this short definition:

Meta data is all physical data and knowledge-containing information about the business and technical processes, and data, used by a corporation.

Now let's expand this definition a little further.

Meta data is all physical data (contained in software and other media) and knowledge (contained in employees and various media) from inside and outside an organization, including information about the physical data, technical and business processes, rules and constraints of the data, and structures of the data used by a corporation.

When we talk about meta data, we are really talking about *knowledge*. We are talking about knowledge of our systems, of our business, and of our marketplace. On the other hand, when we talk about a meta data repository, we are talking about the physical database tables used to store the meta data that will be delivered to its business and technical users (see Figure 1.1). While the physical implementation of a meta data initiative requires many activities, the meta data repository is the backbone of the physical implementation.

a good anology is wikipedia

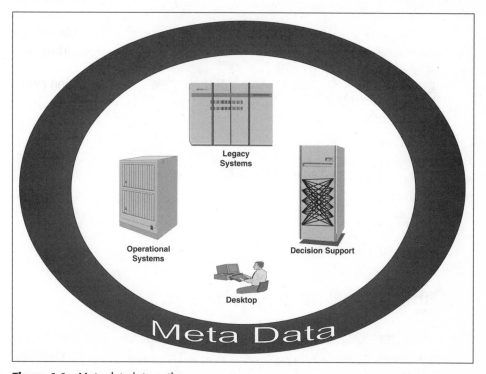

Figure 1.1   Meta data interaction.

Meta Data—The Beginnings

Many people believe that meta data and meta data repositories are new concepts, but in fact their origins date back to the early 1970s. The first commercial meta data repositories that appeared then were called *data dictionaries*. These data dictionaries were much more *data* focused than *knowledge* focused. They provided a centralized repository of information about data, such as definitions, relationships, origin, domain, usage, and format. Their purpose was to assist database administrators (DBAs) in planning, controlling, and evaluating the collection, storage, and use of data. For example, early data dictionaries were used mainly for defining requirements, corporate data modeling, data definition generation, and database support.

One of the challenges we face today is differentiating meta data repositories from data dictionaries. While meta data repositories perform all of the functions of a data dictionary, their scope is far greater (see Figure 1.2).

Commercial Evolution of Meta Data

Computer aided software engineering (CASE) tools, introduced in the 1970s, were among the first commercial tools to offer meta data services.

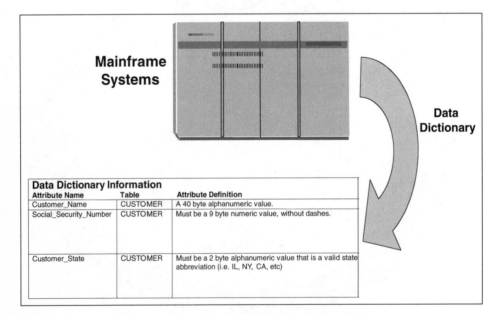

Figure 1.2 1970s: Repositories masquerading as data dictionaries.

CASE tools greatly aid the process of designing databases and software applications; they also store data about the data they manage. It didn't take long before users started asking their CASE tool vendors to build interfaces to link the meta data from various CASE tools together. These vendors were reluctant to build such interfaces because they believed that their own tool's repository could provide all of the necessary functionality and, understandably, they didn't want companies to be able to easily migrate from their tool to a competitor's tool. Nevertheless, some interfaces were built, either using vendor tools or dedicated interface tools (see Figure 1.3).

In 1987, the need for CASE tool integration triggered the Electronic Industries Alliance (EIA) to begin working on a CASE data interchange format (CDIF), which attempted to tackle the problem by defining meta models for specific CASE tool subject areas by means of an object-oriented entity relationship modeling technique. In many ways, the CDIF standards came too late for the CASE tool industry.

During the 1980s, several companies, including IBM, announced mainframe-based meta data repository tools. These efforts were the first meta

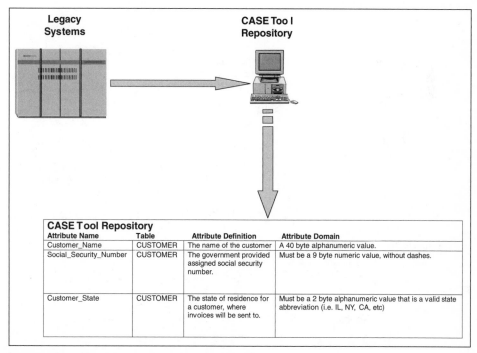

Figure 1.3   1980s: CASE tool–based repositories.

data initiatives, but their scope was limited to technical meta data and almost completely ignored business meta data. (See Chapter 2, Meta Data Fundamentals, for a detailed discussion of business and technical meta data.) Most of these early meta data repositories were just glamorized data dictionaries, intended, like the earlier data dictionaries, for use by DBAs and data modelers. In addition, the companies that created these repositories did little to educate their users about the benefits of these tools. As a result, few companies saw much value in these early repository applications.

It wasn't until the 1990s that business managers finally began to recognize the value of meta data repositories (Figure 1.4).

The meta data repositories of the 1990s operated in a client-server environment rather than on on the traditional mainframe platform that had previously been the norm. The introduction of decision support tools requiring access to meta data reawakened the slumbering repository market. Vendors such as Rochade, RELTECH Group, and BrownStone Solutions were quick to jump into the fray with new and exciting repository products. Many older, established computing companies recognized the market potential and attempted, sometimes successfully, to buy their way

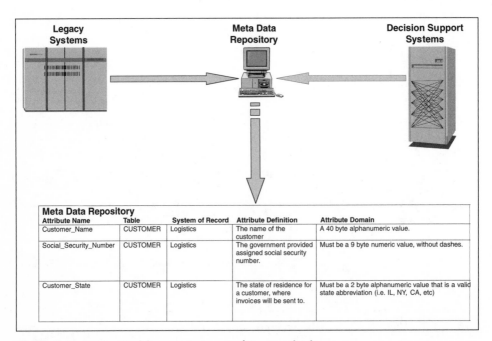

Figure 1.4   1990s: Decision support meta data repositories.

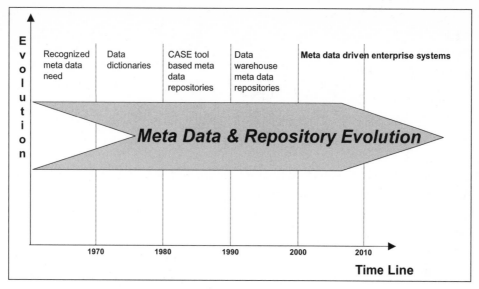

Figure 1.5   Evolution of meta data and meta data repositories.

in by acquiring these pioneer repository vendors. For example, Platinum Technologies purchased RELTECH, BrownStone, and LogicWorks, and was then swallowed by Computer Associates in 1999. As Figure 1.5 indicates, meta data repository technology has come a long way in the past 40 years.

ALIASES

Over the years meta data repositories have had many aliases. The terms *information library, data dictionary,* and *information directory* have all been used to refer to the same thing—a *meta data repository.* Similarly, the teams that build and administer meta data repositories are known by many names too, including:

- Central architecture team
- Data administration team
- Data architecture team
- Data management team
- Data resource management team
- Information architecture team

For our purposes we'll simply call ourselves the "Meta Data Repository team."

Factors Shaping Today's Meta Data Market

Three major factors are shaping the current state of the meta data market:

- Myths and misunderstandings
- Shortage of professionals with real-world experience
- Complex integration architectures

Myths and Misunderstandings

In the meta data industry, a great deal of misleading marketing comes from consultants and software vendors alike. I remember hearing a consulting vendor give a presentation to a large consumer electronics company, in which he proposed building a meta data repository using only three data entry people to type static hyper text markup language (HTML) into a Web page. This type of solution is no solution at all. It's purely a manual effort that is likely to provide limited, short-term value, and virtually no long-term value. (Fortunately I knew the company managers very well and was able to dissuade them from adopting this solution.) It pays to be wary of vendors who are promising a quick fix!

Many vendors claim that their product or suite of products is a meta data solution (and in their limited definition of meta data, this may be true). These types of solutions generally do a credible job of capturing the meta data used in the vendor's products, but not meta data from sources outside these product suites.

Shortage of Professionals with Real-World Experience

One of the biggest challenges facing chief information officers (CIOs) and IT directors today is attracting and retaining qualified IT personnel. The need for qualified IT professionals is growing at a tremendous rate, with worldwide IT spending expected to reach $3.3 trillion by 2002. Many companies are justifiably concerned about locating talented IT people as we experience our most severe workforce shortage ever.

A study by International Technology of America discovered that we currently have a negative 10 percent unemployment rate in IT—meaning that as an industry, we're unable to fill 10 percent (about 346,000 specific jobs) of the available positions with qualified people.

Meta data repository teams are particularly hard-hit by the personnel shortage. The demand for experienced project managers and repository architects is very high, and the number of qualified people is all too low. This situation presents a difficult challenge for any organization attempting to build a meta data repository or extend its existing data warehouse with such a repository.

Complex Integration Architectures

Today's meta data integration architecture does not involve seamlessly integrated products. Instead, it is composed of a series of proprietary vendor products that use the IT equivalent of chewing gum, string, and paper clips to link to one another. Two major initiatives on the horizon do, however, hold hope for resolving this integration issue in the future. One effort is headed by the Meta Data Coalition (MDC) and the other by the Object Management Group (OMG). Both are attempting to define an industry standard version of the meta models. A broadly supported set of meta models would enable data warehousing products from different vendors to share data and information. If successful, these standard models would provide the data warehousing market with an open, common infrastructure across all data warehouse tool vendors. In Chapter 4, Understanding and Evaluating Meta Data Tools, we examine both of these efforts in detail.

Until a standard is established, however, and software vendors adopt and implement it, a complex integration strategy is required to bring the various sources of meta data together. The issue of meta data integration is one of the primary factors that is preventing many organizations from achieving successful data warehouse and data mart implementations.

Why Meta Data Is Needed

Several factors have triggered the need for meta data in businesses today. These include the following:

- Current systems are inflexible and nonintegrated.
- Existing data warehouses and data marts need to grow.
- Business users' needs are not being fulfilled.
- Companies need to reduce the impact of employee turnover.
- Businesses need to increase user confidence in data.

Inflexible and Nonintegrated Systems

Global competition, changing distribution channels, and ever-growing consumer demands are forcing companies to reevaluate and change the methods they use to compete. As a result, businesses are demanding more functionality and shorter development cycles from their IT departments to attain and maintain a competitive advantage in the marketplace. These demands have forced chief information officers and IT directors to take a much closer look at their organizations' information systems.

In the vast majority of cases, this investigation reveals that the great majority of systems were built as "stovepipe" applications. Stovepipe applications form their own system islands and do not communicate easily with each other. Often, these islands have their own hardware platforms, databases, and development languages. As a result, when a systems change is needed in a particular application, it is exceedingly difficult to anticipate and manage the downstream effects of this change on other systems. I recall a situation several years ago in which a company had made a minor change to a field length in its logistics system. Unfortunately, the developers were not aware that the table they had modified was being used by the inventory management system to calculate the company's ability to fulfill future customer orders. This minor table modification triggered errors in the interfaces between the logistics system and the inventory management system, causing the inventory management system to lose all data on future overseas shipments. Because this error occurred in production, the company was forced to inform its customers that it could not fulfill their orders as scheduled. Needless to say, this situation is not good for business!

We are all aware of the Year 2000 (Y2K) problem. When we stop to think about it, Y2K is merely a date field that was designed without proper regard for future requirements. The solution to the problem is merely a change in a field's length to hold a four-digit year (e.g., 2000). When we consider the problem in these terms, it doesn't appear to be highly significant. So, how significant *is* this problem? Federal Reserve Chairman Alan Greenspan estimated that businesses spent several hundred billion dollars trying to fix the computer glitch. David Wyss, chief economist of consultants Standard & Poor's DRI, was quoted by Rich Miller in *USA Today* as saying the computer bug could reduce economic growth by $66 billion in a two-year span (i.e., 1999 and 2000). So much for an insignificant problem. Personally, I was happy that the Y2K issue occurred, because it revealed the inflexibility of our existing systems' architectures.

Similarly, the current mergers and acquisitions craze also helps to illuminate the weaknesses in our systems architectures. Corporations look for merger and acquisition opportunities to enhance shareholder value. The concept is that a sound merger or acquisition offers a quick and easy method of enhancing a company's core strengths or of correcting weaknesses. Mergers or acquisitions enable companies to avoid substantial internal capital outlay and costly start-up business phases and often allow them to reduce IT spending by consolidating their IT infrastructure and resources. These concepts are solid, but the task of achieving IT economies of scale is easier said then done. Because there is remarkably little information about a company's systems (i.e., its meta data), the task of integrating the systems with another firm's applications is extremely challenging.

To understand the system impact of a Y2K change requires a careful analysis of the current operational and decision support systems (DSSs). A meta data repository significantly reduces both the time and cost of analysis and development by documenting the data transformation rules, data sources, data structures, and context of the data in the data warehouse and data marts. This information is critical because without the repository, the transformation rules often reside only in the IT staff's collective memory. Because the results of the analysis and developmental changes are captured and retained in the meta data repository, the benefits are long-lasting, helping to reduce the costs of future releases and the likelihood of developmental errors.

Growth of Existing Data Warehouses and Data Marts

Meta data provides a corporation's IT department with the ability to maintain and grow its systems over time. During the past several years, many companies have built decision support systems to help them make better strategic decisions. And, although there is no question of the value of these decision support systems, their proliferation puts a great deal of stress on an organization's IT department. Decision support systems and the data warehouses that typically serve as their foundations are organic structures; they grow very quickly and in directions that are difficult (or even impossible) to predict, which makes the IT department's task of maintaining and extending them very difficult.

Decision support systems and their underlying data warehouses and data marts are likely to continue to grow in size and complexity as corporations become more customer-focused and demand a better understanding of their competitors and their customer base in order to reach sound strategic decisions.

The proliferation of decision-support systems across all enterprises caused the average data warehouse budget to increase by 150 percent (see Table 1.1) from 1996 to 1998. And, the Palo Alto Management Group projects that the decision support market will grow to $113 billion by the year 2002.

Table 1.1   Data Warehouse Project Budgets

COMPANY SIZE	1996 ACTUAL	1997 ACTUAL	1998 ACTUAL
$10M to < $100M	$1,145	$450	$2,110
$100M to < $500M	$890	$1,415	$3,820
$500M to < $1B	$2,065	$1,950	$3,780
$1B to < $5B	$2,535	$1,845	$5,105
$5B to < $10B	$2,905	$2,780	$7,225
> $10B	$3,970	$4,155	$6,370

Source: META Group

Increasing Data Warehouse Size

Data warehouses and data marts do not shrink over time; they only grow. As the databases that manage these systems grow in size, the need for meta data to help manage that data also increases because it is vital for showing what data is used most often and for locating dormant data (i.e., data in the database that is not accessed). The average data warehouse size jumped from 216GB (gigabytes) in 1997 to 834GB in 1998. This trend is not likely to slow down as business users continue to demand more and more detailed analysis. In addition, many data warehouses are being used for *click stream analysis*, which requires storage of a tremendous amount of data. Click stream analysis is the examination of the manner that a user accesses a company's Web site. The data warehouse stores all of the user's clicks, which are then analyzed to identify usage patterns.

Companies have stated that they expect to have an average data warehouse size of 1.6TB (terabytes) by the end of 1999 (see Table 1.2). Even today we are hearing about companies that are planning to store 100TB by the year 2001. With ever-increasing user demands, and improved hardware and relational database technology, we can expect to see the first 1PB (petabyte) data warehouse go online before long.

Increasing Number of Data Warehouse Users

As data warehouse database size increases dramatically, so too does the number of business users (see Table 1.3). As the decision support industry matures, we find that more and more business users need valid, timely information—and those needs continue to increase rapidly. Business users

Table 1.2 Data Warehouse Database Size

SIZE IN GB	1996 ACTUAL	1997 ACTUAL	1998 ACTUAL	1999 PLANNED
<10	36%	40%	14%	5%
10 to <100	31%	29%	33%	14%
100 to <250	13%	12%	13%	22%
250 to <500	6%	4%	9%	8%
500 to <1,000	7%	5%	12%	21%
>1 TB (terabyte)	6%	10%	19%	30%

Source: META Group

are just now beginning to understand the potential benefits of decision support systems, and as that understanding grows, so too do their demands for information.

Poor Decision Support Architecture

Meta data allows corporations a much greater level of knowledge about their decision support architecture. This information enables companies to make better architectural decisions and add greater flexibility to change their decision support systems.

When the decision support movement took hold in the early 1990s, many companies built independent data marts without the proper data warehouse architecture to support these marts over time. Companies tried to

Table 1.3 Data Warehouse Users

NUMBER OF USERS	1996 ACTUAL	1997 ACTUAL	1998 ACTUAL	1999 PLANNED
<10	30%	36%	17%	3%
10 to 49	25%	29%	26%	12%
50 to 99	15%	13%	22%	19%
100 to 499	16%	13%	27%	35%
500 to 999	4%	4%	7%	16%
>1,000	10%	5%	1%	14%

Source: META Group

build their decision support systems in the least expensive manner possible, eliminating many of the up-front steps that are necessary to understand the data as it exists beyond the walls of their individual departments. In addition, in order to sell the concept of building independent data marts, many vendors used the fact that they are easier to implement. The lack of thorough analysis and long-term planning prevented independent data marts from providing an effective and sustaining business intelligence system. All too often, companies built their decision support systems on this architecture that cannot be properly scaled to meet business users' ever-increasing needs.

When these companies attempt to scale (grow) these flawed architectures, they realize that a major development effort is necessary to restructure their decision support system. This effort is greatly simplified when meta data exists.

Building a well-designed and scalable business intelligence system is a complex task that requires sophisticated software, expensive hardware, and a highly skilled and experienced team. Finding data warehouse architects and project leaders who truly understand data warehouse architecture is a daunting challenge, both in the corporate and consulting ranks. In order to build a data warehouse, a corporation must truly come to terms with its data and the business rules that apply to that data. While this task is challenging, it is a necessary step and one upon which the true value of the decision support process depends.

Unfulfilled Needs of Business Users

The reason we exist as IT professionals is to meet the informational needs of our business users. As an industry, we have been less successful than we would like. I remember that during a plane flight I was reading a survey that asked chief executive officers (CEOs), "Do you feel your IT systems meet the needs of your business?" Eighty-four percent of CEOs felt that their IT systems did *not* meet the needs of their businesses. As an IT consultant for more than 12 years, I was truly hurt by this statistic. (In truth, my first impulse was to reach for the airsick bag!) Fortunately, these same CEOs were also asked, "Do you feel your IT systems are important?" Eighty-five percent said "Yes, they are important." Across the board, our systems are not meeting the needs of our business users. These numbers also point to a major trend in our industry: Business executives are forcing CIOs to pay greater attention to the value that IT brings to a business.

Mergers and acquisitions are also fueling the need for IT systems to speak to their business users in business terms. When companies merge or one

LEARNING THE HARD WAY

A large insurance company headquartered in the Midwest relied on a consulting vendor to build its corporate decision support system. Unfortunately, the vendor built the system with little regard to sound architecture. Within a year, the insurance company's decision support manager had accumulated a long list of system modifications and enhancements requested by the business users. Because of the poor architecture and the lack of meta data, the manager could not modify the system. At that point, the company hired me to completely rebuild its decision support system.

Because business users were still relying on the decision support system, we had to maintain the integrity and accuracy of all the existing reports. The facts that (1) there was no meta data of any sort to work from and (2) the consultants who initially built the system had failed to transfer any knowledge to the client compounded the problem immeasurably. We had only one option for identifying the business rules: print out every program and manually walk through every line of code. This task was incredibly time-consuming and tedious, requiring the full-time efforts of four developers over the course of three and a half months just to document about 90 percent of the business rules. We discovered the remaining 10 percent of the rules after a long, drawn-out parallel testing effort. The testing effort required four months to achieve two consecutive clean, parallel system runs.

I believe that if the original data warehouse development team had populated a meta data repository, we could have generated a variety of impact analysis reports that would have let us reduce the design time by more than 70 percent. We also would have had a much more accurate design that would have shortened the parallel testing effort by half—and that's a conservative estimate. Obviously, after this experience, the client was fully convinced of the value of a meta data repository.

acquires another, the business users generally need to be able to use the information generated by the information systems of both, or to merge the information from both systems into a single report. Although company A's business users may know from experience that report XC001AB gives them information on product sales by region, company B's users would not have any idea what report XC001AB is all about, or know how to elicit the information they need on product sales by region.

Meta data holds the key to this challenge. Meta data provides the semantic layer between the technical systems and the business users. In simple terms, meta data translates the technical terminology used in IT systems into terms a business user can understand.

NOT MEETING BUSINESS USER NEEDS

I was brought in to assess a data warehouse for a large financial services company in the Midwest. When I met with their decision support manager, I was told that they had a very good decision support system. However, none of the business users were accessing the reports they had created. The project leader told me they had a report that showed product sales over time by region and by marketing campaign. This sounded like an valuable report, so I asked to see him access it through the system. The project manager clicked on a report entitled "XC001AB." That's right—XC001AB! I asked, "How would a business user know that report XC001AB showed product sales over time by region and by marketing campaign!" Clearly a marketing analyst would much rather see this report titled "Product sales, by region, by marketing campaign, over time." This example illustrates why so few senior executives believe that their company's IT systems meet the needs of their business.

High IT Employee Turnover

One of the major challenges that businesses face today is the high rate of employee turnover in their IT departments. When a company loses an employee, it is losing much more than an individual who has coded Java for the past three years. In reality, it is losing an individual who has accumulated three years' worth of knowledge about the company business and its business systems. Meta data seeks to capture the knowledge—both business and technical—that is stored in our employees, and to make it accessible to everyone in the organization.

Lack of User Confidence in Data

Meta data increases business users' confidence in the data that they rely on in the corporate decision support and operational systems. Meta data accomplishes this feat by providing a semantic layer between these systems and the users. (See the section on meta data–driven business user interfaces later in this chapter for additional discussion of this topic.)

Emergence of Customer Relationship Management

Managing a global company is more difficult than ever before. In today's market, it is not enough to produce a quality product in an efficient manner, and price it appropriately and distribute it effectively. Instead, companies

MISSING META DATA: THE COST OF INCORRECT DECISIONS

Anyone who doubts that users need meta data to describe their data need look no further than the National Aeronautics and Space Administration's (NASA's) 1999 Mars Climate Orbiter mission. The orbiter spent nine months coasting toward Mars. NASA engineers on the ground calculated the size of periodic rocket firings for midcourse adjustments using feet per second of thrust, a value based on the English measure of feet and inches. However, the spacecraft's computer interpreted the instructions in Newtons per second, a metric measure of thrust. The difference (and resulting error) was a whopping 4.4 feet per second. These rockets firings happened 12 to 14 times a week over the nine-month voyage. "Each time there was a burn (rocket firing) the error built up," said Art Stephenson, director of the Marshall Spaceflight Center and head of a NASA investigation team.

As the spacecraft approached its rendezvous with Mars and the engineers prepared for a final rocket firing, there were indications that something was seriously wrong with the navigation, but no corrective action was taken. When the Mars Climate Orbiter did fire its rockets, the craft went too low into the planet's atmosphere—and has not been heard from since. "We entered the Mars atmosphere at a much lower altitude [than planned]," said Ed Weiler, NASA's chief scientist. "It [the spacecraft] either burned up in the Martian atmosphere or sped out [into space]. We're not sure which happened." Stephenson said that the problem was not with the spacecraft, but with the engineers and the systems used to direct it. Obviously the NASA space program could use a meta data repository to provide that semantic layer between its systems and its engineers.

"The spacecraft did everything we asked of it," said Stephenson. He said the mathematical mismatch was "a little thing" that could have been easily fixed if it had been detected. "Sometimes the little things can come back and really make a difference," he said. A little thing like meta data could have saved everyone a great deal of pain and a very significant amount of money. The cost of the misinformation in this case: $300 million!

---

must understand, anticipate, and exceed their customer's needs better than their competition can.

To put it a bit differently, a company's success is determined by its ability to market the right products to the right people, at the right time, in the right place, and at a lower price than its competitors. The old business philosophy of "if we build it, they will come" is not effective in today's business climate (if, indeed, it ever was). Mass production alone can no longer sustain long-term corporate growth, or even survival. Increasing consumer expectations and global competition are demanding that companies differentiate their offerings to individual consumer groups in order to offer relevant products and services to those customers that represent the most value to the business.

Today's companies must deliver goods and services that are directly relevant to their target market. Of course, to do this, companies need to be able to identify who their market is, and understand what needs their product or service can satisfy for that market. In short, companies need to make their products relevant to the consumers who represent the greatest potential value for their business. Making the transformation to this customer relationship management or one-to-one marketing approach is vital to the long-term viability of any company competing in today's market, but the shift requires CIOs and IT directors to radically change their information management strategies to support it.

Making the transformation from a product-centric company to a customer-centric company (as illustrated in Figure 1.6) is impeded by outdated sys-

---

WHAT IS CUSTOMER RELATIONSHIP MANAGEMENT?

A customer relationship management strategy simply states "create products or services that satisfy your individual customer's consumer or commercial needs." This is a key corporate paradigm shift as companies move from being product-centric to customer-centric. Nearly any business can benefit from customer relationship management. The experience of a friend of mine provides one example of a missed opportunity for this strategy. My friend, who recently moved into a new area of the country, went to her local grocer to purchase various food items for her family. This grocer, like many others, provides coupons to entice customers back to the store. Grocers provide different coupons depending on the consumer's purchases. Among other things, my friend purchased her favorite brand of waffles (Brand A), which she has been buying exclusively for the past 20 years. At the checkout, she received a coupon for waffles, but the coupon was for Brand B rather than her favorite waffles. If the store had insight into her buying habits, it would have known that Brand A waffles are the only kind she is going to buy. If it had given her coupons for Brand A rather than Brand B, she would almost certainly return to redeem the coupons, and very possibly begin to buy her family's groceries there on a regular basis. But without consumer information about my friend's buying habits, the grocer was unable to focus on her specific needs and offer the right enticement to lure her back to the store.

Customer relationship management tries to understand our individual buying trends and individual circumstances, and then market appropriately to them. Making the transformation to this new approach is forcing CIOs and IT directors to radically change their IT strategy to support this new customer relationship management strategy.

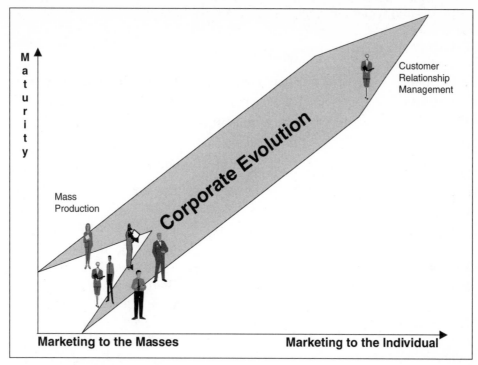

Figure 1.6 Marketing evolution.

tems designed to manage a company's products and day-to-day operations rather than its customer base. These operational systems have evolved over the years to process transactions that produce, deliver, and invoice products/services. Unfortunately, they cannot handle remedial questions like, "Which products are most profitable for us?" or "Which customers buy product X most often?" These systems cannot easily or quickly provide answers to these fundamental questions, which are redefining the world of business. Decision support systems go a long way toward helping companies to get the kinds of information they need for customer relationship management from their operational systems, but they don't provide a complete solution. We'll discuss decision support systems in some detail later in this chapter, and explain what they can and can't do, and how they relate to meta data.

Decision Support Moves to the Forefront

Decision support systems are a key ingredient for effectively meeting the needs of customers as well as quickly responding to changing market conditions. Operational systems, which are primarily designed to produce, deliver, and invoice products or services, are incapable of answering questions like:

- "Which customers are most profitable for our company?"
- "Which segment of our market offers the greatest future potential profit?"
- "Which of our products are complementary (i.e., market basket analysis)?"
- "Which competitors pose the greatest threat to our existence?"
- "Which of our products or services provides the greatest value to our customers?"

Decision support systems, which are designed to manage customer information rather than product information, can handle these types of questions; they provide the link between legacy operational systems and business users' needs to support one-to-one marketing.

Many companies now understand that they cannot compete effectively in today's (and tomorrow's) market without a DSS. I believe that in the near future (i.e., within 5 to 10 years) decision support will be a key component in every major IT initiative. The growth in IT decision support budgets between 1996 and 1998 (see Table 1.4) supports this opinion; note that the expenditure more than doubled between 1997 and 1998. Companies are no longer deciding whether to build a DSS, but determining how quickly they can build it.

Components of a Decision Support System

To understand meta data repositories, you need to understand the various components of a decision support architecture. Because there are many fine books dedicated to this topic, we'll merely summarize the components illustrated in Figure 1.7, and recommend that you research these in more detail on your own if you are not familiar with DSS architecture.

Table 1.4 IT Decision Support Systems Budget ($ in Thousands)

	1996 ACTUAL	1997 ACTUAL	1998 ACTUAL
Consulting	$585 – 26%	$495 – 25%	$1,154 – 24%
Software	$779 – 34%	$656 – 34%	$1,733 – 37%
Hardware	$913 – 40%	$795 – 41%	$1,840 – 39%
Total	$2,277	$1,946	$4,727

Source: META Group

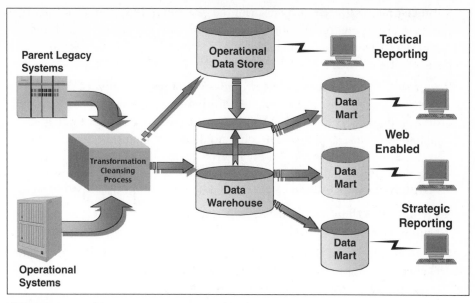

Figure 1.7   Decision support systems architecture.

Data Warehouse

The data warehouse is the foundation of a decision support system architecture (see Figure 1.8). A data warehouse is a single, enterprise-wide collection of data that has the following four key characteristics (taken from the classic book by W. H. Inmon, *Building the Data Warehouse*, second edition, Wiley, 1996, p. 33):

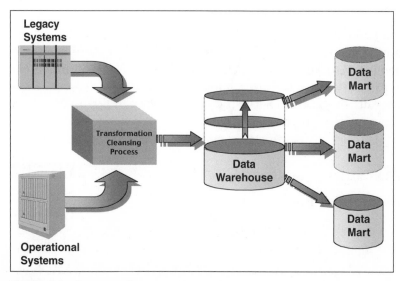

Figure 1.8   Data warehouse components.

Subject-oriented.   By subject-oriented, we mean the "nouns" of the organization (e.g., customers, logistics, manufacturing, finance, marketing, and sales). Companies typically have between 20 and 30 subject areas, depending on their industry and the scope of the DSS.

Integrated.   A data warehouse provides an integrated view of the enterprise's major subject areas. The test for integrating all of this operational data is the usually the largest (and most daunting) task in the decision support lifecycle, because data commonly resides in multiple operational systems. For example, one of my international clients has 28 separate order entry systems around the world, with each of these systems maintaining its own view of the customer, and using different record formats.

Nonvolatile.   Data warehouse data is not updated directly by its users. It is for access purposes only.

Time variant.   Data warehouses hold historical (snapshot) views of data, even as it changes over time. This allows the decision support users to compare sales numbers over the life of the company.

One of the primary uses of a data warehouse is to fulfill the data needs of the data marts that it supports. Data marts, which I'll describe in more detail in the next section, are designed for quick user access but are cumbersome for loading other data structures (i.e., data tables). Data warehouses, on the other hand, provide comparatively slow user access, but contain the detailed, transaction-level corporate data, and are excellent for loading other data structures (i.e., data marts). Most data warehouses limit business user access to one-time or ad hoc queries.

Data Marts

Data marts (see Figure 1.9) are sets of data designed and constructed for optimal decision support business user access. They can be sourced from a data warehouse or directly from a company's operational systems. Data marts are generally designed to serve the needs of a specific, homogenous business user group (e.g., marketing, finance, human resources, etc.). Data in the data marts is usually summarized and designed for specific reporting needs.

Operational Data Stores

An operational data store (see Figure 1.10) is a set of integrated data without history or summarization provided for tactical decision support. Architecturally operational data stores look very much like a data warehouse

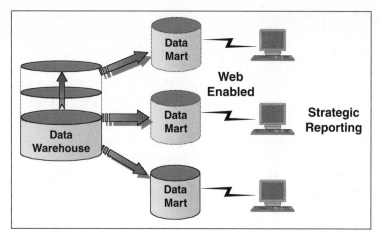

Figure 1.9   Data mart components.

with two key differences: (1) the data in an operational data store is volatile, as it is updated on a real-time or near real-time basis, and (2) the data in the operational data store is current-valued and not historical. This is because historical data is simply too voluminous to store and still have real-time updates (see W. H. Inmon, *Building the Operational Data Store*, second edition, Wiley, 1999, p. 15).

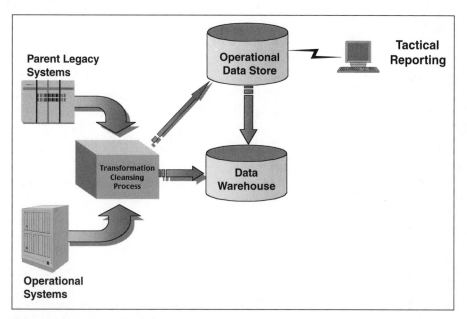

Figure 1.10   Operational data store components.

Meta Data and Decision Support

Meta data defines the contents of the DSS and helps business users locate relevant information for their analysis. Meta data also allows users to trace data from the DSS to its operational source systems (i.e., drill-down) and to related data in other subject areas (i.e., drill-across). By managing the structure of the data over a broad spectrum of time, it provides a context for interpreting the meaning of the information. As meta data is extracted and stored over several years, snapshots of the data exist for each year. To accomplish this, the meta model tables must allow the users to easily trace back through the meta data repository (i.e., the database for meta data) to earlier versions of the meta data.

Decision Support Challenges

It's easy to see the need for decision support systems, but implementing them is anything but easy. The challenges for implementing a DSS come from both the business and technical arenas.

Business Challenges

The most common cause for DSS project failure is that, once built, the systems don't meet the business objectives or needs of the organization. Decision support systems that don't satisfy the business users' needs eventually die from lack of interest.

An enterprise DSS requires consent and commitment from all of the key departments within an organization. Decision support systems pull data from all of the key operational systems from across the enterprise and create an integrated view of the organization. Gaining enterprise-wide support for the initial release can be challenging, especially if the various departments don't agree on what that view should look like.

Defining clear, measurable business objectives is critical for building a DSS and justifying its cost to the organization. Once the initial DSS release can be cost-justified, it is relatively easy to gather management support and funding for follow-up releases. (Note that most decision support systems more than double in size and number of users in their first year of production, so the success of the initial release is crucial for the long-term survival of the system.)

Technical Challenges

Decision support projects technically stress an organization in very different ways than do traditional system projects. Data warehouses typically source data from most, if not all, of an organization's key operational systems. Integrating this data is extremely complex and requires considerable effort on the part of the DSS implementation team and IT staff. For example, most companies want to store customer data in the data warehouse. This data often resides in several of the firm's operational systems, and must be integrated and cleansed before it can be loaded into the data warehouse. The process of integrating the data is, in itself, complicated and requires a significant amount of knowledge about the data just to integrate it.

Decision support systems typically store and access large quantities of data; one or more terabytes is not uncommon. Such massive amounts of data can significantly increase the chance of failure. In addition, massive volumes of data often push the envelope of the database management system (DBMS), middleware, and hardware, and may force developers to use parallel development techniques. The answer to many of these technical challenges comes in the form of a hefty price tag. As a result, adding the dimension of size can be both painful and costly.

Many legacy systems contain redundant or inaccurate data. The lack of data quality in the operational systems has caused more than one decision support effort to fail. In a perfect world, the IT staff would go back to the operational systems and clean the data, but this rarely occurs in the real world. As a result, to ensure its usability, the operational data must be cleaned before it is loaded into the data warehouse. Meta data is critical for monitoring and improving the quality of the data coming from the operational systems. Meta data tracks the number of errors that occur during each data warehouse load run and can report when certain error thresholds are reached. In addition, the DSS data quality metrics should be stored over the history of the DSS. This allows corporations to monitor their data quality over time. See Chapter 8, Implementing Data Quality through Meta Data, for a detailed presentation on this topic.

As Figure 1.11 illustrates, a DSS typically incorporates a wide variety of tools from multiple vendors, including one or more of the following:

- ETL (extraction, transformation, and load)
- Meta data integration
- Data modeling
- Data quality
- Access (OLAP, ROLAP, or MOLAP)
- Corporate information portal
- Data mining

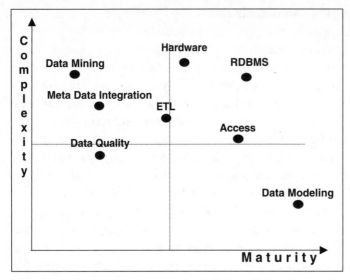

Figure 1.11   Decision support technology.

A company's IT personnel need a thorough understanding of the tools used in the DSS, and they typically require training to achieve this understanding. Multiple levels of training are not uncommon, including initial education to convey the underlying concepts (e.g., data warehouse, data mart, operational data store, star schema design, and meta data), and specialized training for specific DSS roles. For example, data acquisition developers generally need training on an ETL tool, and data warehouse access developers may require training on an access tool (e.g., OLAP, ROLAP, or MOLAP). In addition, users may require training on the Web component used to access the data warehouse and the meta data repository. Remember, these are only the DSS-specific training issues; additional training may be required on the hardware, middleware, desktop, RDBMS, and coding language (e.g., SQL, COBOL, C++, etc.) used for the ETL tool.

Meta Data ROI

Few statistics are available on the deployment of meta data solutions. However, a 1999 Data Warehouse Institute survey of 175 respondents (listed in Figure 1.12) revealed two important statistics. Though the vast majority (86 percent) of companies responding to the survey agreed that meta data is

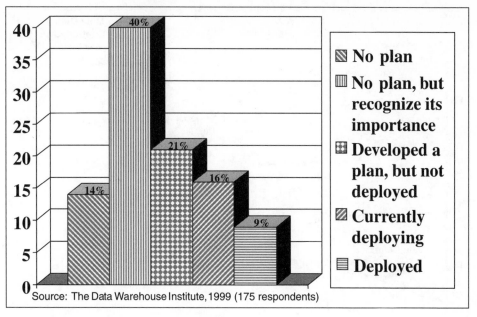

Figure 1.12   Deploying a meta data strategy.

very important, only 25 percent have deployed or are currently deploying a meta data repository solution.

One of the reasons more companies have not implemented meta data repositories is that they do not understand the potential return on investment (ROI) that meta data offers (see Figure 1.13).

In the following paragraphs, we'll illustrate meta data's value by walking through these key solutions to common business problems:

- Data definition reporting
- Data quality tracking
- Business user access to meta data
- Decision support impact analysis
- Enterprise-wide impact analysis

As we look at these solutions, remember that the more valuable the solution, the more complex the meta data initiative is likely to be (as shown in Figure 1.13). Although *meta data–controlled systems* (represented at the top of the curve in Figure 1.13) do not yet exist, major companies are working very hard to make them a reality. We discuss this topic in detail in Chapter 11, The Future of Meta Data.

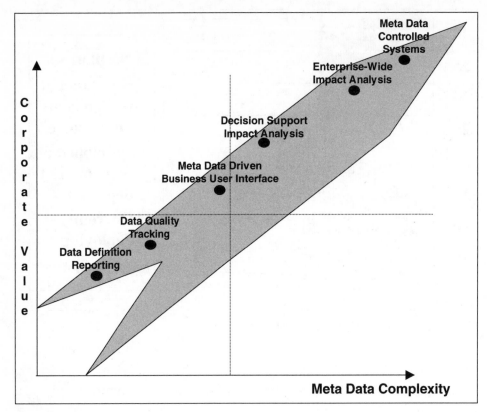

Figure 1.13   Meta data ROI curve.

Data Definition Reporting

Data definition reporting is one of the most basic meta data solutions. In some ways, it resembles the early data dictionary initiatives that attempted to create a central repository for storing and accessing technical definitions for the attributes and entities used in a company's IT systems. Figure 1.14 illustrates a sample data definition report on the *order entry* system for a company.

Database administrators, programmers, data modelers, and business analysts all commonly use data definition reporting. And, while these reports are a good beginning for a meta data initiative, their value to the company is relatively limited because they do not truly target the business. Most IT departments that successfully implement data definition reports experience only mild productivity gains from their experienced developers, but

Question: Show all fields definitions in the "Order Entry" system

System	Table	Table Description	Column	Column Description	Data Type	Length	Domain	Unit	Valid From Date	Valid To Date
							Corporate Data Definitions Report			January 17, 2000
Order Entry	CUSTOMER	Information on a client of a company	CUSTOMER NAME	A customer who has a direct business relationship with this firm or is a subsidiary or affiliate of a client	char	100	N/A	N/A	March 22, 1999	January 3, 2000
			CUSTOMER NAME	A customer who has a direct business relationship with this firm	char	50	N/A	N/A	March 22, 1999	September 2, 2000
			CUSTOMER TYPE	Customer types associated with the firm	char	1	"D" - Direct customer "I" - Indirect customer	N/A	January 3, 2000	January 3, 2000
	PRODUCT	Information on the firms catalog products	PRODUCT NAME	A active product listed in the firm's published catalog	char	100	N/A	N/A	January 3, 2000	January 3, 2000
			PRODUCT PRICE	A active product's list price in the firm's published product catalog	num	18.6	N/A	USD, Dollars	January 3, 2000	January 3, 2000
			INVOICE NUMBER	The firm-generated number associated with the itemized recurring and nonrecurring charges billed to a customer	char	20	N/A	N/A	January 3, 2000	January 3, 2000

Figure 1.14 Meta data ROI—data definition reporting.

less-experienced IT staff members and business users find the reports highly valuable (see Table 1.5).

Data Quality Tracking

Data quality is a significant issue in many, if not all, businesses competing in today's market. Companies realize the strategic value of their IT systems, but if the data in these systems is redundant, inaccurate, or incomplete, it can seriously damage the company's competitive position. Also, mission critical initiatives like e-business, customer relationship management, and decision

Table 1.5 Meta Data ROI—Data Definition Reporting

BUSINESS/TECHNICAL VALUE	ROI MEASURES
Reduce IT staff's learning curves	Cost savings through productivity gains
Reduce IT-related problems	Cost savings through reduction in IT staff errors
Reduce impact of IT staff turnover	Cost savings through better training

support frequently depend on data from the company's existing legacy systems. If the quality of the data in these systems is poor, it will directly impact the reliability, accuracy, and effectiveness of any of these initiatives. The old IT saying of "garbage in, garbage out" summarizes the fact that data quality, or the lack thereof, is critical to any enterprise (see Table 1.6).

Meta data is a critical component to any data quality initiative. Meta data provides the mechanism for monitoring and improving the quality of the data coming from the operational systems into the DSS. Meta data tracks the number of errors that occur during each data warehouse/data mart load run and can report to the IT staff when prespecified error thresholds are exceeded. If, for example, we are loading transactional sales records into a DSS for the Marketing department, we may decide that if more than 2 percent (i.e., our threshold) of the dollar amounts of all of the sales transactions are in error, we need to stop the DSS load processes and investigate the problem. It is important to note that on data records that have dollar amount fields in them, it is generally advisable to set the error thresholds on the dollar values of the records in error rather than on the number of records in error. Let's suppose, for example, that typically 100,000 records, totaling $20,000,000 in transactional sales, are loaded into the DSS every month. If 2,000 of these sales records (i.e., 2 percent), totaling $20,000 (i.e., 0.1 percent of sales dollars), erred out without loading into the DSS, the business users may not feel that this is a large enough error to skew their decision-making process. However, if 10 records (i.e., .01 percent) erred out, totaling $2,000,000 (i.e., 10.0 percent of sales dollars) in sales, then it is

Table 1.6   Meta Data ROI—Data Quality Tracking

BUSINESS/TECHNICAL VALUE	ROI MEASURES
Improved business decision making	Data quality is improved, which provides business users with more accurate systems and reports.
Reduction of IT-related problems	Improved data quality reduces many system-related problems and IT expenses.
Increased system value to the business	DSS business users are likely to make better decisions if they are aware of possible errors skewing report numbers.
Improved system performance	As data quality improves, system errors are reduced, which improves system performance.

WHAT HAPPENS WHEN DATA QUALITY IS SKIPPED?

Unfortunately, companies are often reluctant to spend the necessary time or money to research, evaluate, and resolve their data quality issues. I had one such client, a very large international company, that had multiple DSS projects underway simultaneously. In my initial proposal, I allocated time and resources to conduct a data quality study to gauge the quality of the company's source system data during the feasibility phase of the decision support initiative. However, the client's decision makers did not want to spend either the time or the money on an activity that they felt had minimal value. Despite my urgings to the contrary, the company refused to conduct the evaluation. In its view, there were no data quality issues—so it wasn't worthwhile spending valuable time and money to evaluate the data.

During the course of the project, however, when we were well down the design path for one of the data marts, our development team discovered that the quality of the data in the source system was so poor that the reports were unlikely to have accurate computations. Further, the data was of such poor quality that it did not even have the information necessary to clean it. To make a bad situation even worse, our project sponsor did not have the authority to go back to the IT team responsible for maintaining the source system to ask them to change it.

As a result, I was left with a task that every consultant dreads. I recommended to senior management that the project be stopped. Because of the severity of the data quality problem, senior management supported my recommendation. Our one saving grace was that our other DSS projects met with much better success than this particular effort—but the client lost approximately $225,000 in consulting fees and employee salaries, above and beyond what it would have cost to evaluate the data early in the development process.

highly probable that the business users would be unable to make accurate decisions. Remember that the business must define what the error threshold should be, because this is a business decision. Figure 1.15 illustrates a sample of a detailed data quality tracking report for the ETL process of a company.

In addition, all of the decision support system's data quality metrics should be stored in the meta data repository and retained throughout the life of the DSS. This allows companies to monitor their data quality over time and to determine whether the quality is improving or declining.

Question: Show ETL load statistics and time

ETL Statistics Report											**January 17, 2000**
Target Table	ETL Process	Target Table Type	Source System(s)	Processing Time	Load Cycle	Number of Records Inserted	Number of Records Updated	Records in Error	Total Number of Records	Load Date	Load Time
Customer	cs0001	Dimension	ERP	0:43:12	3	223	196	2	1,194	March 2, 2000	5:18:10
Customer	cs0002	Dimension	Order Processing	0:27:39	3	22	5	0	1,194	March 2, 2000	5:18:10
Customer	cs0003	Dimension	Sales Force	0:18:45	3	51	17	0	1,194	March 2, 2000	5:18:10
Product	pd001	Dimension	Order Processing	0:29:28	3	41	28	1	112	March 2, 2000	5:18:10
Employee	ee001	Dimension	ERP	0:37:55	3	23	15	0	276	March 2, 2000	5:18:10
Time	tm001	Dimension	External Source	0:05:41	3	1	0	0	3	March 2, 2000	5:18:10
Sales	sl001	Fact	Order Processing	2:35:30	3	36,908,928	0	17,172	58,095,382	March 2, 2000	5:18:10
Customer	cs0001	Dimension	ERP	0:41:45	2	287	201	0	898	February 1, 2000	3:36:38
Customer	cs0002	Dimension	Order Processing	0:25:32	2	15	1	0	898	February 1, 2000	3:36:38
Customer	cs0003	Dimension	Sales Force	0:16:48	2	78	24	0	898	February 1, 2000	3:36:38
Product	pd001	Dimension	Order Processing	0:28:34	2	31	24	0	71	February 1, 2000	3:36:38
Employee	ee001	Dimension	ERP	0:34:59	2	9	2	0	253	February 1, 2000	3:36:38
Time	tm001	Dimension	External Source	0:04:13	2	1	0	0	2	February 1, 2000	3:36:38
Sales	sl001	Fact	Order Processing	1:04:47	2	16,130,774	0	230	21,186,454	February 1, 2000	3:36:38
Customer	cs0001	Dimension	ERP	0:49:42	1	334	0	0	518	January 3, 2000	3:47:35
Customer	cs0002	Dimension	Order Processing	0:28:21	1	37	0	0	518	January 3, 2000	3:47:35
Customer	cs0003	Dimension	Sales Force	0:31:09	1	147	0	22	518	January 3, 2000	3:47:35
Product	pd001	Dimension	Order Processing	0:45:33	1	40	0	0	40	January 3, 2000	3:47:35
Employee	ee001	Dimension	ERP	0:50:18	1	244	0	0	244	January 3, 2000	3:47:35
Time	tm001	Dimension	External Source	0:02:21	1	1	0	0	1	January 3, 2000	3:47:35
Sales	sl001	Fact	Order Processing	0:20:11	1	5,055,680	0	0	5,055,680	January 3, 2000	3:47:35

Figure 1.15 Meta data ROI—data quality tracking sample report.

In decision support systems, it is common to compare field values from different time periods. Figure 1.16 illustrates a decision support report that indicates global corporate sales on a monthly basis for a consumer electronics manufacturer. Business users can use this report to compare U.S. sales from October 1998 to November 1998 for the holiday buying season and, during the comparison, determine that the sales figures for November seem a bit low. They could then check the data quality statistics and see that 8.4 percent of the records in the November decision support load run erred out and were not loaded. This would let them know their margin for error when making decisions based on this report.

Data quality tracking is valuable to many people within an organization, including corporate executives, project managers, database administrators, programmers, data modelers, business analysts, and business users in many and varied departments.

Chapter 8, Implementing Data Quality through Meta Data, provides a detailed discussion of the issues associated with using meta data to enhance data quality.

Business User Access to Meta Data

As IT professionals, we need to understand that our users don't care whether the information they need comes from a data warehouse, a data

Corporate Information Access

1999 Monthly Global Sales Report				January 7, 2000
Month	Product Category	Sales $ (in thousands) U.S	Sales $ (in thousands International	Sales $ (in thousands Total
December	TV	22,101	10,200	32,301
	VCR	11,190	4,300	15,490
	Cellular Phone	12,190	7,193	19,383
	Digital	4,002	1,301	5,303
	Miscellaneous	1,209	870	2,079
November	TV	42,000	22,200	64,200
	VCR	21,190	9,878	31,068
	Cellular Phone	28,193	12,193	40,386
	Digital	8,901	2,901	11,802
	Miscellaneous	2,730	1,530	2,730
October	TV	70,100	32,950	103,050
	VCR	31,900	14,878	46,778
	Cellular Phone	41,700	17,550	59,250
	Digital	20,000	4,100	24,100
	Miscellaneous	4,850	2,850	7,700

Data Quality Tracking Statistics
8.4% of the dollar value were not loaded
1.7% of the records were not loaded

Figure 1.16 Meta data ROI—data quality tracking reveals margin for error.

mart, an operational data store, or a meta data repository. They just want to be able to find the information they need quickly and with minimal searching. Meta data can help us to meet our business users' needs and speak to them in business terms they understand by providing a semantic layer between our IT systems and our business users. Figures 1.17 through 1.20 illustrate a Web-enabled DSS that meets this goal. This Web front-end is designed with the business user in mind. If, for example, a business user wants to view the numbers for monthly product sales, he or she need only access the decision support Web site called "Corporate Information Access" (as in Figure 1.17) and indicate a search target, in this case, *Monthly Product Sales* (Figure 1.18).

At this point, meta data comes into play. Meta data in the meta data repository contains business definitions for each of the DSS reports. When the business user searches for reports that have the words *Monthly Product Sales* in their meta data definitions, the system returns a list of reports containing that search string (Figure 1.19).

The user can then select one or more reports for viewing or enter a new query, which would generate a new response meeting the search criteria. In

Figure 1.17   Meta data ROI—meta data–driven business user interface.

this case, let's say our user chooses to display global product sales, by month, by region (Figure 1.20).

This report presumably provides our user with the information he or she is looking for, but it may also raise some questions about just how the U.S. sales dollar figure is calculated. Thanks to meta data, this information is also available. The meta data repository can store business definitions (i.e., calculation for U.S. sales dollars) along with the report totals. Integrating this meta data into the decision support report enables the business user to understand exactly what goes into U.S. sales dollar calculation (as in Figure 1.21). In this case, the report clearly indicates that U.S. sales dollars includes sales from Canada and Mexico, but does not subtract sales dollars from returned product orders.

As the following series of figures illustrates, meta data can significantly improve the value and accessibility of information in the DSS for business users.

A meta data business user interface directly targets the business side of an organization, which is a piece of the puzzle that meta data has been sorely lacking for many years. This functionality is important to many people within the organization, including corporate executives, senior man-

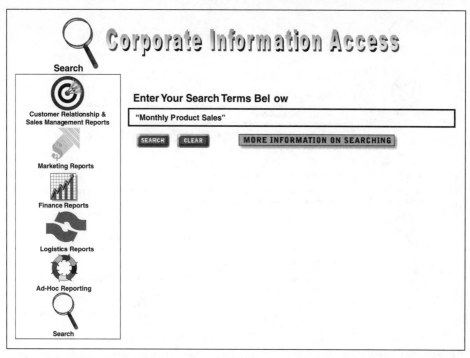

Figure 1.18 Meta data ROI—meta data–driven business user interface search request.

agers of lines of business (i.e., marketing, finance, etc.), business analysts, and business users (see Table 1.7).

Decision Support Impact Analysis

A meta data repository can significantly reduce both the costs and time involved in development by allowing the IT development staff to run tech-

Table 1.7 Meta Data ROI—Meta Data–Driven Business User Interface

BUSINESS/TECHNICAL VALUE	ROI MEASURES
Reduction of IT-related problems	Easier information access, thereby reducing IT-related questions and problems
Increased system value	DSS has greater relevance for the business users, letting them do their jobs more efficiently
Improved business decision making	Users are able to access and specifically understand the information they need to make business decisions

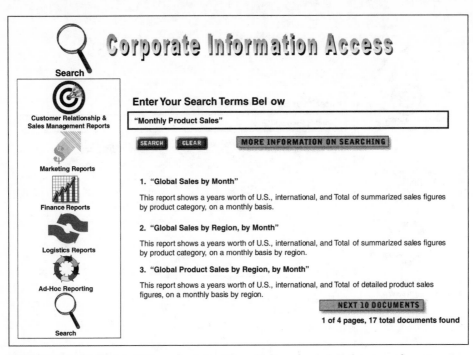

Figure 1.19 Meta data ROI—meta data–driven business user interface search response.

Corporate Information Access

1999 Monthly Global Sales Report				January 7, 2000
Month	Product Category	Sales $ (in thousands) U.S	Sales $ (in thousands International	Sales $ (in thousands Total
December	TV	22,101	10,200	32,301
	VCR	11,190	4,300	15,490
	Cellular Phone	12,190	7,193	19,383
	Digital	4,002	1,301	5,303
	Miscellaneous	1,209	870	2,079
November	TV	42,000	22,200	64,200
	VCR	21,190	9,878	31,068
	Cellular Phone	28,193	12,193	40,386
	Digital	8,901	2,901	11,802
	Miscellaneous	2,730	1,530	2,730
October	TV	70,100	32,950	103,050
	VCR	31,900	14,878	46,778
	Cellular Phone	41,700	17,550	59,250
	Digital	20,000	4,100	24,100
	Miscellaneous	4,850	2,850	7,700

Figure 1.20 Meta data ROI—meta data–driven business user interface target report display.

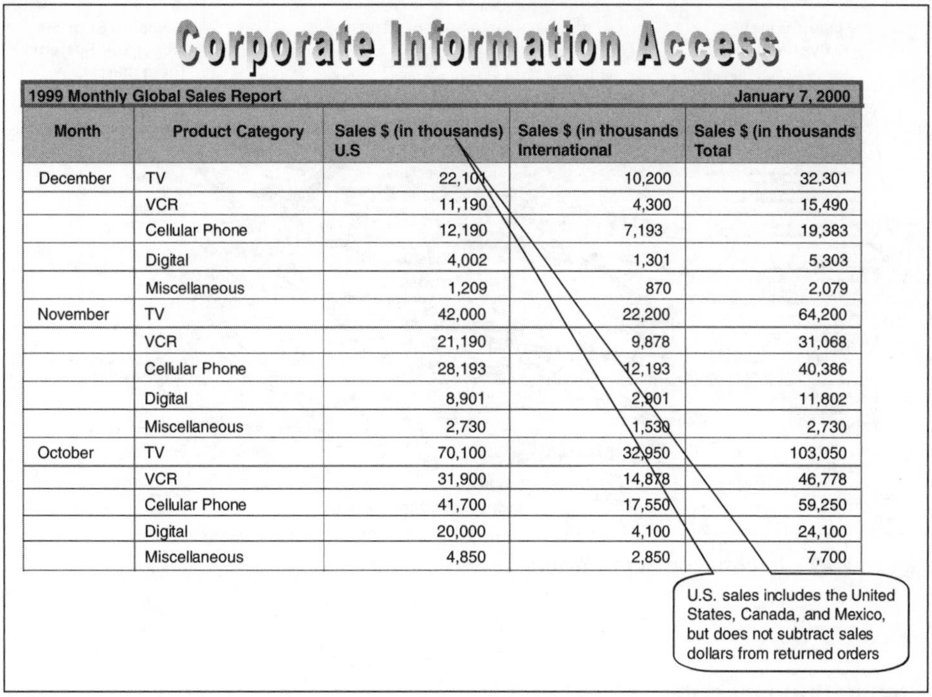

Corporate Information Access

1999 Monthly Global Sales Report				January 7, 2000
Month	**Product Category**	**Sales $ (in thousands) U.S**	**Sales $ (in thousands International**	**Sales $ (in thousands Total**
December	TV	22,10?	10,200	32,301
	VCR	11,190	4,300	15,490
	Cellular Phone	12,190	7,193	19,383
	Digital	4,002	1,301	5,303
	Miscellaneous	1,209	870	2,079
November	TV	42,000	22,200	64,200
	VCR	21,190	9,878	31,068
	Cellular Phone	28,193	12,193	40,386
	Digital	8,901	2,901	11,802
	Miscellaneous	2,730	1,530	2,730
October	TV	70,100	32,950	103,050
	VCR	31,900	14,878	46,778
	Cellular Phone	41,700	17,550	59,250
	Digital	20,000	4,100	24,100
	Miscellaneous	4,850	2,850	7,700

U.S. sales includes the United States, Canada, and Mexico, but does not subtract sales dollars from returned orders

Figure 1.21   Meta data ROI—meta data–driven business user interface integrated business definition.

nical impact analysis reports across all corporate systems stored in the meta data repository. Because many companies are currently trying to implement DSS impact analysis, we'll specifically discuss this functionality, then explain how to roll the concept out into other systems.

Impact analysis reports help developers to thoroughly understand the effect of proposed changes to the DSS environment. This functionality is critical for any company trying to manage its DSS over time. Not long ago, I was working with an East Coast insurance company that has conducted several decision support efforts over a four-year span. During that time, one of the IT managers took the time to map out the flow of data from their operational systems to their data staging areas, and finally to their data mart structures. Figure 1.22 illustrates the actual results of the investigation.

I know when you look at Figure 1.22 it looks and is unreadable. What is interesting is that this data flow chart *is* an accurate representation of this company's decision support architecture! This figure is by far my favorite picture, and I use it in nearly all of the presentations I give on decision support and meta data. In a single image, it manages to communicate several important messages about:

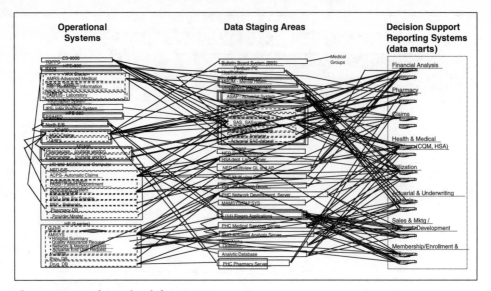

Figure 1.22 Information infrastructure.

- Redundant data
- Redundant processes
- Lack of hardware/software platform consolidation
- Strain on the IT organization
- Maintenance nightmare
- Tremendous waste of money

And, people's response to this image is even scarier than the architecture itself. When I show it to clients, they typically ask me where I got a copy of their information architecture.

Decision support systems collect their data from the operational systems of a business. It is quite common for these operational systems to undergo changes in their business rules and data structures, and these changes can directly impact the decision support systems that they feed. Impact analysis reports help to control the effect of these changes. Let's suppose that the table used to store customer data in a company's order entry system needs to be modified. Meta data in the repository allows me to run an impact analysis (Figure 1.23) to indicate all of the decision support tables/files, programs, and fields that may be affected by a change to the order entry system.

The *table type* field on our sample report can equal one of three values: *S*, *I*, or *T*. *S* indicates that the table is a source table/file from the operational

Question: Show all decision support/files, programs, and fields impacted by a change to the "CUST" table in the "Order Entry" system.

Impact Analysis Report						January 7, 2000
Source System	Source Table	Impact Field	Program Impacted	Tables/Files Impacted	Table Type	Fields Impacted
Order Entry	CUST	Customer_Name	CUSTOMER_PR02	DW_CUSTOMER	T	Cust_Name_First
						Cust_Name_Middle
						Cust_Name_Last
			CUSTOMER_PR01	I02_CUSTOMER	I	Cust_Name_First
						Cust_Name_Middle
						Cust_Name_Last
		Customer_Addr	CUSTOMER_PR02	DW_CUSTOMER	T	Cust_Name_Address
						Cust_Name_City
						Cust_Name_State
						Cust_Name_Zip
			CUSTOMER_PR01	I02_CUSTOMER	I	Cust_Name_Address
						Cust_Name_City
						Cust_Name_State
						Cust_Name_Zip

Figure 1.23 Meta data ROI—sample decision support impact analysis report.

system to the DSS. *I* signifies that the table is an intermediate table/file between the operational system and the DSS, and *T* indicates that the table/file is the target decision support table. The DSS development team can use this data to gauge the effect that the change to the operational system will have on the DSS, thereby reducing the amount of time required for the DSS team to modify the DSS. In addition, the likelihood of development errors is significantly reduced because the impact analysis identifies all programs affected by the change.

Impact analysis reports are available in a very wide variety of flavors. For example, the decision support team may want to analyze how the *sales amount* field in the marketing data mart is being populated. Figure 1.24 illustrates an impact analysis report showing all of the systems, tables/files, programs, and fields used to populate the *sales amount* field in the marketing data mart.

Impact analysis reporting minimizes the costs of the system enhancement and helps to reduce the propensity of new development errors (see Table 1.8).

The decision support team should be able to limit the amount of information contained in the impact analysis by performing record selection on the following report attributes:

Question: Show all systems, tables/files, programs, and fields used to populate the "Sale_Amount" field in the "DM_Marketing" data mart.

Impact Analysis Report						January 7, 2000
DSS System	DSS Table	Impact Field	Program Impacted	Tables/Files Impacted	Table Type	Fields Impacted
DM_Marketing	SALES	Sale_Amount	DW_ORDERS_PR01	ORDERS	S	LINE_AMOUNT
						LINE_QUANTITY
						LINE_DISCOUNT
				I01_ORDERS	I	LINE_AMOUNT
						LINE_QUANTITY
						LINE_DISCOUNT
			DW_ORDERS_PR02	I01_ORDERS	I	LINE_AMOUNT
						LINE_QUANTITY
						LINE_DISCOUNT
				DW_ORDERS	T	LINE_AMOUNT
						LINE_QUANTITY
						LINE_DISCOUNT
			DM_SALES_PR01	DW_ORDERS	T	LINE_AMOUNT
						LINE_QUANTITY
						LINE_DISCOUNT

Figure 1.24 Meta data ROI–decision support impact analysis sample field population report.

- Source system
- Source system table
- Source system field
- DSS table
- DSS field
- Table type

Enterprise-Wide Impact Analysis

Enterprise-wide impact analysis expands the scope of DSS impact analysis to include all of a company's IT systems, not just those involved in the decision support process. We've separated these two topics because it is much easier for a company to build a meta data repository that stores meta data on the DSS. This is because these systems are relatively new and, as such, typically use advanced design and technology, as compared to older operational systems. However, meta data is every bit as important to the older systems as it is to our newer ones.

Understanding the system-wide impact of a major IT change requires a careful analysis of the current operational and decision support systems. A

Table 1.8 Meta Data ROI—Decision Support Impact Analysis

BUSINESS/TECHNICAL VALUE	ROI MEASURES
Reduction of IT related problems	IT staff much less likely to make programming errors when making system enhancements, since all affected programs, tables/files, and fields are identified
Reduce IT development lifecycles and costs	IT development lifecycles are greatly reduced, since all affected programs, tables/files, and fields are identified
Reduce redundant data	IT staff can identify redundant data in systems, and reduce the likelihood of building redundant systems or populating systems with redundant data
Reduce redundant processes	IT staff can identify redundant processes in systems, and reduce the likelihood of building redundant system processes in the first place
Reduce impact of employee turnover	Documents the knowledge that may otherwise be known only by the developer who built the programs, and makes it available to the entire IT staff
Improved system performance	Removes redundant data and processes, thereby improving system performance

meta data repository can significantly reduce both the cost and time frame required for this effort by storing complete documentation on the data transformation rules, data sources, data structures, and the context of the data in the data warehouse and data marts. This information is critical because without the repository, the transformation rules may exist only in the staff's memory. Meta data helps the analysts to understand the effect of proposed changes to the decision support system's environment, thereby reducing the costs of future releases and helping to reduce the likelihood of new development errors (see Table 1.9). For example, let's suppose that a company wants to expand the length of its customer number field to a 30-byte alphanumeric value throughout all of its systems. Figure 1.25 presents an enterprise-wide impact analysis report listing all of the systems, tables/files, fields, and their domains affected by a change to the length of all occurrences of the customer number field. This report clearly identifies those systems and fields that cannot handle a 30-byte alphanumeric.

A meta data repository enables the IT development staff to run a technical impact analysis report across all corporate systems stored in the repos-

Question: Show all systems, tables/files, fields, and their domains impacted by a change to the length of all occurrences of the Customer_Number field.

Impact Analysis Report				January 7, 2000
Field	System	Tables/Files	Fields	Domain
Customer Number	Order Entry	CUSTOMER_BILL_TO	CUST_NAME	Alphanumeric 20
		CUSTOMER_SELL_TO	CUST_NAME	Alphanumeric 20
		CUSTOMER_SHIP_TO	CUST_NAME	Alphanumeric 20
		ORDER_HEADER	CUST_NAME	Alphanumeric 20
		ORDER_DETAIL	CUST_NAME	Alphanumeric 20
	General Ledger	CUSTOMER	Cust_Name	Alphanumeric 35
		EXPENSES	Cust_Name	Alphanumeric 35
		CUST_ACCOUNTS	Cust_Name	Alphanumeric 35
	Data Warehouse	DW_CUSTOMER	Cust_Name	Alphanumeric 20
		I01_CUSTOMER	Cust_Name	Alphanumeric 20
		I02_CUSTOMER	Cust_Name	Alphanumeric 20
		I03_CUSTOMER	Cust_Name	Alphanumeric 20
	Data Mart - Marketing	DM_CUSTOMER	DM_Cust_Name	Alphanumeric 20
		I01_DM_CUSTOMER	DM_Cust_Name	Alphanumeric 20
		I02_DM_CUSTOMER	DM_Cust_Name	Alphanumeric 20

Figure 1.25 Sample enterprise-wide impact analysis report.

itory. This type of functionality is critical for any company trying to ensure that its IT systems are sufficiently flexible and maintainable to support its ever-changing business information needs.

Like DSS impact analysis reports, enterprise-wide impact analysis reports are generally quite technical. This isn't a problem because they are used primarily by the IT staff that supports the company's information systems. The IT staff should be able to limit the amount of information on the impact analysis reports by having record selection on the following report attributes:

- System
- System table
- System field
- Table type

Enterprise-wide impact analysis reports provide a company with the system flexibility to meet its current and future businesses needs. This functionality is important to many people within the organization, including project managers, database administrators, programmers, data modelers, and business analysts.

Table 1.9 Meta Data ROI—Enterprise-Wide Impact Analysis

BUSINESS/TECHNICAL VALUE	ROI MEASURES
Reduction of IT-related problems	IT staff much less likely to make programming errors when making system enhancements, since all affected programs, tables/files, and fields are identified
Reduce IT development lifecycles and costs	IT development lifecycles are significantly reduced, because all affected programs, tables/files, and fields are identified
Reduce redundant data	IT staff can identify redundant data in their systems and reduce the likelihood of building redundant systems containing redundant data in the first place
Reduce redundant processes	IT staff can identify redundant processes in their systems and reduce the likelihood of building redundant system processes in the first place
Reduce impact of employee turnover	Documents the knowledge that may otherwise be known only by the developers who built the programs, and makes it available to the entire IT staff
Improved system performance	As redundant data and processes are removed the performance of the system is vastly improved

Successful business executives realize that knowledge is one of the primary factors that differentiate companies in the information age. Meta data is all about knowledge, and capturing and using it. With meta data and a meta data repository, companies can move from the crawling stage of IT development to the walking stage. The next chapter illustrates the fundamental concepts of meta data that we will use throughout the remainder of the book.

Meta Data Fundamentals

This chapter defines the fundamental concepts of meta data that are at the core of this book. These concepts, which include a meta data repository, business and technical meta data, meta data users, and meta data security, are important for understanding what meta data is and how companies can use it effectively. In addition, this chapter identifies structured and unstructured sources of meta data.

Meta Data and the Meta Data Repository

While the concept of meta data is not new; meta data's role and importance in the decision support environment certainly is. Because meta data captures the historical changes to the data in decision support systems, it enables companies to trace those changes over time and understand both the origins of the data and the trends that shape their business decisions.

For the purposes of this book, we use the term *meta data repository* to refer to the physical database tables that contain the meta data. A meta data repository supports every phase of development of an IT system, from requirements gathering, data model design, data mapping, user access, and data warehouse maintenance through future development and historical data needs definition.

We've all heard that meta data is "data about data," which is a simple enough definition—but what exactly does that mean? To understand meta data's vital role in the data warehouse, consider the purpose of a card catalog in a library (see Figure 2.1). The card catalog identifies what books are in the library and where they are physically located. It can be searched by subject area, author, or title. By showing the author, number of pages, publication date, and revision history of each book, the card catalog helps you determine which books will satisfy your needs. Without the central card catalog information system, finding books in the library would be a cumbersome and time-consuming chore.

Meta data is the card catalog in a data warehouse. By defining the contents of a data warehouse, meta data helps users locate relevant information for analysis. In addition, meta data enables users to trace data from the data warehouse to its operational source (i.e., drill-down) and to related data in other subject areas (i.e., drill-across). By managing the structure of the data over a broad spectrum of time, it provides a context for interpreting the meaning of the information. As meta data is extracted and stored over several years, snapshots of the data exist for each year. To accomplish this, though, the meta model tables need to be captured with a *From* and *To* date on each column. These allows users to easily trace back through the repository to past versions of the meta data.

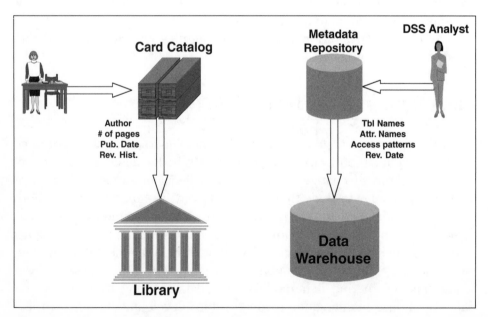

Figure 2.1 Meta data repository and card catalog parallel.

The concept and language of meta data originated in operational systems. However, since operational systems contain a single, correct definition of data, the need for meta data is not as relevant. Decision support systems, on the other hand, contain historical data, which in turn contains multiple structures and content that change over a period of time (see Figure 2.2). Since it is common for a user of the decision support system to look at data over a broad spectrum of time, it is important to understand what changes have occurred, and when. Meta data provides this information.

Technical and Business Meta Data

A meta data repository contains two types of meta data: technical and business. *Technical meta data* is meta data that supports a company's technical users and IT staff, whereas *business meta data* is meta data that supports a company's business users.

Technical meta data provides developers and technical users with information about their decision support and operational systems that they will need in order to maintain and grow these systems over time. If, for example, the company needs to reconfigure its geographic sales regions, the IT managers can use the technical meta data to list all of the programs, tables, and

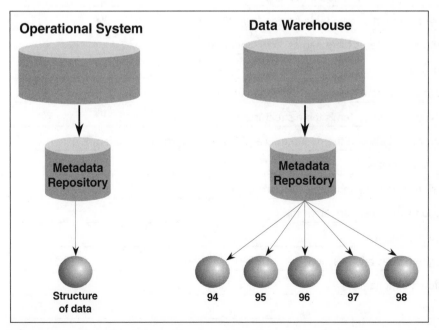

Figure 2.2 Operational versus data warehouse meta data requirements.

systems that contain geographic sales data. This information enables the managers to better and more quickly estimate the amount of development resources and time that their team will need to make the changes. It also helps the managers to identify any other systems that are likely to be affected by the change and bring those managers into the project. The IT developers then use other technical meta data to identify specific lines of

Table 2.1 Examples of Technical Meta Data

EXAMPLES OF TECHNICAL META DATA
User report and query access patterns, frequency, and execution time
Audit controls and balancing information
Technical structure of data
System of record feeding the decision support system
Identification of source system fields
Mappings and transformations from the operational system(s) of record to the decision support system
Encoding/reference table conversions
Data models, both physical and logical
Decision support system table names, keys, and indexes
Operational systems table names, keys, and indexes
Domain values
Operational system's table structures and attributes
Decision support system's table structures and attributes
Relationship between the data model and the decision support system
History of extracts
Decision support system table access patterns
Decision support system archiving
Job dependencies
Program names and descriptions
Version maintenance
Security
Purge criteria

Table 2.2 Examples of Business Meta Data

EXAMPLES OF BUSINESS META DATA
Structure of data as known to the business analyst (product hierarchy may have a meaning to the business user that differs from the IT developer)
Common access routines for the information in the decision support system
Subject areas (e.g., product, sales, customer, etc.)
Business definitions for table names ("CUST" table would become "Active customers that have placed orders in the past two years")
Attribute names and definitions in business terms
Data quality statistics
Decision support system field mappings, transformations, and summarization
Rules for drill-down, drill-up, drill-across, and drill-through
Domain values
Data stewards (who owns the data)
Data location
Decision support system refresh dates

code that will need to be changed to implement the new geographic sales regions. In this way, technical meta data is absolutely critical for maintaining and growing our information systems. It helps the IT staff to plan for additional releases of the decision support and operational systems and helps the developers to actually implement those changes. Without it, the task of analyzing and implementing such changes becomes significantly more difficult and time consuming. (See Table 2.1 for a list of examples of technical meta data.)

Business meta data supports the business users of the operational and decision support systems. Business meta data provides the decision support analysts with a road map for access to the information in the decision support system's underlying data warehouses and data marts. Business users are usually executives or business analysts and tend to be relatively nontechnical, so they need to have the decision support system defined in the business terms that they understand. If, for example, an executive in the sales department wants to look at sales dollars, by product category, by geographic sales region, the business meta data lets him or her locate the various decision support reports that contain this information. The sales executive can then choose the report that best suits his or her needs. For a graphic walk through this process, see the "Meta Data–Driven Business User Interface" section in Chapter 1. In essence, business meta data gives business users a greater understanding of the information in the decision support system and thereby increases their confidence in the data. (Table 2.2 lists examples of business meta data.)

Meta Data and External Data

External data is brought into a company from an outside source, and may come into a decision support or operational system in electronic form (e.g., Dun & Bradstreet and Dow Jones reports) or in nonelectronic form (e.g., white papers, magazine articles, or reports). Companies typically have little control over external data sources, but they do need to capture meta data from the external sources that describes the incoming data, including the following:

- Document ID
- Date of entry into the decision support and/or operational system
- Source of the external data
- Classification of the external data (e.g., marketing, financial, etc.)
- Index words
- Purge date
- Physical location reference
- Length of the external data

Meta Data Users

Meta data users fall into three broad categories: business users, technical users, and power users (see Figure 2.3). All of these groups contain a variety of decision support and operational users and all need meta data to identify and effectively use the information in their company's systems.

Business Users

The majority of business users are not very technical. They typically have a business background and get the information they need from the decision support system's predefined queries and reports. These users typically need

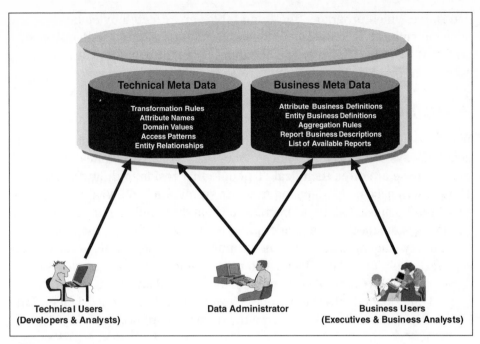

Figure 2.3 Meta data users.

meta data that enables them to identify and locate information in the decision support system, such as business names, definitions of the decision support tables and columns, and descriptions of existing reports. In addition, many business users are interested in receiving estimates of query and report execution times in order to decide if they want to run their query/report. Common examples of these users include:

- Marketing analysts
- Sales analysts
- Financial decision makers

Technical Users

Technical users, like business users, fill many roles within an organization. They may be programmers, data acquisition developers, data access developers, data modelers, senior analysts, or members of the meta data repository team. The IT staff that builds, maintains, and administers the decision support and operational systems use the meta data differently than do business users. They need to understand how the programs extract, transform, and load the data into the data warehouse and data marts. They need to determine which programs, files, and tables are affected by changes to the decision support system. The technical meta data allows the decision support staff to more efficiently and accurately plan for additional development releases of the decision support system.

Power Users

While the majority of business users are not particularly technical, there are nearly always some power business users that are more technically inclined. In fact, these are often technical IT people that reside in the business area. These users access the decision support system on a regular basis, understand the business data, and become intimately familiar with the decision support system tables. They understand relational database concepts, structured query language (SQL), and use sophisticated query tools in the normal course of their jobs. These users also need to understand any changes in the decision support system content, and how the data is extracted, transformed, and loaded into the warehouse so they will have confidence in the information results they derive from the decision support system.

Common Meta Data Sources

One of the biggest challenges with meta data is that it exists in many different sources, and each source has its own meta data repository. While many vendors market their tools as *meta data solutions*, in reality most of the tools are *sources* of meta data rather than solutions. The exception to this rule has traditionally been ETL (extraction, transformation, and load) technology; some ETL tools do have a repository, which can be a meta data solution if the repository has a very limited scope. These tools tend to have limited functionality because typically they can only bring in meta data that comes from other software vendors that they have formed alliances with. When it comes to loading meta data from a source other than these vendors' partners, these tools tend to fall short. As a result, any company that uses an ETL tool's meta data repository technology should understand that it will eventually need to move away from that tool and into a full-scale meta data integration tool (see Chapter 4, Understanding and Evaluating Meta Data Tools). Table 2.3 lists the most common sources of meta data by location.

ETL Tools

ETL tools extract data from operational sources, clean it, transform it, and load it into a decision support system's operational data store, data ware-

Table 2.3 Meta Data Locations and Types

COMMON META DATA LOCATIONS	TYPES OF META DATA
ETL tool/process	Data transformation rules Program job dependencies Decision support system balancing statistics Decision support system load statistics Data lineage
Data modeling tools	Logical and physical data models Technical entity definitions Technical attribute definitions Domain values
Reporting tools	User access patterns Report execution time Business entity definitions Business attribute definitions Business metric definitions
Data quality tools	Data quality statistics Audit controls
Vendor applications	Logical and physical data models Data dictionary
Documents	Business policies Business entity definitions Business attribute definitions Business metric definitions Data stewardship
Employees	Business policies Business entity definitions Business attribute definitions Data stewardship Data lineage

house, or data marts. These tools simplify the largest decision support task, that of data integration, which accounts for 75 percent of the work in a decision support system. The ETL process generates some of the meta data that is most valuable to the technical and power users.

Although ETL tools do a fairly good job of automatically capturing meta data, there are two caveats to consider. First, as the decision support developers use these tools, there are quite a few fields that they will not be required to enter as they build their ETL processes. But the more time that these developers take to enter meaningful values into these fields, the better the meta data will be. Second, these tools have gaps in the meta data that they capture. For example, each of these tools allows the developer to write a custom program, typically called a *user exit*, that the tool can call. Any processes that this program executes are not reflected in the tool's meta data. Decision support developers should be careful to limit the processes in the user exit to only those tasks that the ETL tool does not have the ability to perform.

Examples of ETL tools include:

- Ardent DataStage
- Evolutionary Technologies, Inc. (ETI) Extract
- Informatica Powermart
- Sagent Solution
- SAS Institute

Data Modeling Tools

Data modeling tools assist in logical data and process modeling as well as physical database and system design. These tools enable companies to capture the data requirements of the business, including many of the business rules, that should be incorporated into the meta data repository. It is important to note, however, that companies use these tools differently, which affects the meta data that is actually available in the repository. One company, for example, may store physical models, logical models, indexes, business table definitions, business attribute definitions, and attribute domain values in its data modeling tool. This company would accumulate a wealth of valuable meta data in its data modeling tool. Another company, however, may choose to store only physical data models in its modeling tool, which would result in a repository with much less valuable meta data.

Examples of data modeling tools include:

- Oracle Designer 2000
- Platinum Erwin (at the time of this writing, Computer Associates, which owns Platinum Technologies, has indicated its intention to retain the Platinum name)
- Silverrun

Reporting Tools

When we refer to *reporting tools*, we are speaking about the tools that business users work with in their decision support system. These tools provide access to the underlying data warehouse and data marts, eliminating the need to manually write SQL code. Many reporting tools feature a point-and-click graphical user interface (GUI) that insulates the users from most of the complexities of the decision support system's database.

Although some tools are quite limited in their functionality and are not able to handle complex queries, most allow users to create libraries of predefined queries that they can invoke as necessary. This eliminates the need for most users to write their own queries. In addition, most reporting tools are available in a *Web version* that can be launched from a Web site. This is particularly useful for applications that need remote, extranet access. Many of these tools also have multidimensional capabilities that permit users to analyze the data along multiple dimensions such as customer, time, region, and product. They share all of the features of the query tools and provide additional functions that enable users to slice and dice the data. By *slice and dice,* I mean that users can interactively change the dimensions on a report or query.

Reporting tools are often used to access the data in the meta data repository and enable users to collect information (i.e., meta data) about which meta data in the repository is most frequently used. This meta-meta data (i.e., meta data about meta data) can then be fed back into the repository. Examples of reporting tool software vendors include:

- Brio
- Business Objects
- Cognos
- Hummingbird
- Information Advantage
- Microsoft
- Microstrategy

Data Quality Tools

Data quality tools analyze the source data for noncompliant data values. Noncompliant data values include data that does not match expected data characteristics (e.g., a character value in a numeric field), data outside of acceptable ranges, data that is inconsistent with valid values, data that does not conform to business rules, or inconsistent address data (e.g., Chicago, Il). The task of cleaning data is a highly complex one. Companies often hand code this logic or use an ETL tool to build it. Data quality tools are designed to vastly simplify the common cleansing tasks such as name and address cleansing.

The meta data about the data cleansing activities is very valuable to the repository. Unfortunately, however, the data quality tool vendors have not done nearly as good a job as the ETL vendors have in capturing this meta data and making it available to a meta data repository. Often data quality tools have only limited capabilities for extracting meta data from them. Users must generally perform a significant amount of manipulation in these tools to put the meta data into a form that can be useful to the repository.

Examples of data quality tools include:

- i.d. Centric
- Trillium
- Vality

Vendor Applications

Meta data often exists in third-party applications such as customer relationship management (CRM) systems, various types of e-business applications, Enterprise Resource Planning (ERP) systems, campaign management systems, and health care systems.

While the meta data can differ widely across these applications, there do tend to be some common threads. First, these applications contain a great deal of valuable meta data, including physical table/attribute names, domain values, and business rules. Second, most of these applications use proprietary databases rather than open relational databases such as Oracle, Informix, SQL Server, or IBM DB2. As a result, extracting meta data from these applications and preparing it for the repository is generally quite difficult. In addition, custom coding is generally required because the meta data integration tools cannot directly read from these sources. Examples of vendor application tools include:

- Peoplesoft
- SAP
- Siebol Systems

Miscellaneous Sources

There are two other important but easily overlooked sources of meta data in most companies: documents and employees.

A wide variety of company documents contain important meta data. I've often found valuable meta data in corporate procedures, competitor write-ups, handbooks, and white papers. Typically, this type of meta data exists in Microsoft Word documents, Excel spreadsheets, or on internal or external Web sites.

A company's employees may prove to be its most vital source of meta data. Employees know all of the tricks that the systems don't necessarily tell you and are often the only source for the vast majority of the business meta data. For example, I have worked at several large consumer electronics manufacturing companies that tend to ship 80 percent of their products during the last week of a month. Although this fact is critical for managing the business, it is not something that is readily apparent from studying the information systems.

While employees possess a vast amount of valuable meta data, they are also the most difficult source from which to extract this information. Unfortunately, there is no easy way to extract meta data from employees. The process—which is largely one of identifying key employees and interviewing them to elicit their internal knowledge of business operations—is definitely challenging, but likely to be worth the effort if done correctly, as I discuss later in this chapter in "Unstructured Meta Data Sources."

Structured and Unstructured Meta Data

An organization's technical and business meta data comes from two broad sources: structured and unstructured.

Structured Meta Data Sources

Structured meta data sources are those that the organization's decision makers have discussed, documented, and agreed upon. Meta data from these sources is commonly stored in tools or documents that are maintained, distributed, and recognized throughout the organization. Structured meta data sources populate both technical and business meta data, as the examples listed in Table 2.4 illustrate.

Unstructured Meta Data Sources

Unstructured meta data sources are those that fall outside of standard models and tools. Much of this information is unwritten; it consists of the information that people "just know" and is generally located in the "company consciousness." It may even exist as a Post-It note on a key employee's

Table 2.4 Examples of Structured Meta Data Sources

SOURCE OF STRUCTURED META DATA	COMMON LOCATIONS
Extraction/Transformation tools	Informatica Powermart, Ardent DataStage, ETI Extract, programs and SQL
Logical and physical data models	Data modeling tools (Erwin, PowerDesigner, Silverrun) and vendor applications (SAP, Peoplesoft)
Business policies	Microsoft Word, Microsoft Excel
Data dictionary	Data modeling tools, Microsoft Access, Microsoft Excel

desk, or on a Web site. In fact, most information on the Web is pretty unstructured. Unstructured meta data is often found in business policies, competitor information, and business rules. Because unstructured meta data sources are generally business-related, they are key to compiling good business meta data.

Unstructured meta data sources are not formally documented or agreed upon, but the knowledge derived from these sources is every bit as valuable as that from the structured meta data sources. Capturing meta data from the many and varied unstructured sources is, however, considerably more challenging than capturing meta data from structured sources. Meta data derived from unstructured sources must be documented, formalized, and accurately reflected in the decision support system. In this respect, an unstructured source is transformed to a structured source. Although organizations differ widely and have many unstructured sources of meta data, the following list suggests some of the unstructured sources that warrant consideration:

- Data stewardship (which we discuss later in this chapter)
- Decision support load and refresh history (see Chapter 8, Implementing Data Quality through Meta Data, for a detailed discussion on this topic)
- Business rules
- Business definitions
- Naming conventions
- Competitor product lists
- Some transformations and summarizations

Data Stewardship

Data is the most important asset of any business, but in order for data to have value, it must be delivered promptly, concisely, and accurately, and be formatted in a way that it can be used. Preparing data (that is, cleansing it and integrating it) is a crucial step in constructing a decision support system, and data stewards play a key role in this task.

A data steward acts as the conduit between IT and the business users, aligning the business needs with the IT systems that support them—both decision support and operational. Among other things, data stewards ensure that companies use their data effectively and to its fullest capacity. The goal of data stewardship is to improve the accessibility, reusability, and most important, the quality of the data. Table 2.5 lists data stewardship responsibilities.

Typically, a data steward is assigned to a specific subject area of a company (e.g., customer, product, order, market segment, etc). In some situations, however, an individual may be the data steward for multiple subject areas, or multiple data stewards may be needed for the same subject area. For example, the marketing department may have a completely different definition of customer than the manufacturing department has. As a result, they may require different data stewards.

While a specific data steward needs to have responsibility for specific data, it is generally advisable for the data steward to work with a defined group of key employees that represent all of the facets of the assigned subject area. This group of peers is responsible for working with the data steward on the tasks listed in Table 2.5.

Table 2.5   Data Steward Responsibilities

TASKS
Assigning and maintaining business entity/attribute definitions
Creating and maintaining business naming standards
Defining business rules
Establishing data quality metrics
Creating and maintaining purge and archive rules
Developing business metrics and derivations
Enforcing data security rules
Assigning data aliases

The meta data project leader should initially work with all of the data stewards in an organization, at least until one of the stewards can assume leadership of the stewardship group. In situations where it is not politically wise to have stewards from one department reporting to a steward in another department, the meta data project leader should retain leadership of the data stewardship function.

Identifying Your Data Steward

When I talk about data stewardship, I am often asked two questions: "How do you identify a data steward?" and "We don't have anyone that has sufficient knowledge to do that job. What should we do?" The answer to both questions is the same . . . You *already* have your data stewards. All companies have people that we turn to when we have a question about our customers, products, services, and so forth. These people are our data stewards; most companies just don't formally identify them as such. However, more and more companies are beginning to recognize the critical role that stewardship serves in the overall quest for high-quality, readily available data. Data stewards, whether they are formally recognized as such or not, are critical as information resources for the companies' knowledge workers and operational staffers. Just as the demand for better systems has increased, so too has the need for data stewardship.

Data stewards are typically subject matter experts who come from the business side of the house. They need to have a thorough understanding of how the company works and be well-respected by the business user community. In addition, data stewards must have excellent communication skills. These skills are sometimes overlooked—but they are crucial because data stewards need to work effectively with people from a variety of departments, with a variety of needs and points of view. When push comes to shove, the data steward is responsible for forging agreements between differing factions.

Meta Data Security

Security is vitally important for all aspects of meta data and the associated data warehouse, but all too often companies consider meta data security too late (i.e., after the meta data has been compromised) or in the final stages of the data warehouse development process. It is important to remember that the meta data contains highly sensitive, proprietary information about the underlying data warehouse and the business that it is describing. If this data were to fall into the wrong hands, such as a business competitor, the results could be disastrous.

Meta data security is most likely to be compromised in either of two places. The first area of vulnerability is the physical location where the data is actually stored. For example, a competent thief can access a meta data repository by accessing the physical file that the data is stored in, bypassing all RDBMS security measures. The second area of vulnerability is the data transmission between platforms, such as the data transfer between an MVS (multiple virtual storage) mainframe and a UNIX workstation. Again, a competent thief can intercept the transmission and use the data.

So, planning a security system that integrates tightly with that of the decision support system and communications system is crucial. There are several ways in which to implement such a system—all of which should be considered early in the development phase. There are two prevailing philosophies of meta data security: (1) *proactive* security, which prevents unwanted access before it occurs, and (2) *reactive* security, which audits access on a continual basis to check what accesses have occurred. The sensitivity of the meta data determines the type and extent of security that is required.

In the next chapter we examine the current state of meta data and its marketplace. To accomplish this, we will review the forces driving the meta data industry today and provide an overview of the numerous factors that affect virtually all meta data repository development efforts.

## CHAPTER 3

Meta Data Standards

In this chapter we discuss why the meta data industry needs a standard meta model of the repository. (The term *meta model* refers to the physical data model, either object or relational, that stores the meta data.) We then examine the efforts of two vendor-driven groups—the Meta Data Coalition (MDC) and the Object Management Group (OMG)—to make a meta model standard a reality. These two groups have some very different concepts regarding a meta model, possibly because of the driving forces behind them; the MDC is backed by Microsoft while the OMG is fueled by Oracle. Lastly, we examine XML and its implications for the meta data arena. All of these initiatives are changing the meta data landscape faster than ever before. Anyone involved with IT needs to follow these developments closely because they are changing the way in which we build and integrate computer systems.

Why Are Meta Model Standards Important?

Storing meta data in a standard meta model is crucial for resolving many of the IT challenges that exist in businesses today. Standard meta data models accomplish two important goals:

- Tool meta data sharing
- Tool interoperability

Tool Meta Data Sharing

It would be wonderful to say that tools available today are able to seamlessly integrate all of your company's sources of meta data into one integrated and architected repository. Unfortunately, that utopia just doesn't exist. Today's meta data integration architecture does not involve seamlessly integrated products, but rather a series of proprietary vendor products attached to one another with the IT equivalent of chewing gum, string, and paper clips (see Chapter 7, Constructing a Meta Data Architecture). Most companies purchase best-of-breed tools for use in their decision support projects rather than purchasing integrated tool suites. While this is a sound concept for building a decision support system, it does present some technical challenges. Because best-of-breed tools are not typically integrated with one another, they do not easily communicate data to each other, if at all. Even those tools that can be integrated generally require a good deal of resource-intensive, manual programming to get them to share data. Figure 3.1 illustrates the interfaces that may need to be built to integrate best-of-breed tools in a decision support environment.

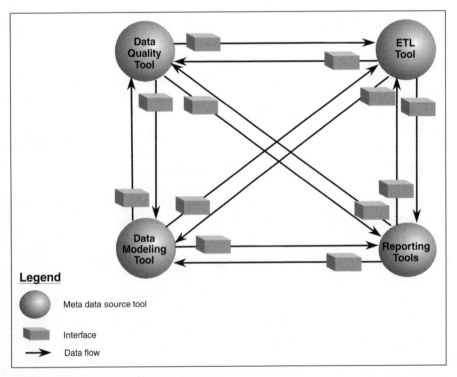

Figure 3.1   Best-of-breed tool interfaces.

To build these interfaces, quite often tool vendors form alliances with other vendors that offer complementary products. While these alliances are certainly valuable, they typically do not provide complete meta data sharing between the tools. This is because it is very difficult for these tool vendors to keep their interfaces up-to-date with each version of their software and with each version of the alliance vendor's software.

Once a meta model standard is established and widely adopted, the number of interfaces needed to allow these best-of-breed tools to share data will be significantly reduced. In fact, it should be reduced enough to allow tool vendors to make these interfaces a standard feature of their tools. (See Figure 3.2 for an illustration of this future architecture.)

Sharing meta data among various repositories and software tools is particularly desirable for global enterprises with dispersed teams using an integrated computing approach to solving similar or related data analysis problems. In such enterprises, coordination is largely dependent on network computing and effective use of knowledge and resources developed by the various teams. The ability to share meta data within and across repositories is extremely important as the repositories become interdependent. Like any

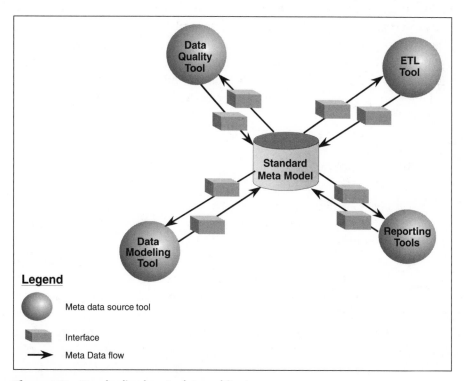

Figure 3.2 Standardized meta data architecture.

other integrated approach to collaboration, information sharing must be managed so as to minimize the duplication of effort while efficiently and accurately capturing and propagating changes to shared information.

Complex software applications such as customer relationship management and decision support generally involve many types of data obtained from a wide range of sources and transformed for various groups with different data needs. Until a meta model standard is established and widely adopted, companies will continue to need an integration strategy to bring the various sources of meta data together. This issue of tool data sharing is a major mitigating factor that has prevented some organizations from achieving successful DSS implementations.

Tool Interoperability

A standard meta model will allow vendor tools to plug into the model to support bidirectional meta data. Today, achieving bidirectional meta data is a very challenging task (which we discuss in some detail in Chapter 7, Constructing a Meta Data Architecture). *Bidirectional* meta data refers to meta data that can be changed in the repository, then fed back into third-party decision support (and potentially other) tools. For example, if a user goes through the repository and changes the name of an attribute in one of the DSS data marts, this change would be fed back into the data modeling tool to update the physical data model for that specific data mart. When meta data is bidirectional, we will be able to manage all of the tools from a centralized data repository, thereby creating true tool interoperability (as illustrated in Figure 3.3).

Meta Model Standards

After several years of disjointed efforts by various alliances and organizations, two major initiatives hold the promise of finally developing a meta model standard capable of resolving this need. The efforts, both of which aim to define an industry standard version of the meta models, would—if successful—enable decision support products from different vendors to share data and information. This, in turn, would provide the data warehousing market with an open, common infrastructure across all data warehouse tool vendors. These two initiatives have brought us closer than ever before to a unified standard for meta data definition and interchange.

The first of these two efforts is the Open Information Model (OIM) from the Meta Data Coalition. This effort was originally spearheaded by Microsoft

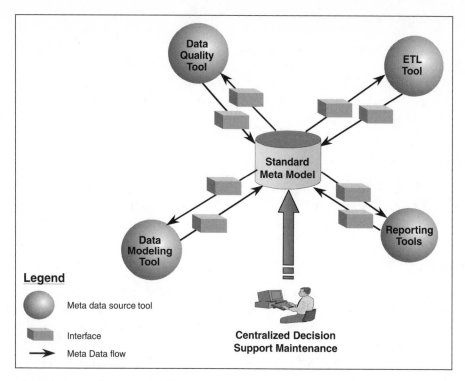

Figure 3.3   Tool interoperability.

and later signed over to the MDC. The second effort was initiated by Oracle, IBM, Hyperion, Unisys, and NCR, and subsequently handed off to the Object Management Group. Before examining these two initiatives, let's first take a look at what makes a good standard in the first place.

What Constitutes a Good Standard?

Many factors contribute to a good standard, and certainly, there is some disagreement within IT as to exactly what those factors are. However, nearly everyone agrees that a standard should be independent of any specific technology, platform, or vendor implementation. These factors are paramount to a good meta model standard.

To be successful (i.e., widely adopted and implemented), the meta model standard must be developed in collaboration with a majority of key software vendors. Just what constitutes a majority of key vendors, however, is also open to interpretation, and the two groups (MDC and OMG) currently attempting to develop such a standard are likely to have very different interpretations.

Technology-Independent

A sound meta model standard should not be based on any specific technology or be required to be implemented on any specific platform. For example, the standard should be able to be implemented on a mainframe, Unix, or Windows NT environment, with nothing more than minimal environment-specific tweaks to the models.

Vendor Neutral

The standard for the meta model must be developed in collaboration with all of the key software vendors. In addition, and most important, the standard must not be designed with any specific vendor in mind.

Realistic In Scope

One of the mistakes that many of the early meta data standards efforts made was trying to be all-encompassing. These efforts spent so much time trying to capture every kind of meta data imaginable that they never could get their standard off the ground. A good standard goes after the big 95 percent of the common meta data that corporations need. That last 5 percent can take forever to accomplish.

Widely Implemented

The most important aspect of any standard is that it becomes widely implemented. More than any of the other factors on this list, the market has always dictated what standard becomes reality (e.g., Microsoft Windows and IBM OS2). No standard is valuable if it just stays on the drawing board.

Meta Data Coalition

The Meta Data Coalition is a not-for-profit corporation composed of approximately 50 industry-leading software vendors and user companies concerned with defining and implementing a meta data interchange format standard. This group, led by Microsoft, has worked for more than two years to define the de facto industry standard for the meta models. The result of this ongoing cooperative effort, the Open Information Model, is intended to be the standard meta model that will house meta data. Microsoft transferred the rights to the OIM to the MDC in 1998 but continues to play an active role in the MDC. To complement its meta model effort, the MDC is also attempting to create standard definitions for business rules and knowledge representation. These efforts are likely to go a long way toward alleviating the pain involved in creating a meta data infrastructure for data warehousing. In an attempt to garner industry-wide support for the OIM, the MDC has released the OIM to approximately 300 software companies for review and comment. To date, the OIM has garnered a wide array of industry endorsements.

The MDC is chartered to maintain and evolve the OIM as a technology-independent and vendor-neutral meta data standard, but the model is intended to extend beyond decision support. The MDC is attempting, over the long haul, to encompass component modeling, knowledge management, and application development in a series of models using SQL as a query language and XML as an interchange format between OIM-compliant repositories. In an early implementation of this effort, Microsoft currently ships OIM as standard with its SQL Server 7 and Visual Studio 6.0.

Evolution of OIM

The MDC released its own meta data standard, the Meta Data Interchange Specification, in 1997. Although MDIS (which uses an ASCII-based interchange format and specifies a lowest common denominator meta model) was a noteworthy attempt, it never gained sufficient industry-wide acceptance to become a standard. Because of this less-than-successful first effort, the MDC eagerly embraced the OIM as its next-generation meta model and interchange specification. A key difference between MDIS and OIM is that OIM provides programmatic access to a meta data repository, giving meta data the power to truly help organizations in their decision support efforts.

The primary purpose of OIM is to support vendor tool interoperability via a shared meta data model. OIM's submodels are grouped by subject area and can be customized. Each submodel is designed to encompass all phases of a project's development lifecycle, from analysis through deployment. Examples of OIM subject areas include Enterprise Resource Planning, online analytical processing (OLAP), data transformation services, and semantic information models. In addition, the MDC is currently reviewing three new models (all originally presented by Microsoft) intended to extend OIM:

Business engineering model.   Provides a means to formally document an organization's structure and processes

Business rule model.   Provides a means to capture, classify, and store business rules used in various applications and business processes

Knowledge description model.   Provides a thesaurus or common vocabulary for describing information contained in a taxonomy of end-user resources

The following section describes some of the specific OIM models in the standard.

Database Model

The Database Model describes information about data maintained in an enterprise's databases and provides mechanisms for extending the information model to support easier evolution. The goal of the Database Model is to make meta data readily available and to provide the infrastructure to enable enterprise-wide data management and tool interoperability.

The Database Model covers the basic elements of a SQL data provider, such as tables, columns, and relationships, and includes a modest amount of deployment information for locating a data provider in a network. It does not, however, address most physical or implementation details.

Through OLE DB, meta data from any relational database can be imported into the Database Model through a single interface. Examples include Microsoft Access, Excel, and Plato.

The Database Model provides mechanisms for extending the meta model to enable easier customization. A set of published interfaces for manipulating the meta data is stored in the repository, independent of the on-disk storage format and completely transparent to the user. It is, essentially, a shared database that spans many database source descriptions, allowing the expression of relationships between different database schemas.

The interfaces of the repository completely encapsulate the stored information. This makes it possible to evolve data in response to information model changes, since tools depend only on the information model, not on the stored representation of data. It also enables vendors to tailor interfaces to support extensions, since extensions do not affect the interface to nonextended objects.

Database Transformation Model

Data warehouses and data marts derive their data from existing production, operational systems. Before this data can be loaded into a data warehouse or data mart, however, it must be integrated and transformed into information that has value to the business users and can be efficiently queried.

The Database Transformation Model, which is an extension of the Database Model, describes the transformations that occurred and the data sources that were accessed. This model is intended to enable sharing of meta data about transformation activities by making that information readily available in a standardized format for third-party ETL tools. This gives the customer a single place to view all of their warehouse transformations, regardless of which ETL tool is in use.

OLAP Model

OLAP is the area of decision support that focuses on the analysis of multi-dimensional data in a data warehouse setting. The OLAP Model supports sharing meta data across vendor tools and applications.

A multidimensional database stores information that is associated with a variety of dimension attributes, such as time, region, product type, and customer type. Such databases are typically used in a DSS setting, where users can explore summaries of the data across each dimension (e.g., total sales by region for each product type or total sales per quarter for each region). The user is essentially exploring a *data cube*, where each dimensional attribute defines one dimension of the cube.

The OLAP Model has several purposes. It provides a place for multidimensional tools to store their schema information, thereby giving the user a single place to view all multidimensional data, regardless of the tool. Database design tools, OLAP query tools, data transformation tools, and OLAP database engines all need schema information about multidimensional databases. The OLAP Model allows any of these applications to store this type of information for reuse or modification by other applications. The OLAP Model also allows the exchange of this multidimensional information.

The OLAP Model covers basic multidimensional schemas based on relational sources, and can be used to store information about MOLAP (multidimensional OLAP), ROLAP (relational OLAP), and HOLAP (hybrid OLAP) tools.

Legacy Model

The Legacy Model stores meta data about legacy system record definitions. These definitions can represent delimited files (like tab, space, and comma), legacy language definitions (e.g., COBOL and PL/I), and record layouts for databases used in legacy systems.

The primary purpose of this model is to allow data warehousing ETL tools to use common (i.e., nonrelational) legacy sources of data transformations. These sources are often sequential files, VSAM files, IMS, or IDMS, and are usually defined using legacy languages.

Semantic Model

The Semantic Model accommodates meta data from linguistic processors and tools that superimpose semantic models onto database schema. The Semantic Model is an extension of the Database Model.

With a semantic or linguistic processor, users can use the English language to interact with the data in databases without learning data manipulation languages. For example, a business user can ask the question, "Give me product sales, by region, by marketing campaign, over time." The linguistic processor takes this sentence and creates data manipulation language to extract the data from the supporting database schema in order to supply the information. The Semantic Model accommodates such English-to-schema mappings.

Because it describes information irrespective of any technology, semantic information is independent of any particular tool. Accordingly, the Semantic Model stores semantic information in a commonly agreed-upon format so that multiple tools can share this information and allows users to employ tools from different vendors. Further, because the Semantic Model inherits information from the Database Model, tools that understand the Database Model can view and access an instance type in the Semantic Model, even if they don't understand the types of the Semantic Model itself.

Object Management Group

The second major initiative to create a meta data model standard, the Object Management Group, was originated by Oracle, IBM, Unisys, NCR, and Hyperion. The meta model standard proposed by this group is the Common Warehousing Metadata (CWM). In early 1999 the group issued a request for proposal (RFP) calling for a decision support meta data standard that conforms with the OMG's Meta Object Facility (MOF), which is a framework for defining meta models, and a meta model interchange mechanism based on the XML Meta Data Interchange (XMI) specification. All responses to the RFP had to be submitted to the OMG by March 2000.

MOF is a subset of the Unified Modeling Language (UML) that defines a set of interface description language (IDL) mappings to meta models and a set of Common Object Request Broker Architecture (CORBA) interfaces that can be used to define and manipulate MOF-compliant meta models. The IDL interfaces automatically generate Java, COM, C, C++, COBOL, Smalltalk, and Ada interfaces to MOF-compliant meta data repositories. The interfaces enable users to automatically generate repository server implementations from MOF meta models or to support repository interoperability. MOF is presently restricted to providing meta data for CORBA-based systems, since the only defined way to interchange MOF meta data is through the CORBA interfaces produced by the MOF's IDL mapping. However, XMI's use of XML provides a way to lift this restriction. Furthermore, because the adopted OMG UML specification defines the UML meta model as a MOF meta model, the XMI proposal could also lead to a model interchange format for UML.

XMI uses the standard means in XML to describe elements and their attributes. In other words, every attribute of a MOF meta model class is represented in the Document Type Definition (DTD) by an XML element whose name is the attribute name. In turn, the attributes are listed in the content model of the XML element corresponding to the meta model class in the same order as they are declared in the MOF meta model. Each association between two meta model classes is represented by two XML elements that represent the roles of the association ends. The multiplicities of the association ends are in turn translated to the XML multiplicities that are valid for specifying the content models of XML elements.

XMI uses three optional attributes—xmi.id, xmi.label, and xmi.uuid—to identify the elements in a document. The id attribute must be unique within a document, but not necessarily unique globally. The uuid attribute, on the other hand, must be globally unique, while the label attribute is intended to hold a user-defined string with any desirable string. XMI requires the use of several XML attributes to enable XML elements to refer to other XML elements using the values of the these three attributes. These attributes allow XML elements to act as simple XLink or to hold a reference to an XML element in the same document using the XML IDREF mechanism.

In October 1998, a detailed specification of XIF was submitted to OMG for review. Shortly after the OMG committee ratified the specification, a group of OMG vendors, including IBM, NCR, and Oracle, demonstrated a prototype of an XIF-based software tool for exchanging UML-based meta data. In the near future, XIF is likely to gain momentum and product support among the non-Microsoft alliance.

The Bottom Line

Several years ago while I was speaking about meta data at a conference in Chicago, an attendee asked me if the latest committee-brokered meta data standard was likely to be successful. My response, then and now, is that a meta data standard will not be successful until one of the major players in the industry decides that such a standard is absolutely necessary. We need a 500-pound gorilla to get all of the vendors moving in the same direction. Microsoft's Open Information Model represents such an attempt.

We have to remember that no effort is perfect, and that no company is going to expend tremendous resources if it is not likely to reap a significant profit. To give credit where it is due, if it were not for Microsoft's participation in the arena, we would be unlikely to have a standard at all. In truth, Oracle and the other members of OMG did not give meta data a second thought until Microsoft recognized the need for a meta model standard. Whether Microsoft's standard is the best is irrelevant—Microsoft has made the meta data market a reality. For the first time, our industry will have a real standard for meta data.

The real question is whether we will have a single standard, two standards, or some combination of the evolving standards. Keep in mind that the oxymoron of two standards would not necessarily be a bad thing. Software vendors could without much difficulty create OIM–CWM interfaces that automatically bridge the two meta models.

I strongly urge, however, that the standards be merged for the good of our industry. A merged standard would accomplish several goals: It would allow both parties to claim victory for making a meta data standard a reality, and the decision support and IT industries would benefit because organizations would be able to efficiently manage their data warehouses and be able to better cost-justify further decision support development efforts. Increased business intelligence efforts translate to increased revenues for all of the software vendors.

The good news is that the MDC and OMG are making overtures to begin the process of aligning the competing standards. To foster this convergence, the OMG has become a member of MDC and vice versa. On the negative side, however, we hear grumbling from both sides; the MDC complains that the OMG standard requires the use of CORBA, and the OMG is gripes that the OIM requires the Component Object Model (COM). Of course, each side disputes the other's claim.

Despite the grumbling, I believe that the groups will eventually put their differences aside and do the right thing—create a single standard for decision support that is both platform and software independent. Maybe I'm too much of an optimist, but I know that the folks on both sides of this fence are highly intelligent people, and I believe that in the end they will do what is right.

The XML Standard

XML is a subset of SGML (Standard Generalized Markup Language), which attempts to define a universal standard for electronically exchanging data. XML maintains the important architectural aspects of contextual separation while removing nonessential features of SGML. Furthermore, XML is an open technology standard of the World Wide Web Consortium (W3C), the standards group responsible for maintaining and advancing HTML and other Web-related standards. This section discusses the potential uses of XML for exchanging meta data across a variety of software systems.

How XML Works

XML offers a text-based mechanism to represent the structure inherent in data in order to author and interpret that data unambiguously. It uses a tag-based approach similar to that of HTML to handle the presentation of the online content. However, because each XML tag name describes the characteristic of the data it specifies, XML is more flexible and extensible than HTML at handling the meta data associated with information content. The following examples, which describe information about a textbook, illustrate this concept. The first is in HTML and the second is in XML:

```
<HTML>
<BODY>
<TABLE>
  <TR>
    <TD>Building and Managing the Meta Data Repository</TD>
    <TD>David Marco</TD>
    <TD>2000<BR>John Wiley & Sons<BR>New York<BR>First Edition</TD>
  </TR>
</TABLE>
</BODY>
</HTML>


<?xml version="1.0"?>
<Book>
  <Name> Building and Managing the Meta Data Repository</Name>
  <Author>
    <Name> David Marco</Name>
  </Author>
  <Year>2000</Year>
  <Publisher> John Wiley & Sons</Publisher>
  <PubCity>New York</PubCity>
  <Edition>First</Edition>
</Book>
```

From these examples, it is clear that HTML is best-suited as a data presentation language, while XML is intended as a tree-based data representation language. In addition to content, each XML element (e.g., Author) may have attributes. An element's attributes are expressed in its opening tag as a list of name value pairs. So, the attributes of the element <Author> would be expressed as:

```
<Author xmx.label="bsj99"> David Marco </Author>
```

The attributes of an element can also be specified by means of the ATTLIST. Using our same example, the following DTD component specifies the optional (keyword #IMPLIED) xmx.label attribute of the Author element consisting of a character data string:

```
<!ATTLIST Book xmx.label CDATA #IMPLIED >
```

XML defines a special attribute called ID, which can be used as a unique identifier for an element within a document. The IDs can, in turn, be used for cross-referencing elements in an arbitrary way beyond the inherent tree-based structure of XML.

The Document Type Definition (DTD) provides a means by which an XML processor can validate the syntax and some of the semantics of an XML document (i.e., the various types of elements that a document can have and the kinds of element nesting that is permitted). Thus, we may have the following DTD declaration for our example:

```
<!Element Book (Name, Author, Year, Publisher, PubCity, Edition)>
```

Of course, a DTD grammar may be more complex than this if it includes, for instance, multiplicities, logical or, and the attribute types permitted for each element. DTDs are often stored in external files and referenced by the XML documents that use them by means of the Universal Resource Identifier (URI), such as:

```
"http://www.EWSolutions.com/xmx.dtd" or simply "file:xmx.dtd"
```

An XML document is *well-formed* if it conforms to the XML's tree-based (hierarchical) structure and its tags are properly nested. If the document also complies with a DTD grammar, it is called a *valid* XML document. The ultimate level of correctness for an XML document is *semantic correctness*, which applies if the data values for each label conform to some criteria that is domain-specific. For our book example, perhaps the values for the publisher label must be within an acceptable range (e.g., John Wiley & Sons). An XML document need not reference a DTD however, even if one exists. The resulting document can be processed more quickly, but at the cost of some loss of confidence in the quality of the document.

XML documents are processed by XML parsers that use XML rules along with any referenced DTD grammars. Such parsers are commercially available from major software vendors, such as IBM and Microsoft, and are part of the most recent releases of the major Web browser programs (e.g., Internet Explorer 5.0).

Unlike HTML, an XML document does not include presentation information. Instead, an XML document may be rendered for visual presentation by applying layout-style information with technologies such as XSL (Extensible Style Language). Web sites and browsers are rapidly adding XML and XSL to their functionality. Finally, DTD is being superseded by DCD (Document Content Definition), which is a proposal to provide data-type support and a new syntax for DTDs. DCD will help to provide richer meta data for data described by means of XML.

Why Use XML for Meta Data Exchange?

XML offers many advantages as a format for meta data exchange. These include:

- XML is already established as an open, platform-independent and vendor-independent standard by an international organization.

- XML supports the international character set standards of extended ISO Unicode.

- XML does not rely on any programming language or proprietary API, and a range of XML APIs are available to create, view, and integrate XML information. Leading XML APIs presently include DOM, SAX, and Web-DAV.

- The cost of entry for XML information providers is low. XML documents can even be created by hand using any text editor. In the future, XML-based WYSIWYG editors with support for XSL rendering will allow creation of XML documents.

- XML's tag structure and textual syntax are easy to read and are clearly superior to HTML for conveying structured information.

- The cost of entry for automatic XML document producers and consumers is low, with the set of available development tools already growing. Major computer vendors, including IBM, currently offer complete, free, commercially unrestricted XML parsers written in Java. A variety of other XML support tools, including implementations of the XML APIs, are available on the Internet.

XML does have two disadvantages that potential users need to be aware of. First, the meta data tags attached to the meta data add a significant amount of overhead to the meta data and to the meta data storage requirements. Second, users need to maintain a listing of the meta data tags, a task which can become problematic for companies that define their own custom tags.

XML-Based Initiatives
for Meta Data Exchange

Several key initiatives have already begun using XML for meta data exchange, further indicating the importance of this emerging standard. Two such initiatives are worth reviewing here: one spearheaded by Microsoft, and the other driven by the OMG.

Microsoft

Microsoft claims to be committed to XML as an open standard and provides support for it in versions 4.x and 5.x of its Internet Explorer Web browser. On the meta data front, Microsoft has proposed the XML Interchange Format (XIF) as the mechanism for exchanging meta data. XIF consists of a set of rules for encoding meta data objects described by OIM in XML. XIF can, in turn, be generated and parsed automatically from any implementation of OIM, which means that all import and export activity is driven by the meta model.

XIF uses various DTDs that correspond to different subject areas of OIM. DTD is not intended to describe higher-level semantic concepts (e.g., cardinality or multiple inheritance). XIF uses DTDs only for documentation purposes to make it easier for developers to understand the structure of an XML document. Furthermore, XIF ensures that all OIM instance information is represented as content, references between objects, and all OIM modeling and support information as begin/end tags and attributes of tags. This ensures that XML browsers and applications are able to process XIF documents, even if they do not understand the semantics expressed by the OIM.

The DTD grammar in turn uses various encoding concepts, such as Character Set and Element, for mapping the OIM interfaces, their properties, and their relationships to the corresponding XML-based syntax. This grammar also extends the standard XML syntax to handle the inheritance model across various subject areas of OIM. Furthermore, relationships and references are resolved by means of the required ID attribute of an element, which must be unique within an XML document.

Microsoft presently provides both an XIF importer and an XIF exporter as COM interfaces for the Microsoft Repository 2.1. These interfaces can be called from any program in C, C++, VB, or Java to import and export XML-based meta data into the Microsoft Repository based on the OIM-compatible DTDs supplied as part of the Microsoft Repository.

With the increasing popularity of XML as the format for representing Web-based and E-commerce data, XML files are likely to become a distinct source of data and meta data for many software products. As a result, the ability to interchange the meta data associated with an XML file while validating some or all of that meta data against predefined (and potentially standardized) grammars is a key requirement for interoperating with the emerging E-commerce and Web-based information systems. Therefore, the ability to effectively manage the meta data sharing and interchange processes with various software tools and by means of standard protocols is a fundamental requirement of any meta data repository architecture for an enterprise solution.

The Bottom Line

XML is fast becoming a standard for information exchange and vendor tool interoperability among different software systems. Its platform independence and vendor-neutral nature, combined with its ease of use and low overhead, make XML a prime candidate for supporting interactions between the growing family of thin-client Web-based applications and their servers. As data warehousing and decision support systems are merging with Web-based applications, particularly for E-commerce, XML is becoming an indispensable part of the new multitier architectures for supporting such systems. The DTD validation rules of XML, in turn, provide a viable framework for creating common vocabularies for exchanging meta data across different classes of software applications and meta data repositories. A number of efforts for standardizing such XML-based grammars, such as Microsoft XIF and OMG XMI, are gaining momentum and are likely to be used to facilitate meta data interoperability across different software systems which operate in heterogeneous computing environments.

In the next chapter, we examine meta data integration and access tools, and illustrate the techniques for evaluating and selecting these tools.

Implementing
a Meta Data Repository

Understanding and Evaluating Meta Data Tools

This chapter explores the requirements that you may have for meta data tools and examines the two types of meta data tools currently on the market: integration tools that let you integrate your various meta data sources into a central repository, and access tools that let you perform inquiries against the repository. Integration is particularly challenging because the tools must be able to interface with the many and varied types of meta data that exist within most organizations. We also look at the current state of the meta data tool market and explore the various components that make up a good tool. Last, we walk through a vendor tool checklist that helps you to organize and document your tool requirements and rate the various vendors' offerings (see Appendix A for the complete checklist, including detailed Comments section).

The Meta Data Tool Market

The meta data tool market has been in a state of flux and not well coordinated to serve the needs of meta data repositories. Tools typically perform specialized integration or access functions for a particular market niche, but no one or even two tools exist that fill the requirements for a majority of meta data repositories. Further, most tools are not integrated with one another and cannot easily share information, which significantly complicates the process of selecting tools. This lack of coordination and integration is largely attributable to the lack of a globally accepted meta model standard (i.e., a physical data model of the repository). As we discussed in Chapter 3, Meta Data Standards, one of the two model standards currently under development (by the Meta Data Coalition and the Object Management Group) is likely to emerge as a de facto standard in the near future. Once this occurs, we are likely to see some cohesion in the meta data tools market, and products from different vendors will be able to share information much more easily.

Two other factors play major roles in the current lack of market coordination and tool integration: the lack of an XML standard and the fact that the meta data tool market is experiencing consolidation. Corporate buyouts are occurring on a regular basis as industry giants like Computer Associates and Compuware swallow previously unknown meta tool vendors and acquire their product lines. Eventually, this consolidation will help to stabilize the market and contribute to standardization, but in the meantime it's difficult to keep track of the vendors and their respective offerings. And, many of the vendors are rushing to add support for XML to their products, but because the XML standard (which we also discussed in Chapter 3) is not yet finalized, each vendor's version of XML varies slightly, causing incompatibilities in the XML and making the tools incompatible with one another. Although the tool vendors have all pledged to support an XML standard when one emerges, vendor support for XML is questionable in the interim.

So, while the wide-open meta data tool market offers lots of opportunities for vendors, it is a complex and constantly changing arena that presents users with difficult choices for acquiring appropriate tools. The market situation is likely to improve, from the users' perspective, in the near future, but few companies can wait for the market to stabilize before selecting tools. The best course in the interim is to select tools that meet your current repository requirements but have sufficient flexibility to change in concert with the market and underlying technology.

Requirements for Repository Tools

Selecting meta data repository tools can be very difficult if you don't do some homework before you begin. To select appropriate tools, you need to consider all of your meta data requirements as well as each tool's capabilities. You have to determine not only what types of meta data you need to capture, but also such factors as how the tools integrate into your system architecture, how the repository data can be accessed and displayed, and how to provide security and maintain the repository. The first step in selecting repository tools is determining what meta data exists within your organization and what sources you need to deal with.

Determining Types of Meta Data

A repository tool must be able to handle the meta data that your business users need; this is key to the success of integrated systems such as data warehouses that depend upon meta data. Identifying what types of meta data your business users need can be difficult, however, given the wide variety of meta data types that exist within an organization. There are two ways to determine what types of meta data your project needs:

Top-down. In the top-down approach, you talk to the users and administrators who are going to work with the repository tools and base your selection criteria on their requirements, regardless of the software or repositories that are already deployed in your organization. This approach is most suitable for a new project that has very little dependency on existing software.

Bottom-up. The bottom-up approach, on the other hand, focuses on satisfying the meta data needs of existing software and repositories, and requires an in-depth study of documentation, such as the data dictionary, or in a worse case, the software code and database catalogues.

It is important for you to understand both the technical and business meta data requirements for your repository in order to accurately evaluate the types and sources of meta data available to you. As we discussed in Chapter 2, technical meta data is meta data about your systems, and business meta data is the business definitions and rules about your organization. Technical meta data contains information about programs and databases, scheduling, and control totals, as well as anything else that pertains to the design, running, and monitoring of your systems. The amount of technical meta data that you need to capture varies depending on your specific requirements. Business meta data is the real-world definitions for the complex systems that exist at your company. Be sure to choose the most important types of meta data first, because you will not be able to gather all of the required meta data in your initial effort. A meta data repository, like any other large DSS project, involves numerous iterations.

Administrative Facilities

Meta data tools must incorporate administrative facilities to allow business users and developers to manage the repository. The primary administrative functions that need to be addressed are:

Security.   Security is extremely important for meta data access and manipulation, particularly when various teams in a distributed environment use the repository. Security is often managed by granting various privileges to different users or classes of users, depending on the type of operations they need to perform on the meta data. The tool must be able to control access to the various types and sources of meta data.

Concurrent access.   If the users and administrators in your project need to concurrently access the meta data, the repository tool must provide the means to manage conflicts that may arise when two or more users attempt to manipulate the same meta data. Conflicts occur when multiple users attempt to update the repository or when two departments differ in their interpretation of a meta data fact. In these cases, the tool should be able to capture the fact that there is a conflict and provide some method of resolving the difference. Most tools provide some type of locking mechanism to ensure that when a user has checked-out a particular piece of meta data for editing, other users can only view that piece of meta data, not change it. Other tools provide an automated alert to notify the meta data administrator when a conflict occurs or generate a report listing all conflicts within a given period of time.

Change management.   Meta data is dynamic and changes frequently throughout a project lifecycle. The repository tool you select should be sufficiently flexible to effectively handle change by providing a means to store and track various versions of the meta data. Furthermore, it is generally very useful to be able to find differences between two versions of the same meta data, thereby facilitating the synchronization process.

Validate integrity and consistency.   Meta data must remain valid and consistent throughout the entire project lifecycle. Any defects in the meta data can have very grave consequences for everyone involved in the project, as well as for the end users of the software products that rely on the repository. Be sure that the repository tool you select has an effective means for regularly checking and validating the integrity and consistency of the repository's meta data throughout the various phases of the project.

Error recovery.   Most meta data repositories rely on some type of database management system for storing and managing the content in a physical medium, such as files. A repository tool should provide the necessary means for recovering from errors that may occur due to problems with saving and restoring the meta data from the physical medium.

Finally, a repository tool that offers a Graphical User Interface can be very beneficial for situations in which data administrators need an easy-to-use interface or scripted language to perform the administrative tasks. If the administrators or users are not comfortable with a tool's administrative facilities, they may neglect many of these very necessary functions, which can have serious consequences if the repository contains sensitive data, such as personnel and salary records.

Sharing and Reusing Meta Data

An effective meta data repository must be able to share the information in the repository among various groups and across teams and software products deployed within the organization. Such sharing saves time and prevents errors and inconsistencies that can occur throughout the project's life cycle, and is, after all, the whole reason for the existence of the repository. By allowing other groups to access the repository, we are able to reuse critical business definitions and calculations and ensure that we maintain a consistent view of the data throughout the organization.

Most large projects require effective reuse of meta data within and across teams and software products deployed throughout the project's life cycle. For example, your project team may decide to create some templates that can be instantiated multiple times in various phases of the project. Chances are good that you'll want to be able to propagate the changes automatically by simply modifying the parent template. The ability to reuse existing calculation logic and business definitions helps to reduce the time it takes for project analysis and increases the consistency with which data is calculated. (If everyone calculates sales totals using the formula that resides in the repository, the apples to oranges syndrome that exists in many companies today can largely be eliminated.) Reuse is one of the holy grails of computing, and a repository can play a major role in helping us to achieve it—but only if the meta data tools support the capability.

If your project requires sharing and/or reusing the meta data in your repository with other groups or repositories in the organization, you'll need a meta data tool that supports these capabilities. Depending on how and with whom you are sharing your meta data, your requirements may be as simple as allowing one or more other parties to access your entire repository, or as complex as writing specific meta data interchange bridges between your repository and another party's software. In any event, a tool's ability to share and reuse meta data is crucial and, therefore, a very important aspect of the selection process. Unfortunately, there is a lot of misinformation about the capabilities of various tools in this regard. Be sure to carefully study and document your meta data sharing and reuse requirements, then diligently evaluate the capabilities of the various repository tools on the market using real-world meta data to test them, if possible.

Extensibility and Compliance with Emerging Standards

For any tool to be successful, it needs to be able to change as industry standards emerge and evolve. This is particularly true of meta data tools because of the ongoing standards battle. The tool that you select must be able to support whichever standard, or blend of standards, the industry ultimately embraces. Because nearly all software projects change over time, the tool must also be able to add extended features and capabilities to cope with such changes. You should, therefore, carefully evaluate the repository tools you are considering to ensure they comply with an open architecture that can be extended easily and effectively without requiring a major overhaul of the system or the purchase of costly upgrades or new products.

Over that past several years, several industry standards have emerged that directly affect meta data repository tools. These standards include meta model content and organization, and delivery. The major new standards in these categories are OIM for the meta model and XML for delivery. If you are planning to deploy your repository tool in an environment that depends (or will depend in the near future) on these standards, be sure that the tool has the appropriate infrastructure and features to properly support these standards. Refer back to Chapter 3, Meta Data Standards, for a thorough discussion of the evolving standards.

Using the Repository

Once it's completed, the repository contains a vast amount of knowledge about your company's inner workings. But the repository doesn't have much value if you can't view its contents. The ability to easily browse the meta data and generate reports is crucial to the repository's success. If possible, you should try to make the repository access tool the same tool that business users currently depend on to access their data warehouse or data marts. Using the same tool eliminates the need for users to learn another tool and helps to ensure that they're comfortable using the repository.

A repository access tool should be capable of easily generating and maintaining a variety of reports. You'll need to evaluate the reporting capabilities of the meta data repository tools you're considering for a number of specific criteria, including:

- Ability to handle different types of data
- Support for various presentation styles
- Ease of use

- Support for Web-based formats (e.g., HTML and XML)
- Ability to be customized
- Interoperability with other reporting tools

Although all of these capabilities are important, some will be more important than others for your specific repository environment, so you need to have a thorough understanding of the user access and reporting requirements in order to effectively evaluate the repository tools that are available. For example, your users may need a tool that can publish one or more reports to a central location for viewing by other users and/or departments. This feature, which is becoming increasingly popular, can help to ensure that all users have the same up-to-date information about the repository contents. Table 4.1 lists some advanced capabilities to look for in a repository access tool.

Many individuals in the company may need to easily browse and interrogate the meta data using user-friendly, Web-enabled access tools. Web access capability is a crucial requirement of a repository tool and, because most tools offer some type of browser access, one that you'll have to care-

Table 4.1 Repository Access Capabilities

CAPABILITY	DETAIL
Data dependency	Because meta data typically contains a complex web of information in which changes to one object are likely to affect one or more other objects, the repository tool should be able to analyze the dependencies among related meta data. The ability to track dependencies allows the developer or business user to examine the affect that a change on one element is likely to have on the rest of the system. This impact analysis helps future development by reducing the number of unknowns in a project.
Lineage analysis	Data lineage lets you follow a data element from its source all the way through the various processes until it reaches its destination. Business users like this feature because it allows them to see exactly what is happening to the data.
Searching	A repository tool should provide effective and efficient means for searching the repository content by name, category, keyword, and other means that are important to your users and administrators. This is particularly important because most projects use a variety of names to refer to different meta data in the repository, and it is often difficult (if not impossible) for users and administrators to remember all of the names and their addresses in the repository.

fully evaluate. Web access facilities vary widely in their capabilities and compatibilities, and many fail to deliver the features that they promise. From a user standpoint, however, Web access is a basic requirement of a meta data access tool and one that can literally make or break your repository project.

Meta Data Integration

Meta data integration is one of the least understood and most misrepresented topics in the entire decision support arena. Despite the many and varied types of meta data that typically reside in different databases, files, and software programs used throughout an organization by many and varied teams, we are constantly assured by tool vendors that a tool seamlessly integrates all of the meta data sources. In reality, however, most tools fall short of delivering on this promise.

This section presents a real-world example of meta data integration and discusses the challenges of today's meta data integration tools market. Before we begin reviewing the strengths and limitations of these meta data integration tools though, I'd like to emphasize that it is much easier to purchase an integration tool and work around its limitations than it is to build custom programs to populate and support the meta data repository.

Meta Data Integration Tools

A dizzying array of meta data repository tools is available today. (See Table 4.2 for a list, and see this book's companion Web site [www.wiley.com/compbooks/marco] for updates.) Most of these tools claim to seamlessly integrate all meta data sources into a repository. Reality delivers a different message, however. Although it is true that most of these tools do a pretty good job of integrating formal meta data sources (i.e., CASE tools, extraction/transformation tools, and other repositories), the majority of them do not have meta models that provide an adequate foundation for business meta data, and they lack an overall vision for the complete data administration process. Specifically, most of the meta models for these tools are strong on the technical side of the meta data equation but relatively weak on the business side. The meta model that eventually emerges as a standard must be equally strong on both sides.

A meta data integration tool must have a fully extensible meta model that will let the tool interface with any source that you have, with little or no modification to the meta model. Most tools do include their own meta

Table 4.2 Meta Data Tools

INTEGRATION TOOLS	ACCESS TOOLS
Ardent MetaStage (Informix)	Brio Enterprise
IBM Information Catalog	Business Objects
Informatica MX2	Cognos Impromptu and Powerplay
Platinum Repository (Computer Associates)	Information Advantage Business Intelligence
Unisys Universal Repository	Microsoft OLAP Services ("Plato")
Viasoft Rochade	Microstrategy DSS Web and Server

model and provide the ability to extend that model as needed, but the task of extending the model is often complex, much like modifying the data model in a decision support system. As a result, many meta data administration teams include a full-time data modeler to handle the model extension chores.

Few repository tools provide a Web-enabled access layer that can satisfy the needs of typical business users. In many cases, the meta data access piece is provided by a "true" reporting tool, such as Microstrategy DSS or Cognos Impromptu. Whichever repository tool is selected, it should be fully Web-enabled, have the ability to capture user access patterns and frequency of report and table use, and be able to store this information in the repository.

Integrating Meta Data Sources

Within any organization, many different sources of meta data exist—each of which requires varying levels of integration complexity and meta model changes. For example, if you may have a CASE tool that stores technical meta data in its own repository, you probably need to write your own extracts in order to get the data out of the proprietary repository. This type of source is considered *nonsupported* because it doesn't fit with any industry standards that facilitate loading into the meta model.

Meta data sources fall into three broad categories of integration:

Certified sources. Certified sources are those that a tool can directly read, properly interpret, and load into the correct attributes of the meta model. These sources are easily integrated and do not require an extension of the base meta model. Because tools are typically designed to accept these sources, there is no need for additional programming or analysis. Common examples of certified meta data sources include technical meta data from CASE tools and transformation rules from extraction/transformation engines. Repository tools are generally certified for several vendor tools in each of these categories.

Generic sources.   Generic meta data sources are those that are in a common format (i.e., tab delimited, space delimited, or comma delimited) that a tool can read. Most tools support one or more generic meta data sources. However, while most tools can easily read the source, programming is often required to map the source elements to the correct attributes in the meta model. It is important, therefore, for a tool to have an interface that can be easily changed to map these sources. In addition, these sources frequently require extensions to the meta model. The process for extending the model can range from simple (i.e., adding an attribute to an existing table) to complex (i.e., building new tables, and/or adding foreign keys for other tables to reference). Common examples of generic sources include the technical and business meta data in databases and spreadsheets, which can be easily extracted into industry-standard formats.

Nonsupported sources.   Nonsupported sources are those that are neither certified nor generic and may require sophisticated analysis for design and programming. These sources present the same challenges as generic sources, along with the possibility of an additional complicated programming step to transform the nonsupported source into a generic source. Nonsupported sources are common sources of informal business meta data and of meta data stored in vendor applications.

It is important to identify all of the various sources of meta data that you need to integrate into your repository. If you classify each of your meta data sources using these three categories, you'll be able to quickly determine the complexity of your project, then determine how well the tools you're evaluating integrate each of the sources. Some tools handle some source categories better than others, so you'll need to prioritize your source categories and find a tool that best addresses those categories.

Meta Data Integration Architecture

You should have a basic understanding of your repository integration architecture when you are evaluating integration tools. Chapter 7, Constructing a Meta Data Architecture, offers a detailed discussion of meta data architecture, but you need to consider the various sources that you'll be integrating as early as possible in the process in order to select an appropriate integration tool.

AN INTEGRATION WAR STORY

Figure 4.1 illustrates an actual integration strategy implemented at one of my company's client sites. This client acquired a vendor tool to integrate its various sources of meta data. As you can see, the client had a dizzying array of meta data sources (see Table 4.3), and the process of integrating all of these sources left us quite light-headed.

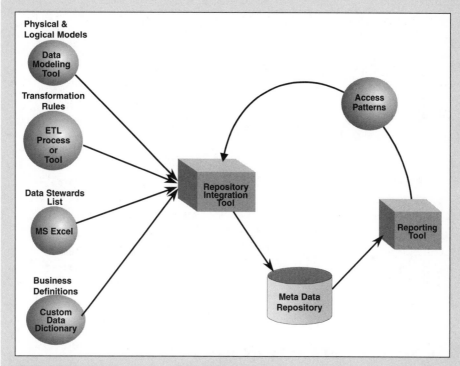

Figure 4.1   Meta data integration architecture.

On the positive side, we verified that the repository tool was certified with both the CASE tool and the integration tool that we used. Integrating the data dictionary, however, was more challenging. Because the data dictionary resided in a third-party application using a proprietary database format, its format was not supported by the integration tool. To resolve this problem we had to design and write two complex programs to extract and manipulate the data dictionary into a generic format (comma delimited) that the repository tool could integrate. This task took one fully dedicated programmer one month to accomplish.

continues

Table 4.3 Typical Sources of Meta Data in an Organization

META DATA SOURCES	META DATA DESCRIPTION	TYPE	MODEL EXTENSION
CASE tool	Physical and logical models, domain values, technical entity definitions, and technical attribute definitions	Certified	No
Extraction Transformation tool	Technical transformation rules	Certified	No
Custom data dictionary	Business attribute and entity definitions	Non-supported	No
MS Excel	Data steward's list	Generic	Yes
Reporting tool	Access patterns and frequency of use	Generic	Yes

The last source of meta data that we addressed was the data stewards' spreadsheet. This source was originally housed in Microsoft Excel and could be extracted in space delimited format, so we manually recreated it. Finally, we used an OLAP tool to access the information in the meta data repository. This tool captured user access patterns and frequency of use, which the data administration staff used to guide them on future repository development phases.

Tool Vendor Interview Process

When you are ready to begin selecting your meta data tools, you'll need to identify the vendors that you want to speak with. You can narrow the field of potential vendors and products by doing some preliminary research. Use product information that is readily available on the Internet and in industry magazines and journals to determine which vendors have tools that meet your general criteria (i.e., perform the functions that you'll need and are compatible with your hardware/software environment). Once you've prepared a preliminary list of potential vendors, you're ready to start interviewing the candidates and evaluating the products. Remember that each of these vendors' tools will have its strengths and weaknesses, so you'll need to thoroughly understand your project requirements and priorities in order to choose the tool or tools that best suit your needs. Nothing is perfect; be prepared to compromise along the way, but if you keep your requirements and priorities clearly in mind throughout the selection process—and manage to ignore the bells and whistles that vendors will wave in front of you—you can't go wrong.

In this section, we present a comprehensive tool selection checklist (Tables 4.4 through 4.15) to help you evaluate the vendors' positions in the market, their long-term viability, and the strengths and weaknesses of the individual tools. This checklist is primarily a guide to help you organize your thinking and compare the vendor offerings on a level playing field. Use this list to begin organizing your own search and translating your repository requirements onto paper. Be sure to tailor this checklist to your own environment, reflecting the points that are relevant for your repository and minimizing or eliminating those that are not.

To help you make an unbiased decision about which tool meets your criteria, the checklist includes a method for assigning a numerical level that corresponds to each item's importance. The *Weight, Percentage Met*, and *Score* columns let you numerically compare how each of the various products ranks. First, assign a weight to each checklist item, using a value between 1 and 5, where 1 is least important and 5 is most important. Then, as you interview vendors, specify the percentage amount that each checklist item satisfies your requirements. The *Score* then reflects the product of the *Weight* and the *Percentage Met* columns. Use the *Comment* column to note any details that may have a bearing on your decision, like an additional feature in the next release, or the results of a product trial—either positive or negative. When the checklist is complete, you can use the scores to determine how well a product fits your priorities.

The first section of the vendor checklist is dedicated to obtaining specific information about the vendor company (see Table 4.4). Information about the company, like the number of years it has been in business and the number of people it employs, can help you to determine whether the company is well established or just starting up. Information about employees is also useful for determining whether the company is likely to dedicate sufficient resources to customer support and product development to meet future needs.

Profit and revenue information is useful for gauging a vendor's financial health and determining whether the company is likely to continue operating long enough to support your long-term needs. While financial health by itself does not ensure a company's long-term survival or its continued support of a particular product line, poor financial health may warn of imminent decline and/or an inability to commit sufficient resources to product support and development. While it may be difficult to obtain solid financials

Table 4.4   Vendor Background Checklist

#	VENDOR BACKGROUND	COMMENTS
1	Full name and business address of vendor.	
2	Parent company.	
3	Number of years company has been in business.	
4	Company structure. Is it a corporation, partnership, or privately held? List names associated with structure if different from Question #1.	
5	Public or privately held company? If public, which exchange is company traded on, and what is company's market symbol?	
6	When did the company go public, or when is it expected to go public?	
7	Total number of employees worldwide.	
8	Total number of U.S. employees.	
9	Web site URL.	
10	Number of developers supporting proposed product solution.	
11	Company profit/loss for past three years (if available).	

on each of the vendor companies (especially in light of the large number of mergers and acquisitions in the market), the more information you can obtain, the better off you are. The last thing you want to do is to purchase a product, only to find that the company is nearly bankrupt and trying to sell off its product lines. Remember that the tool market is changing rapidly and that vendors must be able to change with it.

The next section of the interview checklist (represented in Table 4.5) addresses the specifics of the vendor's proposed solution, which may be a single product or combination of products and services. During the interview process, try to find out as much as possible about the proposed solution, including the number of other clients using precisely the same solution, specifics about any limitations of the solution, and plans for future enhancements or upgrades. Ask the repository architect and infrastructure architect on the meta data administration team to carefully review all the components of the proposed solution and compare them to the repository's technical environment and support structure (Question #13). You'll need to determine how well the various components in the proposed solution com-

Table 4.5 Checklist for Proposed Vendor Solution

#	PROPOSED SOLUTION OVERVIEW	COMMENTS
12	Provide a summary of the vendor's proposed solution and explain how it meets the needs specified in this document.	
13	What are the names and versions of the product(s) component(s) comprising the vendor's proposed solution?	
14	Number of worldwide production installations using precisely this proposed solution configuration.	
15	Number of U.S. production installations using precisely this proposed solution configuration.	
16	What hardware, operating system, DBMS, and Web browser limitations do each of the product(s) component(s) have in the proposed solution on client and server platforms?	
17	What is the release date and version number history of each of the product(s) component(s) over the past 24 months?	
18	What is the anticipated release date and new feature list for each of the product(s) component(s) for the next 12 months?	
19	Provide a list of known software bugs, errors, or other technical issues associated with each of the product(s) component(s).	

municate with one another; and what hardware platforms, DBMSs, Web servers, and communication protocols are required. Last, don't neglect the all-important aspects of migration and security, particularly as they relate to the individual components.

Be especially mindful of any requirements you have for downloading Java applets and/or ActiveX controls (Question #16) to the business users' PCs. This requirement may conflict with either your company's Web policy or your clients', if you intend to deploy the solution externally. You'll also want to know whether your firm is going to be the first to attempt using this solution (Question #15).

No vendor interview would be complete without a look at the costs associated with the tools. The next section of the checklist should help you to understand all of the costs involved with this tool, as well as the costs of upgrades and maintenance (see Table 4.6). Many vendors obtain a significant portion of their revenues from maintenance and product upgrades. Annual maintenance fees associated with a product can be quite substan-

Table 4.6 Checklist for Determining Cost

#	COST OF PROPOSED SOLUTION	WEIGHT	% MET	SCORE	COMMENTS
20	Total cost of proposed solution.				
21	Cost of consulting services required for installation.				
22	Cost of consulting services for initial project setup.				
23	What is the vendor's daily rate for consulting services without expenses?				
24	Annual maintenance cost/fee.				
25	Are all new product component releases/upgrades provided while under an annual maintenance agreement? If not, explain in detail.				

tial, and typically range from 14 to 18 percent (Question #24). Be sure to understand all of these costs before you commit to a tool solution. Hidden costs can make a seemingly attractive solution totally impractical—but you may not discover how impractical until it's too late! Also, try to negotiate consulting time early in the purchase process (Question #21) to get your staff trained and the repository up and running quickly.

The next portion of the checklist (Table 4.7) addresses the specifics of the vendor's hardware and software proposal. First, you'll need to ensure that the proposed tool will work in your environment without requiring any major changes in your existing system architecture. After all, the best tool in the world won't do you much good if it doesn't work with your other system components or if you have to upgrade your existing system components to support the vendor solution. This is the time to determine performance benchmarks, memory and disk requirements, and operating system requirements. Make sure that the proposed tool can support the various DBMS techniques (e.g., parallel threads, dirty reads, and other unique DBMS features) you need to support the DSS environment. Determine whether security can be centrally controlled (Question #32) or distributed; how various DSS projects can be separated; and how access is controlled through the Web. Does the product provide row-level security to allow users to access a repository table (Question #37) but not all rows in the table? Last, be sure to address issues that are likely to affect the user training curve, such as the programming languages (Question #45) used by the repository, so that you fully understand the level of training that will be

Table 4.7 Evaluating the Details of Proposed Solution

#	TECHNICAL REQUIREMENTS	WEIGHT	% MET	SCORE	COMMENTS
26	Are there any database schema design requirements for the DSS data model in order to function with the repository product?				
27	How does the tool control the various versions of the meta data (i.e., development, quality assurance, and production) stored in the repository?				
28	How is meta data from multiple DSS projects controlled and separated? How can various projects share meta data?				
29	Describe how meta data repository contents are migrated from one system engineering phase to the next (i.e., development, quality assurance, and production). How does this processing sequence differ when dealing with multiple projects on various time lines?				
30	What DBMS privileges does the product support (e.g., roles, accounts, and views)?				
31	Can DBMS-specific SQL statements be incorporated into queries?				
32	Describe the security model used with the product.				
33	Can administration and use privileges be assigned at a user, workgroup, project, and enterprise level? Describe.				
34	How does the product use existing infrastructure security systems?				
35	Does the product use any type of single sign-on authentication (e.g., LDAP)?				
36	Are all user IDs and passwords centrally located for all product components? Where?				

continues

Table 4.7 Evaluating the Details of Proposed Solution *(Continued)*

#	TECHNICAL REQUIREMENTS	WEIGHT	% MET	SCORE	COMMENTS
37	Where are user security constraints for the product stored?				
38	Can a user have access to the repository tool for one project but no access for another project?				
39	Can a user view the SQL generated by the product?				
40	Is the product Web-enabled? Describe.				
41	Can the product be fully used through Web browser on the client?				
42	Can the product be fully administered through a Web browser? Describe.				
43	Which Web browsers does the product support? Which Web server products does the product support?				
44	What ActiveX controls and/or Java applets are required on the client PC? How large are these controls and/or applets?				
45	What programming requirements are required to support the proposed meta data repository solution (e.g., script, SQL, etc.)?				
46	What scalability options are available in the solution to determine where processing is performed for optimization?				
47	What collaborative support comes with the proposed solution (e.g., e-mail, pagers, etc.)?				
48	Describe what processing functions run on the client versus the server.				
49	Does the product allow multiple meta data developers to work simultaneously with the same DSS project? Describe facilities.				

Table 4.7 *(Continued)*

#	TECHNICAL REQUIREMENTS	WEIGHT	% MET	SCORE	COMMENTS
50	What scheduling tools does the product interface with (CA-7, CRON, Control-M, JES/2, etc.)?				
51	Does the product use any middleware components? If so, how do they improve overall performance of the product?				
52	Do new upgrades or releases of the product come with automated repository DBMS conversion routines?				
53	What is an average hardware configuration (number of processors, speed of processors, hard disk space, RAM) for the client and server components of the proposed architecture? Specify assumptions.				

required for users and administrative staff. Also be sure to determine the memory and processing requirements for each user desktop and understand how the vendor calculates these needs (Question 53).

Examining the technical information about the tool will help you to assess the impact that the proposed solution is likely to have on your existing environment. If, for example, the tool requires large amounts of network bandwidth and your network is already stressed, then this tool may not be appropriate for your environment. Be sure to walk through this section of the interview slowly and carefully, making sure that the vendor answers your questions. If you miss anything here, it is likely to come back to haunt you. If, for example, you fail to ascertain that the tool supports ActiveX and Java, you'll have a hard time categorizing your Web application. Although this would not have mattered a few years ago, it could be crucial in today's Web-conscious world.

The next section of the checklist (Table 4.8) addresses the tool's meta data management capabilities. Because most tools interact with a large number of systems, the information in this section may be harder to nail down than most of the other sections. As meta data management evolves, tools are providing more and better facilities. A few years ago, we would not have thought to ask about bidirectional meta data or active versus passive

Table 4.8 Meta Data Management Capabilities

#	META DATA MANAGEMENT	WEIGHT	% MET	SCORE	COMMENTS
54	Is the meta data repository tool active or passive in controlling the processes of the DSS environment? If active, explain.				
55	Can the meta data repository tool's meta model be extended to include additional tables or columns?				
56	What types of source system data can the repository directly read and capture meta data from (e.g., DBMS, flat files, DDL, spreadsheets, copybooks, etc.)?				
57	What CASE tools or data modeling tools can the repository tool directly read and capture?				
58	How are business rules captured and stored in the repository?				
59	How are calculations captured and stored in the repository?				
60	What front-end query reporting and/or OLAP tools can access and store meta data directly from the repository?				
61	What data monitoring tools can the repository directly access meta data information from?				
62	Describe the types of user interfaces that the repository tool has for manual entry of meta data.				
63	Can the repository tool read and write CASE Data Interchange Format (CDIF) compliant meta data files?				
64	Describe how data mappings between source operational and target decision support data are captured and maintained in the repository tool.				

Table 4.8   *(Continued)*

#	META DATA MANAGEMENT	WEIGHT	% MET	SCORE	COMMENTS
65	What reporting capabilities does the meta data repository tool include as standard? Can data from the repository be exported externally to other applications (e.g., spreadsheets)?				
66	Does the tool support predefined and/or ad hoc reporting? Describe.				
67	How does the repository share and separate meta data needed for various DSS projects (e.g., atomic data warehouse versus various departmental-specific data marts)?				
68	What facilities does the repository tool have for analyzing the impact of a change on a source operational system to the DSS environment?				
69	What notification or alert utilities does the tool provide in response to changes to operational systems, data mappings, DSS data model, or reports?				
70	How does the tool support the base components of a meta data repository (i.e., operational source system, logical DSS data model, physical DSS data model, source to target data mapping, ETL load statistics, business subject area views, query statistics)?				

systems, but these capabilities are becoming increasingly important as companies try to leverage every last ounce of competitive edge out of their repositories. Be sure to ask about such data management features as agents or triggers (Question #54) to make the repository more proactive. And, because organizations' requirements differ widely, be sure that the tool's meta model can be easily expanded (Question #55) to support any future additions to your repository. You'll also need to have a clear understanding of your firm's current and future meta data requirements to determine the likelihood that you'll need support for advanced capabilities such as closed loop architecture or bidirectional meta data in the future.

Be sure to ask the vendor about any competitive advantages that the tool offers (see Table 4.9). Does this tool offer any features that make it significantly better than others on the market? It is also advisable to ask the vendor to tell you about the tool's shortcomings. If the vendor tells you that the tool doesn't have any shortcomings, you're probably not hearing the whole story—or getting all the information you need. When I conduct vendor interviews, I tell the vendors up front that I expect to walk away knowing about at least three problems with the tool, and that I'm not really comfortable with the tool (or the vendor) unless that happens. Vendors shouldn't be afraid to tell you what they know about the tool, including its weaknesses (and every tool has weaknesses!). After all, it's better for everyone concerned if you hear the whole story during the evaluation process than later, just weeks away from implementation. In any case, whatever you hear from the vendor, it's best to do some additional research and check some third-party information sources such as Gartner Group and Meta Group to hear what these experts have to say about the vendor company and proposed solution.

The next section of the checklist (Table 4.10) addresses an area that is often overlooked in the tool evaluation phase—vendor support. All too often, companies get caught up in evaluating a product's neat bells and whistles and forget to ask about the vendor's ability or willingness to pro-

Table 4.9 Vendor Differentiating Factors

#	DOCUMENTATION:	WEIGHT	% MET	SCORE	COMMENTS
71	Discuss the extent to which the vendor's proposed solution fits the needs of a meta data repository tool for a decision support environment.				
72	Discuss the advantages of the proposed solution has over other vendor products in this DSS market space.				
73	What is the vendor's company's market share in this DSS market space? Source of market share?				

Table 4.10 Evaluating Vendor Technical Support

#	TECHNICAL SUPPORT	WEIGHT	% MET	SCORE	COMMENTS
74	Discuss in detail the technical support offered in the proposed solution.				
75	Where is the primary technical support center located?				
76	What times and days of the week is the support center available for customer support?				
77	Describe the technical support center's guaranteed response time.				
78	Describe the escalation procedures used to resolve customer problems.				
79	Are technical support costs included in the annual maintenance agreements? If not, how are technical support costs charged backed to the customer?				
80	Are all product components comprising the proposed solution supported out of a single technical support center? If not, explain.				
81	Is an online database(s) of previously closed issues and/or frequently asked questions (FAQs) and their solutions available for customer review?				
82	Describe how upgrades can be installed in parallel with existing versions.				

vide ongoing support. The questions in this section are designed to help you determine what support is available from the vendor, and how readily the vendor provides support when you need it. For example, does the vendor offer on-site problem resolution? Is this type of support included in the basic product price? If so, for how long? What happens if a problem cannot be resolved in a timely fashion? Is support available on holidays or weekends if your repository suddenly will not load or if data corruption occurs? Good support is invaluable when you need it. Try to determine what type of vendor support you can expect before you actually need it.

Product documentation is another aspect that is often overlooked during the evaluation and selection phase (see Table 4.11). Always be sure to determine what types of documentation the vendor supplies with the tool(s) and what supplemental information is available. Very often, vendors provide only a single CD-ROM with user and technical documentation. If you're going to need multiple copies of the documentation or printed copies, find out if there is an additional charge for these. You should also ask about the availability of other types of documentation, such as Internet documentation, newsgroups, and fax-back support.

Most vendors provide some type of training facilities with their products, even if they're only computer-assisted courses or hard copy manuals, but you'll need to determine (Table 4.12) just what is included as standard with the product and what is optionally (i.e., for additional cost) available. This is particularly important if you've determined from answers to questions in earlier portions of the questionnaire that the product may involve a significant amount of user or staff training or multiple levels of training. I remember one client that had purchased a great tool and proceeded to implement it, only to

Table 4.11 Evaluating Vendor Documentation

#	DOCUMENTATION:	WEIGHT	% MET	SCORE	COMMENTS
83	Discuss the quality and availability of all forms of software documentation (i.e., user, technical, and installation).				
84	What media/format is documentation provided in (e.g., online, CD-ROM, or hard copy)? Are multiple copies or alternative media/formats available at no charge?				

Table 4.12 Evaluating Vendor Training

#	TRAINING	WEIGHT	% MET	SCORE	COMMENTS
85	What training classes are included in the cost of the proposed solution? How many students does the solution include?				
86	What is the training cost for each class?				
87	Where are training classes held?				
88	Are any computer-based training (CBT) courses available? If so, what is the CBT cost?				
89	What training classes are recommended for the repository architect, data administrator, infrastructure developer, and business users, based on the contents of the proposed solution?				

find that the users required one type of training, the developers another type, and the administrators yet another type of training. To top this off, the product involved separate training courses for beginner, intermediate, and advanced levels of each training track. The client, who had failed to investigate the training requirements and offerings during the product selection phase, was understandably unhappy with the prospect of spending thousands of dollars and untold numbers of staff hours just to get the tool into general use.

Selecting a tool is, of course, only the first step. Lots of other questions may arise when you actually begin to implement the tool into your environment. If you ask the right questions up front (see Table 4.13) during the selection process, you're less likely to encounter some nasty surprises during the implementation phase. For example, you may want to ask the vendor to supply copies of sample implementation plans (Question #91), then compare them to your environment to determine whether this product is really appropriate for your firm.

Ask the vendor to provide you with a skill set list so that you know precisely what types of skills are required to implement this tool. If your current staff does not possess the necessary skills, ask if the vendor can supply skilled per-

Table 4.13   Evaluating Product Implementation

#	IMPLEMENTATION	WEIGHT	% MET	SCORE	COMMENTS
90	Describe the sequence of events and level of effort recommended for clients to consider in planning their implementation strategy.				
91	What is typical duration of implementation cycle?				
92	How well does proposed product solution handle the number and types of data sources described in this document?				
93	How many DSS database schema dimensions and facts can the proposed product solution handle?				
94	Provide a sample project plan for implementing the proposed solution for a single DSS project.				
95	What repository implementation reports can the proposed product solution generate?				
96	What client resource skill sets need to be in place for installation and implementation?				

sonnel on a temporary basis to help you get through the implementation cycle, and what cost is involved in renting the necessary skills. Also, ask the vendor about the likely duration of the implementation cycle for a company and configuration similar to yours. If the vendor can't provide this information, you may want to research the implementation issues more closely to get a thorough understanding of the time and personnel requirements.

The vendor may have alliances and/or partnerships with other companies that may be beneficial to your firm. Be sure to ask about these arrangements (Table 4.14), as well as any strategic partnerships that the vendor has

Table 4.14 Evaluating Vendor Partnerships and Alliances

#	STRATEGIC PARTNERSHIPS	WEIGHT	% MET	SCORE	COMMENTS
97	Identify and describe the vendor's strategic partnerships with computer aided software engineering (CASE) or data modeling tool vendors.				
98	Identify and describe the vendor's strategic partnerships with DSS extraction, transformation, and loading (ETL) tool vendors.				
99	Identify and describe the vendor's strategic partnerships with DSS data cleansing tool vendors.				
100	Identify and describe the vendor's strategic partnerships with DSS query reporting and/or OLAP vendors.				
101	Identify and describe the vendor's strategic partnerships with DSS data monitoring tool vendors.				
102	Identify and describe the vendor's strategic partnerships with hardware vendors.				
103	Identify and describe the vendor's strategic partnerships with DBMS vendors.				
104	Identify and describe the vendor's strategic partnerships with value-added resellers (VARs).				
105	Identify and describe the vendor's strategic partnerships with integrators.				
106	Identify and describe the vendor's strategic partnerships with consulting/implementation providers.				

with other meta data specialists. Does the vendor work closely with other tool vendors or industry associations to continue product development within the framework of emerging standards? Can the vendor offer an end-to-end solution comprised of other vendors' tools? Being aware of partnerships and alliances also helps you to avoid those sticky situations in which a vendor may recommend another company's tool just because the two organizations have a strategic alliance, not because the tool is necessarily appropriate for your environment. You want to make sure that the tools you select are the right ones for *you*, not the right ones for the *vendor*.

Finally, at the end of the interview process, you'll need to obtain references from each of the vendors under consideration (see Table 4.15). The best way to get a good feel for a tool is to talk to people who use it. Ask the vendor to provide references of other companies (Question #107) that use the tool in an environment similar to yours. You may be able to meet other users (current or previous) at trade shows and industry conferences; this too is an excellent source of hands-on information. Understandably, vendors typically provide references to customers who are satisfied with the products; the users you meet and speak with at conferences and seminars may not fall into this category. These users, as well as those that the vendor references, may help you to avoid a lot of pitfalls. They may have already been down the road you're on and can offer sound advice for selecting or implementing the product. In addition, you may want to see if there are any organized user groups for the product in your area and try to talk to people there.

Table 4.15 Evaluating Customer References

#	CUSTOMER REFERENCES	WEIGHT	% MET	SCORE	COMMENTS
107	Obtain from vendor at least three customer references that may be contacted regarding quality of software, upgrades, proper sizing, implementation, and training. Each should include the following: ■ Company name and address ■ Contact name, title, and phone number ■ Type of services offered ■ Modules installed (names of modules) ■ Installation date(s)				

Look on the Internet for any information on the tool. Search engines like www.deja.com can help you find discussions about any number of things.

When all of the vendor interviews are complete, I like to lay out all the pluses and minuses of each tool on a white board. This helps me to determine which products meet our specified needs and offer the best solution. Be sure to spend sufficient time to find out all you can about all of the tools. The more information you have now, the better off you will be in the long term.

Now that you have a firm grasp of what is required to select your repository tools, we're ready to move on to the next important aspect of building a repository—organizing and staffing, which are every bit as important as tool selection. Remember, a tool is only as good as the people who use it.

## CHAPTER 5

Organizing and Staffing the Meta Data Repository Project

Researching the needs of repository users and understanding how to incorporate the types and sources of meta data that they need is crucial for successfully implementing a repository. But understanding the need for these factors is much easier than actually accomplishing them. Many repository projects fail, not for lack of understanding, but for lack of organization and implementation expertise. In the first part of this chapter, I discuss several of the common mistakes that companies make in implementing meta data repository projects and explain how to avoid these pitfalls. Then I examine the specific roles and skill sets required to staff and organize the meta data repository project team, as well as the organizational support that these team members need. Last, I discuss some of the generic qualities that are necessary for developing a real working team.

Why Meta Data Projects Fail

Too often, companies believe that they can purchase a tool that will make a fully functional meta data repository magically appear. If only it were that simple! A meta data repository, like any other significant IT initiative, takes a great deal of knowledge and investment, as well as a methodical development approach.

The fact is that meta data management is not a project; it is a cultural shift that requires the active participation of its users. If users are not actively involved in the process of capturing and maintaining meta data, the overall quality of the meta data is likely to be poor, and the meta data repository will not be able to provide the value that business users—and CEOs and CIOs—demand.

In my experience, companies that fail make several common mistakes when starting their meta data projects. Although there is certainly wide variation in the ways that repository projects can go awry, the following list summarizes the most common mistakes that companies—especially those that lack experience implementing data warehouse architectures—are likely to make:

- Failing to define objectives
- Evaluating meta data tools prior to defining project requirements
- Selecting meta data tool(s) without a thorough evaluation
- Failing to create a meta data repository team
- Failing to automate meta data integration processes
- Allowing a meta data tool vendor to manage the project
- Failing to appoint an experienced meta data project manager to lead the effort
- Trivializing the meta data repository development effort
- Failing to create standards that supporting teams can follow
- Failing to provide open access to the meta data

I'll describe each of these common mistakes in detail in the following pages, explaining the effect that they typically have on the overall project, and ways to avoid the pitfall.

Failing to Define Objectives

The meta data repository team often fails to clearly define the specific business and technical objectives of the meta data repository. Because these objectives serve as a guide for all project activities, it is essential to clearly define them at the beginning of the project.

Good business and technical objectives are both definable and measurable. They not only serve as a guide for implementing the repository; they are also imperative for justifying the cost of the entire project. If the initial release of the repository can be cost-justified, the challenge of attaining funding for the inevitable follow-up releases is greatly simplified. And, the repository will inevitably grow to support the ever-expanding role of the associated data warehouse/data marts and the increasing demands of its users. Remember, like a data warehouse, a meta data repository is not a project, it is a process. (See the "Project Scope Document" section in Chapter 6, Building the Meta Data Project Plan.)

Evaluating Meta Data Tools Prior to Defining Project Requirements

This is *the* most common mistake that organizations make when beginning meta data repository projects. I am always surprised by the number of phone calls I receive from companies asking me to suggest a meta data tool for their repository project. My standard response is, "What are your repository's requirements?" Typically, the reply from the other end of the line is silence. This situation is very disturbing. Meta data repository requirements must guide the tool selection process, not precede it. Meta data requirements determine which tools should be purchased and what functionality is required from each tool. Selecting the tool (or tools) before defining the project requirements often leads companies to purchase unnecessary tools, which then become "shelfware," or—even worse—cause the companies to implement their repositories with the wrong tools, severely limiting the capabilities of their meta data repository.

Chapter 6, Building the Meta Data Project Plan, contains a detailed description of the requirements definition process and explains where in the project lifecycle meta data tools should be evaluated and purchased.

Selecting Meta Data Tools without a Thorough Evaluation

All of the major meta data tools maintain and control repositories in different ways. Finding the tool (or tools) that best suits your company requires careful analysis. Educated consumers are likely to be most satisfied because they understand exactly what they're buying and how it's likely to operate in their systems environment. They also understand what it is that they're *not* buying, which eliminates a lot of misunderstanding in the future.

It is important to remember that no matter how careful you are in the selection process, no meta data tool can make the repository effort easy, despite what the tool salespeople or marketing literature may say. A successful meta data project requires knowledge, discipline, talented employees, and good old-fashioned hard work—just like any other major IT endeavor. While none of the tools eliminate these needs, most companies are still better off purchasing a tool and working around its limitations than trying to build everything from scratch.

In Chapter 4, Understanding and Evaluating Meta Data Tools, I present a step-by-step approach for selecting the best tool for your company.

Failing to Create a Meta Data Repository Team

Companies often fail to form a dedicated team to build the meta data repository. This team, which should include members from other IT teams as well as business users, should be responsible for building and maintaining the meta data repository, and for managing access to the repository. In my experience, companies use a variety of organizational structures for these teams and assign a wide variety of names, but for the most part the employees are not dedicated solely to the meta data repository initiative.

After the meta data team is formed, its leader should report to the same manager as the head of the decision support team, so that the two teams can operate on a peer level with one another. If the meta data project manager reports to the decision support manager, the meta data repository often becomes a subset of the decision support system and all too often is neglected. The meta data project team and the decision support system team must work together as equals because each team's work directly affects the other. A muddled data warehouse architecture directly (and negatively) affects the quality of the technical meta data in the repository, and, conversely, a poorly designed repository can greatly reduce the effectiveness of the decision support system.

The second half of this chapter provides detail on establishing and administering an effective meta data repository implementation team.

Failing to Automate the Meta Data Integration Processes

The process of loading and maintaining the meta data repository should be as automated as possible. All too often, meta data repositories contain many manual processes in their integration architectures, and these repositories are almost sure to be less than successful. The task of manually keying in meta data is far too time-consuming for the meta data repository team, and it typically makes the repository nonscalable and impossible to maintain over time. With careful analysis and some development effort, the vast majority of manual processes can be automated.

A significant portion of business meta data resides within the employees of a company. As a result, some manual processes may be required to initially capture this type of business meta data. If this is the case, it is advisable to build a front end to enable the business users and analysts to directly modify their business meta data. This front end *must* be kept simple. I often build the front end using Microsoft Excel or Visual Basic because most business users are comfortable with this technology.

Remember that you want the business users to take an active role in maintaining their meta data. The meta data repository manager should not require an IT person to approve changes that are input by business users. When this occurs, the IT person becomes the data steward of the business meta data and the business users do not feel like they own it. As an IT person, you really don't want to be the data steward of the business meta data.

Allowing the Meta Data Tool Vendors to Manage the Project

Tools vendors often convince companies to let them manage the meta data repository project. Doing so is nearly always a critical mistake because the tool vendors become far too focused on using their particular tool or tool suite for the project rather than focusing on building a solution to deliver value to the business. After all, the tool vendors are not true integrators; they are tool experts—and the same is true of consultants employed by the tool vendors. They are most concerned with making their tools work (which is what they *should* be focused on). While the meta data integration tool is at the heart of the meta data process, much more than a tool is required to create a fully functional, scalable repository.

Failing to Appoint an Experienced Meta Data Project Manager

An experienced meta data project manager keeps the vision of the project in concert with the realities of meta data and decision support. This may sound obvious, but is really quite difficult when implementing a repository in a real-world environment. The repository architect must be knowledgeable about building a robust, maintainable repository that can suit immediate needs and be scalable to accommodate the ever-expanding and changing user requirements. These fundamental challenges typically require a highly-experienced, senior-level individual.

In some cases, it may be practical to hire an outside consultant to get the repository project up and running, but the person should be highly skilled at knowledge transfer and work closely with an in-house employee right from the onset of the project. Be wary of consultants without real-world, hands-on experience. Writing or speaking about meta data is very different from having the necessary experience to navigate through the political quagmires and the knowledge of actually designing and implementing a meta data repository.

I describe the various project roles in detail later in this chapter and offer some suggestions for filling the required positions.

Trivializing the Meta Data Repository Development Effort

Too often, companies underestimate the amount of work required to build a meta data repository. All of the tasks required to build a data warehouse—including defining business and technical requirements, data modeling, source system analysis, source data extraction and capture, data transformation and cleansing, data loading, and user data access—are also required to build a meta data repository. An iterative approach usually provides the best hope of keeping the scope of the data repository project under control. You don't have to do everything at once, but you do have to keep the end result in mind at all times, because it will be your guiding light.

Like most other major IT efforts, a meta data repository project often involves significant political challenge that should not be overlooked in the planning phase. Politics can cause the best-planned meta data and DSS projects to go astray. Remember that you'll need cooperation from multiple IT and business teams to support the meta data effort, and be sure to keep the other players in mind as you begin to plan and implement the repository.

Failing to Create Standards That Supporting Teams Can Follow

The meta data repository team must develop standards for capturing the key business and technical meta data. These standards should be clear, concise, and easy for business users and members of the data warehouse team to follow. If the meta data repository team creates standards that are too complex and tedious for other teams to easily follow, the meta data repository team will be perceived as a bottleneck to the decision support development process. Once this happens, it is probably only a matter of time before the meta data repository team is disbanded.

KEEP IT SIMPLE

I was contacted by a midsized health care company on the East Coast to help it improve the business users' satisfaction with their meta data repository and to conduct an assessment of the meta data repository team. During the assessment, I met with the meta data project manager and asked him if he had implemented any corporate meta data standards for the development teams to follow. At this point he got very excited and opened his desk drawer and proceeded to hand me a binder that was more than two inches thick! He then said, "Just read through the binder. It tells you all you need to know about our standards and how to follow them." I asked if he handed this same binder to the project managers of the development teams. He answered yes. I then discovered that none of the development teams were following the standards (which wasn't any surprise). Why should a project manager, who already is working 50 or 60 hours a week, take time out to read a two-inch-thick manual on something that he is not aware can help him? I also wasn't surprised when I spoke to the development team leaders and discovered that they viewed the meta data project manager as a roadblock to their success.

The golden rule is to keep the standards exceedingly simple to understand and follow. Then meet with each of the team heads and personally show him or her how to follow the standards. In addition, keep the amount of time needed to complete each of the procedures to a minimum, and do not neglect to create a feedback loop so the other teams can let you know how you're doing.

Failing to Provide Open Access to the Meta Data

A key goal for all meta data repository projects must be to provide open access to the meta data, permitting any and all business and technical users to access it with little or no effort. Many of the early meta data repository efforts did a decent job of integrating valuable meta data, but got side-tracked by failing to roll the meta data out to the users. In some cases, users had to go to the meta data repository team to beg for access to the information that they needed. Clearly, this technique is doomed to failure.

Meta Data Repository Team Responsibilities

A meta data repository team functions best as a dedicated group reporting directly to the CIO. It is important for the team to reside at a high level in the IT organization because it has to work with other IT teams to define procedures that everyone must follow. The meta data repository team has many responsibilities, including:

- Building and maintaining the meta data repository
- Selecting meta data integration and access tools
- Working with tool vendors
- Working with the data stewards to define business meta data
- Administering meta data procedures for other teams to follow

Organizing the Meta Data Repository Team

Although meta data repository efforts differ in size and scope, there are 10 key roles that must typically be filled in order for a project to be successful. These roles require specific, qualified resources assigned to them, and an interactive organization that has the confidence and support of executive management, as well as cooperation from end user departments that may not be directly involved in the implementation. (Figure 5.1 illustrates a typical hierarchy for a meta data project implementation.) The 10 key roles are:

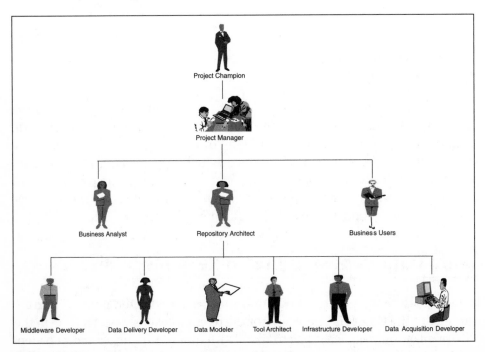

Figure 5.1   Meta data repository project team hierarchy.

- Project champion
- Project manager
- Repository architect
- Data modeler
- Business analyst
- Data acquisition developer (back-end)
- Data delivery developer (front-end)
- Middleware developer
- Infrastructure developer
- Tool architect

In large repository implementations, each role is likely to require a dedicated full-time resource, and multiple resources may be required for some roles, such as the data acquisition and data delivery developer roles. Some roles may be filled from the central IT group—for example, the middleware developer and infrastructure developer. In many repository implementations, certain key roles can be combined and served by the same resource. Table 5.1 presents some typical role combinations that have proven effective in implementing repository projects. In most cases, however, it is not advisable to assign more than two roles to the same resource.

Whether you are just beginning a meta data repository project or maintaining an existing repository, you need to assign at least one resource to each of these roles. The biggest difference between developing a repository and maintaining one is that during the maintenance period more roles can be filled by the same resource.

The following sections describe the functions and responsibilities of the key roles and summarize the position requirements and recommended skill sets for each.

Project Champion

The project champion, who is typically part of executive management (e.g., a vice president or director of a key line of business) is usually the person who attains the initial funding for the repository project. This individual is responsible for articulating the value of building a meta data repository, using business terms to convince the relevant departments and upper management that the project can help the company to achieve its major goals. Table 5.2 lists the professional and technical skill sets required for this position.

Typically, the project champion does not initiate the meta data concept within the organization. A business manager or member of the IT group may

Table 5.1 Typical Role Combinations

Project manager Repository architect
Repository architect Data modeler
Project manager Business analyst
Data modeler Business analyst
Data modeler Data acquisition developer
Data modeler Data delivery developer
Middleware developer Infrastructure developer
Tool architect Repository architect
Tool architect Data acquisition developer
Tool architect Data delivery developer
Tool architect Data modeler
Data acquisition developer Data delivery developer

Table 5.2 Project Champion Skill Sets

PROFESSIONAL SKILLS	TECHNICAL SKILLS
Ability to articulate the benefits of meta data to the organization	None
Ability to acquire funding for the project and ongoing maintenance	
Ability to obtain a capable, experienced project manager to lead the effort	
Ability to rally support from other departments	
Ability to remove political obstacles to the repository's success	

bring the concept to the attention of executive management and enlist the support of a project champion. Sometimes the meta data project may be initiated from outside the organization, with a consultant or software vendor introducing the idea to an IT or business manager, who then presents the idea to executive management and seeks a project champion. Organizations often enlist the aid of a consultant to help cost-justify a repository project and prepare the initial proposal to executive management.

The role of the project champion is crucial in helping the development team enlist support and assistance from other departments that may initially be unwilling to commit resources to the meta data repository effort. Any major, cross-departmental IT initiative, whether it's a decision support system or customer relationship management (CRM) package, requires the support of executive management as well as the departmental managers that will be called upon to commit resources. Executive-level support is imperative for overcoming the barriers and ivory towers that exist in all corporations. Any substantial project that lacks executive-level support and interdepartmental cooperation has a high probability of failure. Table 5.3 summarizes the requirements of the project champion role and the project phases in which this role participates.

Project Manager

The meta data repository project manager role is very similar to that of any project leader in a major IT implementation, with one key difference—the meta data repository project manager's work does not substantially

Table 5.3 Project Champion Requirements Overview

DESCRIPTION	REQUIREMENT
Number of resources required	1
Years of work experience	10+ years
Difficulty filling position	Medium to high
Experience required	Prior experience with major system development efforts
Orientation and feasibility phases	Yes
Design phase	No
Construction phase	No
Rollout phase	Yes

decrease once the repository is rolled out to production. On the contrary, as is common in any DSS initiative, the responsibilities of the project manager typically increase over time. Meta data repositories, like decision support systems, grow in an organic manner (very rapidly and in directions that are seldom anticipated), thereby presenting the repository project manager with a continuum of new challenges and tasks. Table 5.4 summarizes the professional and technical skills that a project manager should possess, and Table 5.5 lists the requirements for the project manager position and the project phases in which he participates.

The project manager should have prior experience leading successful meta data repository implementations. This individual is responsible for planning the project phases, configuring and assembling the staff, and establishing the short- and long-term strategies for the repository. The project manager needs to have strong communication skills, both written and verbal, and the ability to select and develop an effective repository staff. It's important to realize that the project manager's job is not to make a star out of everyone on the team, but to assign the team members to the roles that best fit their experience, skills, and professional goals, thereby getting the most out of each employee.

The project manager should be capable of managing outside vendors, both software and consulting. The importance of this ability cannot be

Table 5.4 Project Manager Skill Sets

PROFESSIONAL SKILLS	TECHNICAL SKILLS
Ability to articulate the benefits of meta data to the project team and the organization	Familiarity with the major meta data tools and vendors
Ability to obtain and mentor staff	
Ability to manage software and consulting vendors	
Excellent written and verbal skills	
Good organizational skills	
Concern for quality and be a quick study, a team player, and highly motivated	
Ability to define and maintain project scope	
Ability to identify positive ROI opportunities that can be served by the meta data repository	

Table 5.5 Project Manager Requirements Overview

DESCRIPTION	REQUIREMENT
Number of resources required	1
Years of work experience	8+ years, including significant project planning and control
Difficulty in filling position	High
Experience required	Prior experience leading successful meta data repository implementations
Orientation and feasibility phases	Yes
Design phase	Yes
Construction phase	Yes
Rollout phase	Yes

understated. While there are many software and consulting companies that do not oversell their products or services, many others do not have such admirable ethics. The best vendors are usually the ones that tell you about the challenges, as well as the potential benefits, of their product. In general, if the vendor doesn't mention any product limitations, you're probably hearing marketing speak. A project manager needs to be able to differentiate between the good vendors and the less-than-good vendors, and partner only with those firms that fit the needs of the company and have high ethical standards. In selecting a vendor or consultant, it is important to remember that just because a firm is large, it is not necessarily good or the best choice for your particular implementation. When a project manager is able to select the best vendors for the project and work closely with them as part of a team, everyone benefits from the win-win situation.

The project manager must also be able to manage user expectations, keeping users informed throughout the project life cycle to ensure that they are prepared to take advantage of the repository when it is available and that they thoroughly understand what the repository can—and can't—do. In addition, the project manager needs to provide for end-user training, either by hiring an outside vendor or by training appropriate trainers within the organization.

Additionally, the project manager should be able to define standardized procedures for other IT and business teams to follow to prepare data for the repository. This is where the project manager's communication skills are crucial. He or she must work closely with the other departments to develop procedures that are easy to understand and follow. If the need for standardization and the standards themselves are not clearly communicated to other members of the organization, they are likely to be misinterpreted, or worse yet, simply ignored. If the repository team and its emphasis on standardized procedures is perceived as an obstacle to success by other members of the organization, the repository project is probably doomed to failure. An old meta data repository joke (actually I believe it is the *only* meta data repository joke) emphasizes the need to communicate rather than dictate to users:

> Q. What is the difference between a data administrator and a terrorist?
> A. You can negotiate with a terrorist!

Change Management

The project manager is also responsible for implementing a change management process. Despite everyone's good intentions, project scope creep is as certain as death and taxes. Projects that do not maintain scope are usually doomed to fail. To prevent this, the project manager must create a process to capture any desired changes to the repository. These changes need to be analyzed to gauge their impact on the project's schedule and staff. The project champion and the key decision makers must then decide whether the change should be (1) implemented in the current release of the repository, (2) implemented in the next release, (3) implemented in some future release, or (4) rejected because it is not cost effective and/or beneficial for the majority of users.

Repository Architect

The repository architect is responsible for the technical architecture that the physical meta data repository and its access schema is based upon. Because the architect is responsible for defining and enforcing the construction standards that the data acquisition and data delivery developers will use during implementation, prior experience designing successful meta data repositories is mandatory. (The development standards define how the meta data will be extracted, transformed, loaded, and accessed.) Also, the repository architect should know how to evaluate the physical data model used to store the business and technical meta data so as to be able to provide the data modeler with sound feedback on the proposed model. The architect must be knowledgeable about trends in the meta data industry, and understand their implications for the future. This is especially true of the ongoing battle between the Meta Data Coalition and the Object Management Group for meta model standards, since the outcome of this controversy is likely to shape the meta data landscape in the future and provide direction for meta data tool developers. (See Chapter 3, Meta Data Standards, for a detailed discussion on the battle for meta data standards.) On this same note, the repository architect must also have a thorough understanding of the various meta data tools, including both integration and access tools, and understand how each of the tools plugs into the overall architecture that is required to sustain the meta data repository. Table 5.6 summarizes the recommended skill set for a repository architect, and Table 5.7 lists the basic requirements for this position.

Data Modeler

The data modeler's responsibilities include the initial design and construction of the meta model (i.e., the physical data model) that will hold the business and technical meta data. This individual requires significant experience in data modeling, although not necessarily in modeling meta data. Anyone with a thorough understanding of multidimensional and third-normal modeling can be quite successful when working with an experienced meta data project manager and repository architect. The data modeler should, however, have a firm grasp of third-normal, star, and snowflake modeling tech-

Table 5.6 Repository Architect Skill Sets

PROFESSIONAL SKILLS	TECHNICAL SKILLS
Ability to mentor data developers and data modeler	Familiarity with major meta data integration and access tools and data modeling techniques
Ability to work with software, hardware, and middleware vendors	Ability to design and build the meta data architecture
Concern for quality and be a quick study, a team player, and highly motivated	Knowledge of meta models and ability to review them in detail
Good communications skills	Understanding of the various extraction, integration, and load strategies
	Knowledge of programming languages and platforms, and understanding of which work best together
	Knowledge of data quality controls and ability to implement them in the meta data load process

Table 5.7 Repository Architect Requirements Overview

DESCRIPTION	REQUIREMENT
Number of resources required	1
Years of work experience	8+ years
Difficulty in filling position	High
Experience required	Prior successful experience building a meta data repository
Orientation and feasibility phases	Yes
Design phase	Yes
Construction phase	Yes
Rollout phase	Yes

niques, since these strategies generally form the basis of the meta data repository model and each of these modeling techniques has advantages and disadvantages that the data modeler must consider. Even if an organization purchases a meta data integration tool that incorporates its own meta model (as many do), the data modeler will have to analyze this model to ensure that it meets the requirements of the data repository implementation team.

The data modeler also needs to understand the database technology used for the physical table implementation and the indexing strategies used for table loads and access. For example, most tables require some sort of B-tree index; however other tables may be better served by bitmap indexing, unless there is a centralized database administrator group that can perform this function. Also, the data modeler needs to be familiar with the functionality and quirks of the RDBMS so that he or she can assist the data acquisition developers with their SQL load scripts if necessary. The data modeler also works closely with the data delivery developers to modify the meta data table designs to facilitate faster and more efficient access. This task may also include adding or modifying indexes and tuning the SQL script used to access the meta model to load the end user reports.

Last, in order to construct the meta models, the data modeler needs to work closely with the business and technical end users and the business analyst(s). Here, the data modeler's communications skills are crucial. He or she must ask the right questions to elicit the complete and accurate responses that are necessary for building meta models that will meet the repository's present and future requirements. Table 5.8 lists the recom-

Table 5.8   Data Modeler Skill Sets

PROFESSIONAL SKILLS	TECHNICAL SKILLS
Ability to work well with the business analyst and end users	Thorough understanding of dimensional modeling, including third-normal, star, and snowflake strategies
Good communications skills	Familiarity with RDBMs, especially the one being implemented during the project
	Experience in transitioning business requirements into a data model that can fulfill them

mended professional and technical skills for a data modeler, and Table 5.9 summarizes general requirements for the position.

Business Analyst

The business analyst's primary responsibility is to meet with the business and technical users to define the reporting requirements of the meta data repository. Because joint application design (JAD) and workgroup sessions are generally the most effective method for defining the end-user requirements for the project, the business analyst should have experience leading such sessions. In addition to defining user requirements, the sessions can be useful for shaping the users' expectations for the repository. More than one

Table 5.9   Data Modeler Requirements Overview

DESCRIPTION	REQUIREMENT
Number of resources required	1
Years of work experience	6+ years
Difficulty in filling position	Medium
Experience required	Significant DSS modeling experience, preferably with meta models
Orientation and feasibility phases	No
Design phase	Yes
Construction phase	Yes
Rollout phase	Yes

repository project has failed because the end-users' expectations for the system were unrealistically high.

The business analyst must also be able to translate the requirements that come from the JAD and workgroup sessions into technical solutions that the data modeler, data acquisition developers, and the data delivery developers can use to guide them during the physical meta data repository implementation. It is an added bonus if the business analyst is well versed in the company's business operations so that he or she can speak to the business users in the business language they understand. Last, the business analyst needs to have excellent communication skills and the ability to work closely with the business and technical end users, as well as the development team for the meta data repository. Table 5.10 summarizes the recommended skill set for the business analyst position, and Table 5.11 lists the position requirements and project involvement.

Data Acquisition Developer (Back-End)

The data acquisition developer for the *back end* of the meta data repository (i.e., the process of getting data into the meta data repository) is responsible for extracting the meta data from its sources, programmatically integrating it, and then loading it into the meta data repository. Because this role is primarily a programming one, the data acquisition developer typi-

Table 5.10   Business Analyst Skill Sets

PROFESSIONAL SKILLS	TECHNICAL SKILLS
Ability to work well with the data modeler, data developers, and end users	Experienced in transitioning business requirements into detailed, technical design documents
Ability to organize and facilitate workgroup and JAD sessions	
Ability to manage and control end user expectations	
Strong organizational skills and detail orientation	
Excellent written and verbal communication skills	
Concern for quality and be a quick study, a team player, and highly motivated	

Table 5.11 Business Analyst Requirements Overview

DESCRIPTION	REQUIREMENT
Number of resources required	1
Years of work experience	5+ years
Difficulty in filling position	Low
Experience required	Experience in information gathering and transitioning into meaningful requirements documents
Orientation and feasibility phases	No
Design phase	Yes
Construction phase	Yes
Rollout phase	No

cally should have a strong background in programming and SQL. In some cases, however, an individual with minimal programming experience can fill this role if a meta data integration tool is being used to build the repository. In this event, the data acquisition developer needs to become intimately familiar with the tool and its use for loading the repository's tables. In addition, because the repository tables are usually loaded into a relational database (e.g., Oracle, Informix, SQL Server, DB2), the data acquisition developer needs to be familiar with the particular RDBMS. In all cases, it is crucial for this individual to have a strong concern for quality and the ability to work well with the repository architect.

The data acquisition developer should also have experience in system testing and be thoroughly familiar with the various testing strategies. All too often, organizations neglect the testing phase of the meta data repository implementation, thereby failing to discover problems until the system is rolled out into production. It is important to remember that shortchanging the testing or design phases of the implementation project does not reduce the project's lifecycle; any immediate time savings are more than offset by rework and redesign during the production rollout phase. Table 5.12 summarizes the recommended skill sets for the data acquisition developer, and Table 5.13 lists the general requirements for the position.

Data Delivery Developer (Front-End)

The data delivery developer for the *front end* of the meta data repository (i.e., the means for accessing the repository) is responsible for extracting the

Table 5.12 Data Acquisition Developer Skill Sets

PROFESSIONAL SKILLS	TECHNICAL SKILLS
Conscientious about meeting project timelines	Knowledge of the programming language, and/or integration tool being used to implement the meta data repository
Ability to anticipate potential technical problems	Strong SQL background
Concern for quality and be a quick study, a team player, and highly motivated	Excellent testing skills
	Familiarity with the operating system used by the hardware platform(s) where development is taking place

meta data from the meta data repository and presenting it to the technical and business users. If a meta data access tool is being used to prepare the meta data for presentation to the users, the data delivery developer must be thoroughly familiar with the tool and its strengths and weaknesses. In better meta data implementations, the meta data repository access tool is the same as that used to access the data warehouse and/or data marts. This is important because the reports that have the greatest value to end users typically incorporate both meta data and data warehouse and/or data mart data.

The data delivery developer must have a strong background in programming and SQL, because the meta data generally comes from a relational data-

Table 5.13 Data Acquisition Requirements Overview

DESCRIPTION	REQUIREMENT
Number of resources required	1–3
Years of work experience	2+ years
Difficulty in filling position	Low
Experience required	Programming and systems development experience
Orientation and feasibility phases	No
Design phase	No
Construction phase	Yes
Rollout phase	Yes

base. Most meta data repository projects use a meta data access tool that can generate its own SQL to present the meta data to the end users. Even if one of these tools is used, the data delivery developer is likely to have to tune the SQL that the tool generates. In addition, the individual in this role needs to understand how to create user-friendly reports that present the meta data and data warehouse or data mart data in a clear and logical manner that end users can apply to their business decisions. Last, the data delivery developer must have solid communications skills in order to work well with the business analyst and the repository's end users. Table 5.14 lists the skill sets for the data delivery developer role, and Table 5.15 summarizes the general requirements and phase involvement for this position.

Middleware Developer

This commonly overlooked role is often staffed from a centralized IT department. In today's development environment, it is usually necessary to source meta data from a variety of hardware platforms (i.e., mainframe, PC, or UNIX). Quite often, this task is significantly more difficult than expected, particularly when speed is of the essence (e.g., when the meta data is being sent to populate a business user report). Middleware often provides the solution for linking these diverse platforms. This middleware developer must be able to work well with the infrastructure developer and the repository architect, and have a thorough understanding of the various hardware and software platforms being used to source the meta data. Table 5.16 summarizes the recommended skill sets for this position, and Table 5.17 lists the general requirements for a middleware developer.

Table 5.14   Data Delivery Developer Skill Sets

PROFESSIONAL SKILLS	TECHNICAL SKILLS
Conscientious about meeting project timelines	Familiarity with the programming language, and/or the meta data access tool being used to implement the meta data repository
Ability to anticipate potential technical problems	Strong SQL background
Concern for quality and is a quick study, a team player, and highly motivated	Excellent testing skills
	Familiarity with the operating system used by the hardware platform(s) where development is taking place

Table 5.15   Data Delivery Developer Requirements Overview

DESCRIPTION	REQUIREMENT
Number of resources required	1–3
Years of work experience	3+ years
Difficulty in filling position	Low–Medium
Experience required	Programming and systems development experience
Orientation and feasibility phases	No
Design phase	No
Construction phase	Yes
Rollout phase	Yes

Infrastructure Developer

The infrastructure developer position, like that of the middleware developer, is often staffed from a centralized IT team. The infrastructure developer is responsible for making sure all of the user PCs have the capacity (e.g., memory, CPU, and operating system) to support the software that is being used in the meta data repository. The infrastructure developer should be a proactive individual who is able to work well with other team mem-

Table 5.16   Middleware Developer Skill Sets

PROFESSIONAL SKILLS	TECHNICAL SKILLS
Proactive approach to implementation and problem resolution	Experience implementing middleware products (e.g., ODBC, JDBC, EDA SQL, etc.)
Concern for quality and is a quick study, a team player, and highly motivated	Thorough understanding of such fundamental middleware concepts as: ■ Asynchronous RPC ■ Synchronous RPC ■ Publish/subscribe ■ Message-oriented ■ SQL-oriented ■ Object request brokers
Ability to anticipate and resolve technical challenges	

Table 5.17 Middleware Developer Requirements Overview

DESCRIPTION	REQUIREMENT
Number of resources required	1
Years of work experience	5+ years
Difficulty in filling position	Medium
Experience required	Significant experience using middleware to link multiple, diverse hardware/software platforms
Orientation and feasibility phases	No
Design phase	Yes
Construction phase	Yes
Rollout phase	Yes

bers, particularly the middleware developer and the repository architect, at the onset of the implementation project to ensure that the hardware, software, and middleware work in concert to support the repository architecture. Meta data repository projects often experience problems because the end users' desktop PCs do not support the access tools being used or the platform that the meta data is sourced from.

Table 5.18 summarizes the recommended skill set for the infrastructure developer, and Table 5.19 lists the general requirements involved for this position.

Tool Architect

An experienced tool architect is required for each meta data tool that is being used in the repository project. Like most other software tools, the meta data integration and access tools involve significant learning curves, which have contributed to the failure of more then one repository initiative. An individual who is intimately familiar with each tool and knows how to use it to its best advantage can greatly reduce the risk of this happening.

The role of tool architect(s) may be filled from inside the organization, hired from outside, or, as is most common, staffed on a temporary basis by the tool vendor. Each of these options involves some advantages and some disadvantages. Hiring an experienced tool architect or borrowing one from the tool vendor can significantly shorten the development cycle because there is little or no learning curve involved, but it can also be expensive.

Table 5.18   Infrastructure Developer Skill Sets

PROFESSIONAL SKILLS	TECHNICAL SKILLS
Proactive approach to implementation and problem resolution	Prior experience implementing hardware software, and middleware technical solutions
Concern for quality and is a quick study, a team player, and highly motivated	Understanding of fundamental hardware platforms and operating environments (e.g., mainframes, Unix, Microsoft Windows, AS 400, and client/server architecture)
Ability to anticipate and resolve technical challenges	Familiarity with fundamental software implementation concepts (e.g., hardware tuning to aid software performance, installation requirements, and backup and recovery techniques)
	Familiarity with fundamental middleware concepts (e.g., asynchronous RPC, synchronous RPC, publish/subscribe, message orientation, SQL orientation, and object request brokers)

Experienced tool architects, especially those familiar with the most popular meta data tools, are in high demand and command a hefty fee. But the investment in a top-of-the-line tool architect can save a considerable amount of time and effort in the development phase, thereby justifying the expense. Borrowing a good tool architect from the vendor can save money as well as time and effort, but the vendor's tool architect is liable to be somewhat short-sighted. Remember, these individuals are experts in their particular tools, not in your meta data repository project. They use the tool(s) to implement your meta data repository, then move on to the next project. Because borrowed tool architects are not likely to see the big picture of the repository in your organization or look toward the repository's future requirements, the repository architect and developers need to work closely with these individuals to ensure that their implementation specifically meets the organization's current and future requirements.

The best time to determine how you're going to fill the role of tool architect is *before* you purchase the meta data tool(s). Ideally, the project manager should have the opportunity to interview the prospective tool architect before signing any contracts for the tool(s), then—if the person seems like a good fit for the project team—make his or her participation a condition of the sale.

Table 5.19 Infrastructure Developer Requirements Overview

DESCRIPTION	REQUIREMENT
Number of resources required	1
Years of work experience	6+ years
Difficulty in filling position	Medium
Experience required	Significant prior experience using hardware, software, and middleware to support major technical implementations
Orientation and feasibility phases	Yes
Design phase	Yes
Construction phase	Yes
Rollout phase	Yes

Regardless of how the role is filled, it is vital for the tool architect to work closely with the meta data repository architect during the initial implementation of the repository and during the knowledge transfer phase. The repository architect must consider the specific tool and its strengths and weaknesses when designing the repository's technical architecture. And, the tool architect is the best person to reveal those strengths and weaknesses. For that reason, it is important for the tool architect to be honest as well as knowledgeable. He or she needs to thoroughly describe the tool's strengths and weaknesses to the other members of the meta data repository project team as early in the development lifecycle as possible. Table 5.20 summarizes the recommended skill set for the tool architect, and Table 5.21 summarizes general requirements for the position.

Table 5.20 Tool Architect Skill Sets

PROFESSIONAL SKILLS	TECHNICAL SKILLS
Ability to mentor repository project team in effective use of the meta data tool	Understand the meta data integration/ access tool inside and out, including future releases
Concern for the success of the project, rather than merely the success of the tool	Experience with successful implementations with the tool
Concern for quality and is a quick study, a team player, and highly motivated	
Good communications skills	

Table 5.21   Tool Architect Requirements Overview

DESCRIPTION	REQUIREMENT
Number of resources required	1 per tool
Years of work experience	5+ years
Difficulty in filling position	High
Experience required	Prior successful experience implementing the tool at multiple client sites
Orientation and feasibility phases	No
Design phase	Yes
Construction phase	Yes
Rollout phase	Yes

What Makes a Good Team?

Now that we've presented the 10 key roles of the meta data repository project team, we need to look at the qualities that transform these individual role players into a real team. First, five qualities are critical to all of the roles that we've described:

- Excellent organizational skills
- Team player
- Strong motivation
- Quick study
- Concern for quality

Personally, I've always preferred a team that has these qualities to a team that has the technical know-how but is lacking in these areas. In my experience, **"Great talent finds a way!"** If the people on your team are quick studies, hardworking, team-oriented, with a strong concern for quality, they *can* and *will* overcome any technical obstacles they encounter.

Second, it is important for all of the project managers and architects to take the time to invest in the other members of the team. In other words, the experienced members of the team should spend some time imparting their knowledge to the other members. In addition, all of the team members should have the opportunity to attend conferences and spend some time just learning about the project and the underlying technologies. It is always

BUT, WE DON'T HAVE THE RESOURCES!

Because most companies have severe resource constraints, I'm often asked, "How can we build a repository using only three resources?" If necessary, it is possible to build a repository with a fairly decent project scope using only three resources. In this situation, I would assign each of the resources to the following roles:

- Resource #1: project manager, business analyst

- Resource #2: repository architect, data modeler, data acquisition developer and/or data delivery developer

- Resource #3: data acquisition developer, data delivery developer, tool architect

As we look at these resources, Resource #1 would be responsible for all of the project management, and the business side of the development of the repository. Resource #2 would handle all of the technical architecture and data modeling, and would fill in as an additional programming resource. Resource #3 would be strictly a heads-down programming resource. Lastly, the team roles of infrastructure developer and middleware developer can be filled by a centralized IT team.

important to remember that people, and their inherent knowledge, are an organization's greatest assets. The paybacks are greatest when you invest in them wisely, and treat them honestly and with respect.

Investing in the skills of the team members is particularly important in projects like a meta data repository because experienced people are difficult to find and keep (especially the project manager and repository architect). If you hire an outside consultant to guide the project, be sure that he or she is willing and able to share knowledge with the other team members so that they will be able to maintain and grow the repository long after the consultant has moved on to other clients.

In the next chapter, we describe the process of building a meta data project plan, providing step-by-step guidelines for planning and implementing the repository project, and assigning responsibilities for each of the steps and deliverables.

Building the Meta Data Project Plan

In this chapter, I take you step-by-step through the process of creating a project plan for implementing a meta data repository. First though, I discuss the initial activities that you'll need to complete before beginning the repository project and describe some of the pros and cons of the two prevailing development methodologies. Then I describe each of the five major phases of a typical repository project, explaining in detail the specific tasks, dependencies, resources, and deliverables involved in each phase, and share some of the techniques that I've used to accomplish the requisite tasks. This chapter is intended for everyone working on a meta data repository implementation project, even nonproject managers.

Identifying the Initial Activities

Before you can create a good project plan, you need to assess the goals of the project and determine what activities must be completed before you can achieve those goals. Typically, the initial activities include:

- Educating the clients and/or prospective users
- Adjusting the plan to staff capabilities
- Funding and scheduling the project
- Selecting a project methodology

Educating the Clients

Does the company have a solid understanding of meta data and decision support concepts? This is the first question I ask myself when I begin working at a client site. This is not to imply that the key personnel and the development staff need to be experts in this area; it's just to assess their understanding of the key concepts that surround the project we're about to undertake. For example, when I speak with a client, I often ask some or all of the following questions:

- What is the difference between a data warehouse and a data mart?
- What is meta data?
- Why is meta data important?
- What makes a data warehouse successful?

Typically, there is a need for education of some sort in any meta data development effort. Education is important to provide a clear picture of what meta data does and doesn't do. Training courses are often necessary to ensure that everyone understands the basic concepts. When a company skips this step, the end result is usually less than favorable.

Education provides two major benefits: (1) It helps the members of the meta data implementation team and the people that they will be working with in the organization to speak the same language, and (2) it can help the project champion and project manager sell the idea of the meta data repository to their executive management. The individuals working on the implementation project often come from different departments and backgrounds. It is important for these people to use the same terms to refer to the same things and to have a common view of the fundamental tasks involved in the project. We discuss these benefits and techniques for realizing them in the orientation phase of our project plan.

Adjusting the Plan to Staff Capabilities

A good staff is the key to any successful project. It is also the key to a good project plan. If you are a data administrator, it is important for you to be able to step back and honestly assess your team. I generally write out my team's strengths and weaknesses, in accordance with the major project phases. Then I use this assessment as direct input for the project plan. After I've completed this analysis, I adjust the project plan according to my findings. For example, if the team is strong on the business analysis side, I may reduce the allocated amount of time for the design phase by as much as

PRACTICING WHAT I PREACH

An honest analysis of the team's skill sets is crucial in that it can have a major impact on the timelines of the project. The most dramatic case of this that I've experienced was at a large retail business in the Midwest. As I was building the detailed project plan, I decided to increase the construction phase of this project by 100 percent above my typical estimate. This company had hired me to perform high-level project management, but it was apparent to me very early on that the project was headed for rough water. The business team and the development team were involved in a fierce political struggle, and the people responsible for the detail work were very green and did not seem amenable to training. Unfortunately, I had the unenviable task of explaining this to the CIO who had asked me to work on the project. Giving a client this type of news is not easy, but I felt strongly about the situation and prepared an estimate to correspond with my negative impressions, confident that it would be accurate. As things turned out, my estimate was within 3 percent of the actual number of hours the project required.

There is an important lesson to be learned from this situation. Don't be afraid to give bad news. The CIO was not happy with the news I gave him, but he accepted it after I demonstrated the reasoning behind my assessment. Because we knew early in the development cycle how long the project was likely to take, we were able to manage our business users' expectations and direct our efforts effectively. If I had not convinced the company to modify the timelines for the project, the end users would have been disappointed and the project would have floundered—or worse—as we continually moved the project date further and further out. Remember, bad news only gets worse over time. The sooner you deliver it, the less painful it is likely to be.

20 percent. Conversely, if, the programmers are a little raw and not accustomed to working with one another, I may increase the time allowed for the construction phase by 15 percent.

People often ask me if the hour estimates in a project plan should be tailored to the specific people on the development staff. If you are 100 percent sure of who will be doing the work, there is nothing wrong with estimating for the specific individuals, and in many cases it is the smart thing to do. For example, a developer in my company typically completes his work 65 percent faster than most of the other developers I know. This developer has worked on more than 15 data warehouse projects, so his skill set is truly unique. When I estimate for him, I tend to cut his timelines by as much as 50 percent, depending on the stability of the design specification and development environment. Fifty percent may seem like a high number, but because he typically works 60 to 70 percent faster than other good programmers, it is actually a rather conservative estimate.

One of the key things to keep in mind when evaluating your team's skill sets is how well its members work together. Systems development requires a great deal of interaction between staff members. Even if you have a group of wonderfully talented individuals, if they can't function well as a team your project is likely to run into difficulties. Team dynamics and communication are absolutely vital to the success of the project.

Funding and Scheduling the Project

Projects rarely have soft timelines and open funding. In fact, I've never encountered this situation. Throughout my career, consulting at many sites for many clients, someone—usually a director, CIO, or vice president—has provided me with project timelines and budgets, or guidelines for developing these variables. Typically, funding and timelines are predetermined, since they can have a major impact the scope of a project. Companies often restrict new development systems from being rolled out during certain peak business periods (e.g., the holiday buying season, end-of-fiscal year, etc.).

It is not uncommon for a company to say that it has $200,000 to purchase tools and $500,000 for consulting, and the project must be finished before the end of the fiscal year—now go build a repository. Constraints like these affect the number of requirements that can be included in the first release of the project. When they exist, it is best to be conservative about the amount of functionality that can be squeezed into the first release of a project. Realize that unexpected events will arise to consume the available time and money. By being conservative, you can provide the meta data implementation team with the necessary flexibility to adapt.

Selecting a Project Methodology

There are two general methodologies for project development:

Big bang.   This methodology, which is sometimes also referred to as a *Waterfall* technique, involves building an entire, fully functional meta data application in one huge development effort. This approach requires completing each step of the process before moving on to the next step. In addition, it mandates a major prototyping effort to identify the end user requirements. Because this methodology tries to implement all of the known user requirements in one development effort, it tends to be very expensive to undertake and significantly increases the probability for project failure.

Table 6.1 Big Bang versus Iterative Development Methodologies

METHODOLOGY	ADVANTAGES	DISADVANTAGES
Big bang	Provides the fastest development path to fulfill all meta data requirements	Requires a large-scale development team effort
		Requires tremendous coordination
		High complexity
		Highest risk
Iterative	Reduces risk of project failure	Long development cycle to fulfill all meta data requirements
	Lessons are learned and leveraged	
	Allows for proof of concept	

Iterative.   This methodology, which is sometimes also referred to as a *Spiral* technique, delivers software functionality in incremental (i.e., iterative) releases. Improvements are identified by successful deployments of the software, with tight controls but continually increasing functionality. Managers make decisions about the feasibility of a project, the resources allocated to it, and the risks associated with development. At each cycle of the spiral, a fresh decision is reached as to the purpose and value in doing another cycle. The motto for this methodology is to "think enterprise, plan enterprise, then implement in small iterations."

Table 6.1 summarizes the advantages and disadvantages of each of these two approaches.

The project plan that we will walk through in this chapter uses the iterative development method, since this is the methodology that I usually try to implement. Table 6.2 summarizes the environmental factors that dictate which development method is most appropriate for a particular environment.

Creating the Project Plan

The project plan that we will walk through is intended to be full lifecycle plan for implementing a meta data repository (and is presented in its entirety in Appendix B and the accompanying CD-ROM). This plan contains all of the major sections that most meta data projects require. Although this project plan focuses on implementing a new repository, the steps for enhancing an

Table 6.2   Selecting an Appropriate Methodology

METHODOLOGY	OPTIMAL ENVIRONMENTAL FACTORS
Big Bang	Minimal internal politics
	IT and business groups must work well together
	Company has a strong understanding of meta data
	Executive level support exists
Iterative	Significant pressure from internal politics
	High corporate exposure
	Repository requirements are highly complex
	Limited funding

existing repository are much the same. Remember that you can use all of the plan, or just the sections that apply to your specific requirements.

A typical meta data implementation project involves the following five phases, which we'll discuss in detail in the following sections:

1. Orientation
2. Feasibility
3. Design
4. Construction
5. Rollout

The timelines for a meta data repository project differ widely according to the functionality required and the available staff. After the initial phases are complete and funding is allocated, the design and construction phases for the first repository iteration typically take about 80 to 90 workdays to complete. The first iteration generally is relatively small but involves a significant amount of work that, at its completion, provides definable value to the company. Obviously, if the first iteration involves numerous or complex requirements, the project timelines need to be extended.

Reading the Project Plan

Before we begin walking through the various phases of the sample project plan, I'll explain a bit about how I've organized this particular plan. Your own plan may differ somewhat from this one, but it will need to represent the same basic entities to determine what tasks need to be completed and in what order, how long those tasks are likely to take, and what resources are required to complete them. The sample project plan uses the following fields to capture this information:

- Task ID
- Duration
- Dependency
- Resource name

Task ID

The Task ID field represents the hierarchy of specific tasks of the meta data repository project plan. Our project plan has four levels in its hierarchy (*phase, activity, task,* and *subtask*), with *phase* at the top of this hierarchy.

Phase refers to a related group of major project endeavors (e.g., *orientation, feasibility, design, construction,* and *rollout*). The Task ID field uses a one-digit numeric (e.g., 1, 2, 3, etc.) to represent a phase. Each phase involves a series of activities, which are represented in the Task ID field by a two-digit numeric, with values separated by a decimal point (e.g., 1.1, 1.2, 1.3, etc.). Activities, in turn, are composed of one or more tasks. Tasks are represented in the Task ID field by three-digit numeric with values separated by decimal points (e.g., 1.1.1, 1.1.2, 1.2.1, etc.). Lastly, a task may involve multiple subtasks, which are represented by a four-digit numeric, with each value separated by decimal points (i.e., 1.1.1.1, 1.1.1.2, 2.1.1.1, etc.). Figure 6.1 illustrates this hierarchy.

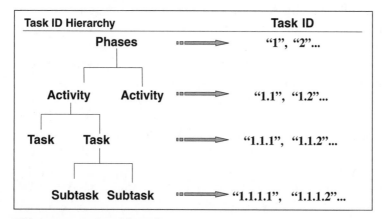

Figure 6.1   Task ID hierarchy.

Duration

The Duration field estimates the number of workdays it will take to complete each phase, activity, task, and subtask. Each value in the duration field is expressed in eight-hour business days, and no task has a duration of less than one day, unless the activity, task, or subtask is a *milestone*. Milestones are represented by the value of "0 days" in the duration field.

It is important to note that the duration for a Task ID that has subordinate Task IDs (e.g., phases that have activities, activities that have tasks, etc.) may not equal the sum of all of the subordinate Task IDs' duration because some of the subordinate Task IDs can be performed concurrently. For example, Table 6.3 presents a Task ID (Phase 1: Orientation) with subordinate Task IDs (Activities: 1.1, 1.2, 1.3, 1.4, and 1.5). Task ID 1 has a total duration of 13 days, even though the sum of Task IDs 1.1, 1.2, 1.3, 1.4, and 1.5 equals 14 days. This is because Task IDs 1.1 and 1.2 do not have any dependencies so they can be performed concurrently.

Dependency

The Dependency field indicates the Task ID for any activity or task that must be completed before work on the current Task ID can begin.

Resource Name

The Resource field lists the names of the resources that will be required for the particular Task ID. When a resource is named to a Task ID, assume that the resource will need to allocate the number of days shown in the duration field to complete the Task ID. The exception to this case is when the resource name is followed by brackets (e.g., []). Brackets indicate the amount (percentage) of this particular resource that will be required. For example, if a resource name field shows "Project Champion [.5]" and the duration of the Task ID is 5 days, then only 2.5 days or 20 hours of the project champion's time will be required for the Task ID. On the other hand, if a resource name field shows "Data Acquisition Developer [2.0]" and the duration for the Task ID is 5 days, then this means that two full-time data acquisition developers need to be assigned to this Task ID in order to complete it on time (i.e., within five days in this example).

Although I described most of the meta data repository project team roles in Chapter 5, Organizing and Staffing the Meta Data Repository Project, there are a few additional individuals who may play a role in developing and implementing the project plan:

Database administrator. This individual is responsible for the physical implementation of the relational and object databases. This role typically includes physical design, capacity planning, monitoring response time and resource usage (i.e., CPU and disk I/O), and identifying and evaluating performance problems, as well as tuning the databases, and reviewing the complex SQL statements written by the data acquisition and data delivery developers.

Key executive management. These are the individuals within an organization who provide budgetary and/or political support for the repository implementation and who therefore are critical to its success. While a repository project can succeed without the support of all of the following individuals, the more they lend their active support to the project, the greater the chances will be of the initiative succeeding. Individuals who typically fall into this category include the chief executive officer (CEO), chief information officer, line-of-business managers, and senior business executives.

Key IT team leaders. Key IT team leaders are the managers of the major IT projects. These individuals are vital to the success of the meta data repository because the repository usually needs to capture meta data from the IT systems that these managers maintain. The cooperation and assistance of these individuals is crucial for ensuring that the repository captures the meta data accurately from the correct sources. Key IT team leaders generally include the decision support manager, operational systems managers (e.g., logistics, invoicing, accounting, and order fulfillment), customer relationship systems manager, and Internet systems manager.

Subject matter experts. Subject matter experts usually come from the business side of the organization and are responsible for the various subject areas (e.g., customer, product, order, market segment, etc.) of a company. Subject matter experts are very similar to data stewards in that they act as conduits between IT and the business users, aligning the users' business needs with the IT systems (i.e., decision support and operational) that support those needs. Subject matter experts are heavily involved with determining the requirements of the meta data repository and establishing priorities for those requirements.

Orientation Phase

The orientation phase (see Table 6.3) is the first phase of the meta data repository's lifecycle. The goal here is to ensure that key people in the com-

Table 6.3   Orientation Phase

TASK ID	TASK NAME	DURATION	DEPENDENCY	RESOURCE NAMES
1	Orientation phase	15 days		
1.1	Gauge organization's understanding of meta data	1 day		Project manager
1.2	Obtain meta data course instructor	7 days		Project manager [0.25]
1.3	Design customized course	3 days	1.2	Trainer, project manager [0.25]
1.4	Conduct executive training	1 day	1.3	Trainer, project champion, subject matter expert, end user committee, project manager, key executive management, key IT team leaders
1.5	Conduct training for key developers	4 days	1.4	Trainer, subject matter expert [0.5], project manager, database administrator, data modeler, repository architect, business analyst, data acquisition developers, data delivery developers

pany understand the fundamental concepts of meta data and the value of a meta data repository. If I feel that the key people understand meta data and its value and are likely to allocate funds to the project, I skip this phase. This happy situation rarely occurs, however, because most companies are still discovering meta data's intrinsic value. The orientation phase also gives the project manager or project champion the opportunity to sell the concept of meta data to the executives in the company. It is almost always necessary to sell the meta data concept to the company before any funding is allocated. This is why the orientation phase must occur before the feasibility phase.

If the project manager has a strong background in meta data and repository implementation, then he or she may be a fine instructor for an orientation class. In most situations, however, it is advisable to bring someone in from outside the company to teach the class. This is primarily because a good meta data course (or any course for that matter) requires about 4 to 6 hours of development time for each hour of class time. Because it usually takes a total of about 24 hours of class time to prepare a company for a meta data repository implementation (i.e., 8 hours for executive training [Table 6.3, Task ID # 1.4] and 32 hours for detailed developer training [Table 6.3, Task ID # 1.5]), the project manager would need between 160 and 240 hours (i.e., 4 to 6 hours × 40) to prepare for the executive and developer courses. This time can be decreased slightly if the development team is familiar with meta data; in this case, 8–16 hours of training should be sufficient.

Of course, finding a qualified meta data course instructor (Table 6.3, Task ID # 1.2) also takes time; figure on spending about seven days to find the right instructor for the course, to negotiate the statement of work, and to sign any necessary paperwork. It's very important that the instructor has actual experience building meta data repositories and not just a theoretical background. In addition, it is best if the instructor is a senior individual, since part of the training task is to sell the concept to executive management. Many companies make the mistake of letting a meta data tool vendor conduct these training sessions. In my experience, a trainer who is borrowed from the tool vendor makes the course very tool-focused and far too technical for management. On the other hand, if the person comes from the vendor's marketing department, the training is likely to be relatively nontechnical—but still very tool-focused. These individuals tend to greatly oversell the ease of building a meta data repository. As we know, any major IT effort takes a good deal of work.

The subject matter expert may attend both courses, or just developer training (Table 6.3, Task ID # 1.5). If this individual will be working on a day-to-day basis with the business analyst, then he or she should attend both sessions.

Feasibility Phase

The purpose of the feasibility phase is to ascertain whether it is cost beneficial for the company to build a meta data repository. There are two key deliverables that occur during the feasibility phase: the *project scope document* and the *high-level project plan* (see Table 6.4).

Create Project Scope Document

The project scope document is the first, and possibly the most important, deliverable in the meta data repository project. Unfortunately, it is also the deliverable that many companies fail to produce. The project scope document should define the specific business and technical drivers for implementing the meta data repository. It serves as the project's compass and drives all subsequent project development work, thereby minimizing the phenomenon of *project creep*. Project creep is a very common cause of project failure; it occurs when the end-user requirements increase or change significantly during the design and development phases. In creating the project scope document, remember the three "Ss" of development: *Staff*, *Scope*, and *Schedule*. These three elements are tightly integrated (as Figure 6.2 illustrates); if you change one, you have to change them all. If you don't, then the quality of the project will suffer.

Creating a project scope document typically requires between three and four weeks (as shown in Table 6.5). If your company sign-off policy calls for multiple signatures and/or there are strong political pressures among the decision makers, then it may take as much as seven weeks to complete this deliverable. On the other hand, if the company is essentially a dictatorship and requires only a single high-level signature, the entire project scope document process can be completed in as little as two weeks.

Table 6.4   Feasibility Phase—High-Level Tasks

TASK ID	TASK NAME	DURATION	DEPENDENCY	RESOURCE NAMES
2	Feasibility phase	26 days		
2.1	Create project scope document	17 days		
2.2	High-level planning and estimating	9 days		

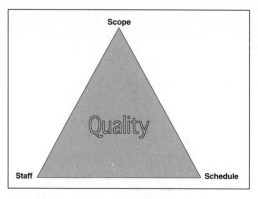

Figure 6.2 Project quality triangle.

I'll discuss each of the major sections of the project scope document in detail on the next several pages, but briefly, the major sections are:

- Project definition
- Future meta data repository releases
- Project scope
- Critical success factors
- Risk factors
- Assumptions
- Issues
- Sign-off sheet

Create Interview Questions and Conduct Interviews

You'll need to conduct interviews (see Table 6.5, Task IDs # 2.1.1 and # 2.1.2) with each of the key technical and business people in the company to determine the critical technical and business drivers that will comprise the project scope document. The first steps, then, are to identify these individuals, then compose questionnaires that focus on the key information requirements that would help these people to perform their jobs more efficiently. (Table 6.6 presents some sample interview questions.)

In many ways, these interviews are similar to a trip to the doctor's office. At the doctor's office, the physician pokes you all over to find out what hurts. After the physician has identified the top two or three things that are

Table 6.5   Feasibility Phase—Create Project Scope Document

TASK ID	TASK NAME	DURATION	DEPENDENCY	RESOURCE NAMES
2.1	Create project scope document	17 days		
2.1.1	Create interview questions	1 day		Project manager, business analyst
2.1.2	Conduct interviews with key personnel	10 days	2.1.1	Project manager [0.5], business analyst, subject matter expert
2.1.3	Evaluate requirements	3 days	2.1.2	Subject matter expert, business analyst, project champion, project manager
2.1.4	Generate project scope document	2 days	2.1.3	Business analyst, project manager
2.1.5	Meet with key personnel to approve document	5 days	2.1.4	Business analyst [0.5], project champion [0.25], project manager [0.5], key executive management [0.25], subject matter expert [0.5]
2.1.6	Obtain sign-off	1 day	2.1.5	Project champion, project manager, subject matter expert

Table 6.6 Sample Interview Questions

QUESTION	PURPOSE
What aspects of your current decision support systems do you find most beneficial and why?	Provides a good gauge as to what really benefits the end user.
What aspects of your current decision support systems could use improvement?	This is an opportunity question that begins to reveal the user's "pain."
What information would help you be more effective on your job?	Another way of asking the previous question (but some people find it easier to respond to a more broad-based question).
What limits your effectiveness on your job?	This type of question tests the skill of the interviewer. Most of the answers are not likely to be technology related, so the interviewer must be able to hear broad answers and understand how meta data technology could aid in the situation. The reason for the broadness of these questions is to discover possible opportunities.

wrong with you, he or she can begin treating the problems. In much the same fashion, the project manager or business analyst who typically conducts these interviews asks questions to discover the information needs of these key individuals, then probes further to determine how well these needs are being met and how improving the information flow would help them do their jobs better.

Keep in mind that the key to a good interview process is not just asking questions. You must also be sure that the interviewee gives concrete answers. For example, if an individual says that the information on a particular report is difficult to understand, a good interviewer follows up with another question like: "Why is it difficult to understand?" Is the information poorly formatted? Incorrect? Or are users not aware of what they are looking at? Follow-up questions are actually more important than the base questions.

The interviewers also need to be able to recognize meta data requirements when they hear them. If, for example, an interviewee says "Our analysts often make incorrect decisions because we don't know how our report metrics are calculated," the interviewer should recognize that meta data definitions may address this problem. I would suggest asking the interviewee what percentage of errors does he or she feel that this problem creates. Ideally, an empirical number can then be placed on this (e.g., approximately

40 each month or at least 2 a day), and a cost attributed to these mistakes from the standpoint of expense (i.e., money lost) and/or opportunity lost (i.e., money that could be made). If, however, the interviewer cannot elicit hard numbers (as is often the case), he or she should continue to probe the issue, asking questions like, "Would business definitions eliminate these errors and make your life *significantly* better?" If interviewees are not willing to state that fulfilling such needs would significantly improve their work performance, the requirement may not be urgent.

Generate Project Scope Document

After the information gathering and requirements evaluation steps are complete, you can begin putting the project scope document together, starting with the project definition section. Remember, you should tailor the project scope document to your particular project; include all of the sections or only those that are directly relevant to your implementation.

Project Definition

The project definition section should set the scope for the first phase of the meta data repository project. As such, it typically lists the specific business and technical drivers and benefits that the meta data repository should accomplish, along with the specific high-level technical project deliverables that need to occur to satisfy these drivers.

When identifying business and technical drivers, it is important to highlight exactly how the driver will benefit the company. Because companies typically increase their profitability by reducing expenses or increasing revenues, each driver should show how it accomplishes either or both of these goals. Examples of the most common technical and business drivers include:

- Reduce future IT development costs and shrink the system development lifecycles

- Improve the business users' access to the decision support information by creating a meta data–driven decision support front end to help them find the information that they need

- Reduce turnaround time for production-related problems

- Provide business user access to historical changes in the decision support system to enable users to make better business decisions

After you have determined the business and technical drivers, it is important to list the specific high-level technical deliverables that will be needed to satisfy these drivers. Some examples of typical technical deliverables and the activities required to create them are:

- Technically integrate all of data models (physical and logical), data transformation rules, and data sources

- Implement a meta data access tool capable of capturing user access patterns and frequency of use

- Implement data administration standards, including data naming standards, application descriptions, and business definitions

- Create a front end for business users to define their report and field definitions

- Create a technical infrastructure capable of providing access to technical and business meta data

- Capture historical changes to the decision support system

- Construct predefined meta data reports for the business and technical users

Although it is important to capture the business definitions for business fields and reports, it is usually very difficult to get a company to take the necessary time to construct all of them. I deal with this situation by telling the business managers that the meta data implementation team will create the initial definitions, but will need assistance from the data stewards assigned by the various business units to review and, if necessary, modify the definitions. I have found this strategy to be quite successful. If the definitions are not created at the beginning of the project, the business is likely to fail to recognize their value and never create them. On the other hand, repository implementation teams often create the definitions, but fail to assign data stewards and/or fail to create a good front end to support the definitions. If business users don't agree with some of the definitions, they should be responsible for changing them, but they need an easy-to-use front end to ensure that the definitions remain complete and consistent. A good front end also eliminates the need for the repository implementation team to review and approve all changes, thereby minimizing the team's ongoing support efforts.

Future Meta Data Repository Releases

This section of the project scope document is vital because it sets the future vision for the meta data repository team. This section presents the ultimate goals for the meta data repository and emphasizes the need to implement a flexible infrastructure that can grow as user needs change and expand. For example, the future vision for the repository may be to incorporate publish and subscribe capabilities, and roll the repository out to the entire enterprise, providing access through a corporate portal. This section also identifies the development activities that must be accomplished in each of the project phases to attain the project vision.

I believe it is valuable to list some key high-level business and technical drivers for Release 2 of the project in this section. While these drivers may change in the project scope document for Release 2 of the project, it is often helpful to state the drivers here to ensure that the repository that is created in Release 1 considers the needs of the future releases.

Project Scope

This section of the project scope document defines, at a high-level, the technical plan for the first phase of the project. It presents the initial meta data integration architecture that will be used, along with the meta data needs that the repository will fill, and the meta data sources. Lastly, the project scope section should list the meta data repository standards that need to be established. These standards are very important because other groups may need to follow them, and a signed document that clearly lists the standards is extremely useful for ensuring compliance.

Figure 6.3 illustrates a high-level architecture for a meta data repository that is not directly integrated into a data warehouse or data mart.

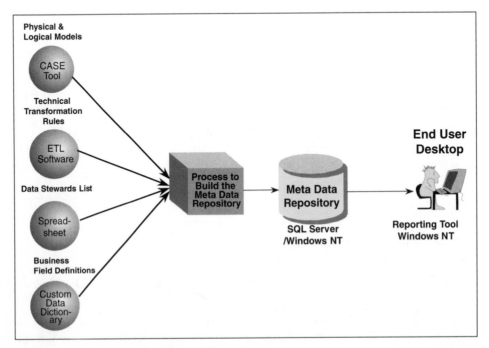

Figure 6.3   Meta data integration architecture 1.

If the first phase of the repository involves modifying new or existing data warehouse reports and uses the same front end as the data warehouse, then the architecture would be similar to that illustrated in Figure 6.4.

Critical Success Factors Section

This section states the items that will be crucial for determining the success of the implementation project. I include it on most of the project scope documents that I create, and generally include such items as:

- Lay the groundwork for an enterprise-wide meta data repository
- Automate repository loading process
- Establish scope control
- Roll out the repository

I include the last three items on this list (automate repository loading process, establish scope control, and roll out the repository) on *every* project scope document that I write because they are critical in all projects. Unfortunately, automating the process for loading the meta data sources into the repository is something that many meta data implementation teams overlook. It is very important to limit the number of manual processes for

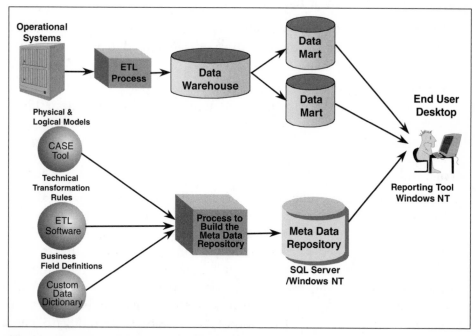

Figure 6.4 Meta data integration architecture 2.

the meta data repository. Although a few manual processes are quite common during the initial load of the repository, these should be one-time efforts. Subsequent loads should be automated with a user friendly front end to automate the process.

Scope control is critical to the success of any effort, IT or otherwise, because most changes in scope have a direct effect on the schedule and staffing needs of a project. As a result, I always include a statement in the project scope document emphasizing the need for a change management process, which is a set of procedures that must be followed in order to trigger any change to any defined phase of the repository project. The change procedures should be easy to follow, but should be mandatory for any change that is requested after the project scope document is signed off. After the change process is complete, it should be subject to approval by the same individuals that signed off on the original scope document.

The critical success factor of rolling out the repository is self-explanatory. If we don't roll the repository out to the end users, we don't have a success.

Risk Factors Section

This section of the project scope document states the potential major roadblocks to the success of the meta data repository project. I include this section on nearly all of the project scope documents that I prepare. Some typical risks that might be listed include:

- Support from other project teams is vital to the success of the meta data project. This section lists the teams that need to assist the meta data repository team.

- Resource allocation and skills refers to the importance for the company to allocate the necessary resources to build and maintain the meta data repository. In addition, these resources need to have the proper skill sets. These points help to attain better resources.

Assumptions

This section usually lists the basic environmental and operating conditions that exist when you begin the repository project and that you assume will remain unchanged during the course of the initial implementation. For example, you may specify the hardware and software platforms that the integration architecture will be based on, or list the key personnel resources (by position or name) who are assigned to work on the repository project. While these factors may seem obvious, even a small change in the operating system environment or the RDBMS that supports the DSS (e.g., upgrading to a new version) or losing a project developer to some other assignment can have a significant impact on the delivery schedule for the repository. (See "Obtain-

Table 6.7 Project Scope Document—Sign-Off Sheet

NAME	SIGNATURE	DATE

ing Clear Management Direction" in Chapter 7, Constructing a Meta Data Architecture, for an example of assumptions that failed to materialize.)

Issues Section

This is a catchall section for any issues that arise during the creation of the project scope document. If, for example, the implementation team intends to use a standard data modeling tool, but is not sure if it can extract meta data from the tool, that question would be noted in this section.

Sign-Off Sheet Section

The very last page of the project scope document is a sign-off sheet for the company's decision makers to indicate their review and approval of the document (see Table 6.7 for an example).

Perform High-Level Planning and Estimating

The high-level project plan is the second key deliverable of the feasibility phase. (Table 6.8 defines the tasks that lead to this deliverable.) This plan uses information from the project scope document to lay out all of the activities and tasks that must be completed in each phase of the project and estimates the costs involved in the initial release of the meta data repository based on projected resource requirements. This plan is vital for ensuring that company executives and IT managers understand the level of commitment and resources that are required for implementing the meta data repository and for cost-justifying the design and construction phases of the project. Table 6.9 illustrates a sample high-level project plan.

After the project plan is approved by the project champion, the meta data repository project manager will have to obtain the resources to staff the plan. Ideally, the resource requirements can be filled from the company's existing staff, but if the IT department does not have sufficient resources to meet the demands of the project plan, the project manager has three options for obtaining the necessary resources: (1) hire additional IT staff, which can extend the project timelines; (2) extend the project timelines so that the available staff can meet its requirements; or (3) hire a consultant to partner with on the project.

Table 6.8   Feasibility Phase—High-Level Planning and Estimating

TASK ID	TASK NAME	DURATION	DEPENDENCY	RESOURCE NAMES
2.2	High-level planning and estimating	9 days		
2.2.1	Develop high level project plan	3 days	2.1	Project manager
2.2.2	Determine resource requirements	2 days	2.1	Project manager
2.2.3	Approve project plan, resource requirements, and funding	2 days	2.2.2	Project champion, project manager
2.2.4	Obtain resources (internal and external)	5 days	2.2.3	Project manager
2.2.5	Initial project plan and resourcing complete	0	2.2.4	

DETERMINING PROJECT COSTS

Some project planners include the orientation and feasibility phases in the cost estimates for the high-level project plan because these phases have already occurred and are considered *sunk* costs. Sunk costs are cash outlays that have already been committed for a project and are irrecoverable regardless of whether the project is accepted or rejected. Some senior managers believe that these costs need to be shown in the high-level project plan to fully understand the project's return on investment.

In my experience, the costs incurred during the orientation and feasibility phases do not need to be considered in the decision to fund the project. However, these costs do need to be included when calculating the project's final ROI. The only exception to this is when the orientation and feasibility phases have taken an inordinate amount of time. For example, let's suppose that an inexperienced project manager wasted a great deal of time and effort during these phases on activities of little or no benefit to the project. In this case, the costs of these phases should probably be considered in the high-level project plan just to give an accurate picture of the project's overall cost to the company.

Table 6.9 Feasibility Phase—Sample High-Level Project Plan

TASK ID	TASK NAME	DURATION	DEPENDENCY
	Meta data repository project plan	81 days	
1	Orientation phase	15 days	
2	Feasibility phase	26 days	
2.1	Create project scope document	17 days	
2.2	High-level planning and funding	9 days	
3	Design phase	36 days	2
3.1	Meta data tool evaluation and selection	26 days	
3.1.1	Meta data integration tool	26 days	
3.1.2	Meta data access tool	26 days	
3.2	Construct integration architecture document	10 days	
3.3	Create detailed design document	17 days	2
3.4	Train development staff (if tool is being used)	10 days	3.1
4	Construction phase	77 days	
4.1	Build meta model	10 days	3.3
4.2	Design meta data security process	6 days	3.3
4.3	Develop meta data integration processes	12 days	3, 3.4, 4.5.3
4.4	Develop meta data reports/access method	10 days	3, 3.4, 4.5.3
4.5	Meta data infrastructure	9 days	4.1
4.5.1	Desktop setup and configuration	9 days	3.1.2
4.5.2	Select and implement RDBMS	5 days	
4.5.3	Meta data tools setup and configuration	3 days	3.1.2
4.6	User acceptance testing (UAT)	11 days	4.3, 4.4
4.6.1	Business user training	6 days	
4.6.2	Technical user training	6 days	
4.7	Conduct user acceptance testing	5 days	4.6.1, 4.6.2
5	Rollout phase	4 days	4.7

MY STRATEGY FOR OBTAINING SIGN-OFF

Information technology development is as serious a business initiative as there is, but it sometimes involves a little bit of humor, too. This can be particularly true of the senior executive sign-off procedure.

Anyone who has ever had to obtain these signatures understands how difficult the task can be. One of my business law professors in graduate school once asked the class to provide the definition of a cosigner. A couple of students tried to answer the question, but the instructor told each of them that their definition was inaccurate. According to the professor, the definition of a cosigner is "an idiot with a pen." I have to say that his comment has greatly limited my desire to ever cosign. This attitude shows that people do not like to sign their names to anything, especially a project scope document that they believe may come back to haunt them.

I have a process for attaining signatures that has proven to be invaluable over the years. I first call a meeting of all the key decision makers to review the document and suggest changes. This meeting typically needs to be scheduled well in advance because the executives typically have very full schedules. The agenda for this meeting is to walk through the project scope document and make any changes that are necessary for its approval. At the end of the meeting, I ask the decision makers to sign off on the document. At this point, they usually ask to have an opportunity to review the revised document with some of their key people. I generally commit to revising the document no later than 24 hours after the meeting and emphasize the importance of gaining approval within five business days from the date of the meeting. Then, I add that anyone who does not request additional changes or corrections within this time frame is giving implicit consent to the document. In other words, "silence is consent."

As soon as the revised document is available (always within my promised time frame) I personally hand a copy to each of the key decision makers. Everyone has one week to review the document and return it to me with changes or corrections. During that week, I seek out each executive and ask, in person, for his or her signature on the document. Sometimes decision makers sign off on the document just to keep me from asking them again. If, however, by the end of the week I haven't received signed documents or feedback from each of the decision makers, I send e-mail reminding everyone that silence is considered consent and that at this point everyone has consented fully to all of the sections of the project scope document. This strategy forces the decision makers to actually make decisions and helps to retain the integrity of the project timelines.

Getting the Decision

The two major deliverables of the feasibility phase—the project scope document and high-level project plan—should provide executive management with sufficient justification to approve (or reject) the meta data repository project. If approval is obtained, it's time to move into the design phase, which brings the development team into the implementation. If, however, the company's decision makers do not approve the repository project at this point, the project manager needs to discover the reason for the rejection. In my experience there are two common reasons why a project proposal is rejected after the orientation and feasibility phases are complete:

Budgetary constraints.   Companies often have budgetary constraints that prevent executive management from funding the meta data repository. In this situation, it is advisable to try to position the repository effort to attain funding during the next fiscal year. In most cases, this means representing the repository project to executive management when funds for the following year's IT initiatives are allocated, which may require reworking some of the resource and cost estimates.

Repository is not perceived as valuable.   Key management is likely to reject a repository project if the majority of managers do not perceive the repository's value to the organization. In this situation, the repository project manager generally has three options: (1) reduce the cost of the project by reducing its overall scope or scaling back on the initial implementation, thereby reducing the amount of risk to the organization while still meeting the major requirements for meta data; (2) expand the scope of the project to fulfill specific needs expressed by key executives, thereby satisfying a key executive's particular interest; or (3) try to resell the concept of meta data, convincing the key executives of the benefits of the repository project or, if necessary, enlisting the aid of a new or additional project champion.

Design Phase

The purpose of the design phase is to document the specific processing and reporting requirements of the meta data repository project, fleshing out the activities and tasks enumerated on the high-level project plan. The key deliverables in this phase are (1) the meta data tools evaluation; (2) an integration architecture document; (3) detail design documents, which include delivery specifications; and (4) a development staff training plan. (See Table 6.10 for details of the design phase.)

Table 6.10 Design Phase

TASK ID	TASK NAME	DURATION	DEPENDENCY	RESOURCE NAMES
3	Design phase	36 days	2	
3.1	Meta data tool evaluation and selection	26 days		
3.1.1	Meta data integration tool	26 days		
3.1.1.1	Identify major integration tool vendors	2 days		Data acquisition developers, repository architect [0.25], project manager [0.25], data modeler
3.1.1.2	Create weighted checklist and interview	5 days		Data acquisition developers, repository architect [0.25], project manager [0.25], data modeler
3.1.1.3	Send checklist and interview to vendors for completion	0	3.1.1.2	Data acquisition developers, repository architect [0.25], project manager [0.25], data modeler
3.1.1.4	Receive completed vendor checklist and interview	10 days	3.1.1.3	Data acquisition developers, repository architect [0.25], project manager [0.25], data modeler
3.1.1.5	Receive tool demo (check demo to checklist answers)	5 days	3.1.1.4	Data acquisition developers, repository architect [0.25], project manager [0.25], data modeler
3.1.1.6	Check vendor references	1 day	3.1.1.4	Data acquisition developers, repository architect [0.25], project manager [0.25], data modeler
3.1.1.7	Select tool	5 days	3.1.1.6	Data acquisition developers, repository architect [0.25], project manager [0.25], data modeler
3.1.1.8	Create contract and obtain vendor signoff	5 days	3.1.1.7	Project manager [0.25], legal department [0.5], project champion [0.25]
3.1.2	Meta data access tool	26 days		

3.1.2.1	Identify major integration tool vendors	2 days	Business analyst, data delivery developers, repository architect [0.25], project manager [0.25]
3.1.2.2	Create weighted checklist and interview	5 days	Business analyst, data delivery developers, repository architect [0.25], project manager [0.25]
3.1.2.3	Send checklist and interview to vendors for completion	0	Business analyst, data delivery developers, repository architect [0.25], project manager [0.25]
3.1.2.4	Receive completed vendor checklist and interview	10 days	Business analyst, data delivery developers, repository architect [0.25], project manager [0.25]
3.1.2.5	Receive tool demo (check demo to checklist answers)	5 days	Business analyst, data delivery developers, repository architect [0.25], project manager [0.25]
3.1.2.6	Check vendor references	1 day	Business analyst, data delivery developers, repository architect [0.25], project manager [0.25]
3.1.2.7	Select tool	5 days	Business analyst, data delivery developers, repository architect [0.25], project manager [0.25]
3.1.2.8	Create contract and obtain vendor signoff	5 days	Project champion [0.25], project manager [0.25], legal department [0.5]
3.2	Construct integration architecture document	10 days	
3.2.1	Identify sources of meta data to be integrated	3 days	Repository architect [0.5], project manager [0.5]
3.2.2	Identify meta data needs each source shall provide	2 days	Repository architect [0.5], project manager [0.5]
3.2.3	Detail the specific integration method each source of meta data will need	3 days	Repository architect [0.5], project manager [0.5]

continues

Table 6.10 Design Phase (Continued)

TASK ID	TASK NAME	DURATION	DEPENDENCY	RESOURCE NAMES
3.2.4	Map out hardware/software architecture	2 days	3.2.3	Repository architect [0.5], project manager [0.5]
3.3	Create detailed design documents	17 days	2	
3.3.1	Identify business users of the repository	1 day		Subject matter expert, business analyst, data modeler [0.5], project manager [0.25], data delivery developers
3.3.2	Identify technical users of the repository	1 day		Subject matter expert, business analyst, data modeler [0.5], project manager [0.25], data delivery developers
3.3.3	Meet with users to define specific reporting needs (business and technical)	10 days	3.3.1, 3.3.2	Business analyst, data modeler [0.5], project manager [0.25], data delivery developers, subject matter expert
3.3.4	Review and approve user requirements	1 day	3.3.3	Subject matter expert, business analyst, data modeler, project manager, data delivery developers, project champion, repository architect
3.3.5	Create detailed data delivery specifications	5 days	3.3.4	Subject matter expert, business analyst, data modeler [0.5], project manager [0.25], data delivery developers
3.4	Train development staff (if tools are being used)	10 days	3.1	
3.4.1	Train development staff on meta data integration tool	10 days		Data acquisition developers, repository architect, tool vendor
3.4.2	Train development staff on meta data access tool	10 days		Repository architect, data delivery developers, tool vendor

Evaluate and Select Meta Data Tools

One of the primary activities of the design phase (Task ID 3.1 in Table 6.10) is evaluating and selecting appropriate meta data tools—both access and integration tools. Although all meta data tools have some drawbacks, I believe that such tools are beneficial for nearly all meta data repository implementation projects and generally advise my clients to purchase and incorporate these tools in their meta data architecture. However, if a company is relatively small and/or has a limited IT budget, purchasing such tools and spending sufficient time and effort to learn them may not be practical. In this situation, it may be beneficial for the company to manually integrate all of its meta data sources and build custom reports.

Chapter 4, Understanding and Evaluating Meta Data Tools, provides detailed guidelines for evaluating and selecting meta data tools, but you should be aware that this can be a lengthy process that requires considerable effort on the part of the business analyst, data developers, and repository architect. The entire evaluation and selection process (i.e., access and integration) typically requires close to a month for each type of tool.

Be sure to document the reasons for each tool's selection. All too often, after tools are selected, the technical environment changes and the tools are no longer appropriate. Questions then arise as to why the tool was selected in the first place. Having an official record of the reasoning behind the selection goes a long way toward protecting the credibility of the implementation project team and provides a foundation for selecting a different tool.

Create Meta Data Integration Architecture Document

The repository architect is responsible for creating the integration architecture document (Task ID 3.2 in Table 6.10), which provides a detailed technical outline of the repository architecture. Because meta data tools play an important role in the repository architecture, this document should be created in concert with the tools evaluation process. The major sections of the integration architecture document are nearly identical to those of the project scope document, with the exception of the first two sections, which I describe in the following pages:

- Meta data integration architecture
- Future meta data repository releases
- Critical success factors
- Risk factors

- Assumptions
- Issues
- Sign-off sheet

Meta Data Integration Architecture Section

The meta data integration architecture section is the key portion of this document. It presents the technical meta data architecture for the initial release of the repository, along with detailed descriptions of the various sources of meta data and an explanation of how they will be technically integrated (see Figure 6.5 for an example).

This section walks through each of the meta data sources and specifically explains what meta data is being brought into the repository, how the meta data will be integrated, and how often the meta data will be updated in the repository. Let's use the sample integration architecture from Figure 6.5 as an example. In the meta data integration architecture section, I would describe the data dictionary portion of the architecture as: "The custom data dictionary contains business field definitions that are embedded in a

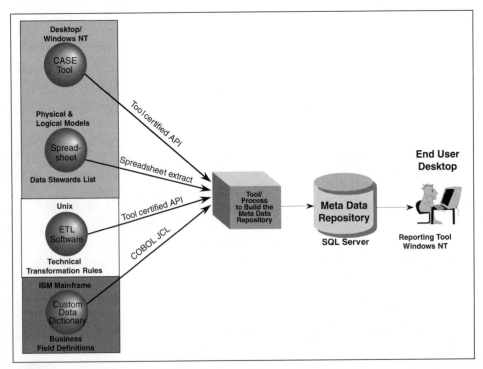

Figure 6.5 Detailed meta data integration architecture.

third-party packaged application which uses a non-open database structure and is located on an IBM mainframe. The meta data repository team will use COBOL (Common Business Oriented Language) and JCL (Job Control Language) to extract the data and FTP to transfer the information to the Windows NT directory where we will integrate it into the meta data repository."

The meta data integration architecture section of the integration architecture document also describes any manual integration processes that are involved in the integration effort and explains why they exist. If a manual process is a one-time occurrence, the integration architecture document should say so. Similarly, if there are manual processes that are not one-time occurrences, the document needs to describe how these processes will be converted to automatic processes in the future.

This section also describes any meta data tools that are being used, including an explanation of the tool(s) strengths and weaknesses, and a brief explanation of why the tool was chosen.

Future Meta Data Architecture Section

Because the first release of a meta data repository project does not usually implement all of the desired functionality, it is necessary to document the plan for handling the remaining requirements in future project releases. This section provides a picture of the future meta data repository.

While this section does not have to include a detailed discussion of each projected meta data source, it is vital to highlight any anticipated future changes to the architecture. These changes may include moving from the current front end to a corporate portal concept or plans to technically integrate new sources of meta data into the repository. This section is intended to focus on the future of the repository and to reduce as many throw-away efforts as possible. Even if the architecture changes during the next release, this section is helpful for keeping future releases of the repository in mind while designing the architecture for the first release.

The critical success factors, risk factors, issues, and assumptions sections are similar to those in the project scope document. For details on these sections, refer back to the description of the project scope document. The sign-off section for this document differs somewhat from the project scope document sign-off in that only the project champion, project manager, and repository architect need to sign off on this document.

Create Detail Design Documents

The repository's front-end report specifications and back-end program specifications are also constructed during the design phase and, along with the delivery specifications, constitute the third deliverable of the design phase (Task ID 3.3 in Table 6.10). While the process for capturing detailed designs has been around for a long time and is well understood, I want to share a couple of techniques that I use to reduce the likelihood of extending this process longer than necessary and to avoid scope creep:

1. Always bring a copy of the project scope document to each design session with the end users to ensure that all design work relates directly to the business and technical drivers listed in the project scope document.

2. When the design documents are complete, obtain signature approval from the end users who have attended the design sessions. All too often, users suffer from *analysis paralysis* during the design sessions; they are unwilling or unable to commit to firm requirements that are necessary for good design. Try to overcome their reluctance to make hard decisions by citing executive-level support and through judicious scheduling. If all else fails, try my *wear them out* technique (see sidebar), which I developed after spending too many hours in unproductive design meetings where users were unable—or unwilling—to make decisions about their reporting requirements.

Develop Detailed Data Delivery Specifications

The detail design documents should include delivery specifications for all of the field-level elements necessary to satisfy the repository users' requirements. These delivery specifications serve as guidelines for the data delivery developers to build the actual report/query programs. The major elements of these specifications include:

- Input tables/files
- Output tables/files
- Detailed processing summary
- Report prototypes
- Issues

Prepare Training Plan for Development Staff

If the meta data repository is going to use data access or integration tools that the development staff is unfamiliar with, the implementation plan should include sufficient time to train the staff to use these tools effectively.

THE "WEAR THEM OUT" TECHNIQUE

I developed this technique while working with a client whose end users were extremely reluctant to make decisions about their requirements. After leading numerous, lengthy detail design meetings (i.e., three to four hours each) in which users rambled on endlessly about unrelated business issues without reaching any meaningful decisions, I resorted to this technique to finally capture their requirements.

When I use this approach, I schedule a design meeting to begin in the afternoon, usually about 1:00 P.M. or later, and make sure that all attendees understand that the goal of the meeting is to capture all of the end user reporting requirements. I also inform all attendees, up front, that the meeting won't end until all of the requirements are captured. My standard warning is that if I'm the only one left in the room making decisions at 3:00 A.M., then that's how the decisions will be made. In this case, my meeting with the end users began like all of the others. There were petty discussions and great deal of talk about business processes, but no decisions about requirements. When dinner was delivered at 5:00 P.M. (no reason to starve anyone to death), we had accomplished absolutely nothing and the attendees began to realize that the meeting really would not end until we had defined the requirements. By 6:00 P.M., an amazing metamorphosis occurred; people stopped arguing and began to make decisions about their requirements. In the next two or three hours, we reached a consensus regarding the user reporting requirements and made the design decisions. The meeting concluded by 10:00 P.M., which is usually the case with this technique. We managed to define all of the requirements, and as a good warden, I finally let my prisoners free to see their families. This technique has served me well, and I've used it many times over the years with wonderful results.

In general, it is advisable to plan on at least two weeks of intensive training on each tool(s), and training must be completed before the staff can begin to use the tools to build the repository. And, a word of warning: If the tool vendor tells you that it offers an intensive three-day boot camp–style course that teaches the developers everything they need to know, don't believe it! I've attended many of these courses, and every one of them was more like summer camp than boot camp. The vendor should, however, be willing to create a really useful course targeted specifically at your development staff. Just be sure that the course instructor is an on-site implementer with real hands-on experience, rather than a full-time trainer who is familiar with the tool but knows little or nothing about your particular repository project. Full-time trainers often lack the necessary expertise to make the tools function effectively in a real-world situation.

Construction Phase

After the design phase is complete, and the detailed design documents are approved and signed off, it is time to begin constructing the back-end programs that will populate the meta data repository and the front-end programs that will present this information to the end users. During this phase, the project manager must ensure that the developers adhere to the repository implementation schedule as spelled out in the delivery specifications. At the same time, the repository architect must work closely with the developers to ensure that all of the programs that they build run efficiently and are maintainable. Table 6.11 summarizes the major endeavors in the construction phase.

User acceptance testing is a key activity in the construction phase and can be crucial to the ultimate success of the project. User acceptance testing is intended to gain end user approval for the meta data repository. It

Table 6.11 Construction Phase

TASK ID	TASK NAME	DURATION	DEPENDENCY	RESOURCE NAMES
4	Construction phase	77 days		
4.1	Build meta model	10 days	3.3	
4.2	Implement meta data security process	6 days	3.3	
4.3	Implement meta data integration processes	12 days	3, 3.4, 4.5.3	
4.4	Implement meta data reports/access method	10 days	3, 3.4, 4.5.3	
4.5	Implement meta data infrastructure	9 days	4.1	
4.6	User acceptance testing (UAT)	11 days	4.3, 4.4	
4.6.1	Conduct business user training	6 days		
4.6.2	Conduct technical user training	6 days		
4.6.3	Conduct user acceptance testing	5 days	4.6.1, 4.6.2	

should closely follow the completion of user training so as to ensure that business and technical users fully understand how and when to use the repository. It is important not to skip or gloss over this step. The success of the repository implementation project depends as heavily on user support as it does on the technical design and construction of the system. The repository project manager needs to work closely with the business and technical users before, during, and after acceptance testing to ensure that the repository meets their ever-changing needs and that they understand what the repository can—and can't—do.

MANAGEMENT AND USER SUPPORT IS CRITICAL TO SUCCESS

At one time I was part of a team hired to implement a new, enterprise-wide, order entry system for a large, global conglomerate with multiple, wholly owned subsidiaries throughout the United States. The implementation team spent two years building the system, which we planned to initially roll out to one of the conglomerate's smaller U.S. companies (we'll call it Subsidiary A for convenience). Subsidiary A was relatively large, with annual revenues of about $1 billion, but its management and end users were reluctant to institute any change and viewed the new system as a threat to their jobs. Management and users joined forces to oppose the implementation effort, and eventually convinced the conglomerate not to implement the system. This decision was highly unfortunate because the system was designed to help Subsidiary A overcome one of it's major problems—a lack of customer service. Features such as automated product pricing, which was designed to calculate price when a clerk keyed in the customer, product code, and quantity, would have helped to compensate for this shortcoming and would have increased Subsidiary A's revenues.

Having failed in our implementation effort at Subsidiary A, the team moved on to Subsidiary B, the largest of the conglomerate's U.S. companies, with annual revenues of about $7 billion. A month before we began rolling the system out at Subsidiary B, the conglomerate initiated a major reorganization of all its U.S. holdings, which had a major negative impact on our system and its internal hierarchies and caused many problems during user acceptance testing. Fortunately for us, the end users at Subsidiary B were absolutely the best I have ever worked with. They spent little or no time looking to assign blame. Instead they stayed focused on the problems and worked as true partners. The result was a highly successful system implementation for Subsidiary B. Sadly for Subsidiary A, it never did implement the new system and experienced poor financial returns, which resulted in major employee layoffs. I firmly believe that if it had been more amenable to change, it might have avoided those layoffs.

Rollout Phase

The rollout phase is the final step of the meta data repository development effort. Three key tasks occur during this phase (as illustrated in Table 6.12):

1. The repository is rolled into production and is accessible to end users (Task ID 5.1 in Table 6.12).

2. The meta data repository team, the project champion, and key executive management conduct a postimplementation review (Task ID 5.2 in Table 6.12) to compare the meta data repository with the objectives of the original project scope document. If the "live" repository matches the scope document and any change requests that occurred during the development phase, the project should be considered a success. If there are differences between the two, the review should reveal where and how the discrepancies occurred and determine what effect (if any) they had on the success of the repository. Of course, the results of the review should be thoroughly documented

Table 6.12   Rollout Phase

TASK ID	TASK NAME	DURATION	DEPENDENCY	RESOURCE NAMES
5	Rollout phase	4 days	4.6.3	
5.1	Roll out repository to clients	0		
5.2	Postimplementation review	4 days		
5.2.1	Plan review agenda and materials	1 day		Project manager
5.2.2	Conduct review	2 days	5.2.1	Project manager, project champion, subject matter expert, key executive management
5.2.3	Publish results	1 day	5.2.2	Project manager, project champion
5.3	Meta data repository in production	0	5.2	

and, if possible, the results of the project quantified. This information is extremely helpful in obtaining funds for subsequent project releases.

3. Planning begins for the next release of the repository project (Task ID 5.3 in Table 6.12), using the original project scope document and the meta data integration architecture document as the foundation for the second release.

In the next chapter, I describe the fundamentals of meta data repository architecture and discuss how the architecture relates to that of the data warehouse. In addition, I touch on some of the advanced meta data techniques that are likely to drive the use of meta data in the future.

## CHAPTER 7

Constructing a Meta Data Architecture

This chapter describes the key elements of a meta data repository architecture and explains how to tie data warehouse architecture into the architecture of the meta data repository. After reviewing these essential elements, I examine the three basic architectural approaches for building a meta data repository and discuss the advantages and disadvantages of each. Last, I discuss advanced meta data architecture techniques such as closed-loop and bidirectional meta data, which are gaining popularity as our industry evolves.

What Makes a Good Architecture

A sound meta data architecture incorporates five general characteristics:

- Integrated
- Scalable
- Robust
- Customizable
- Open

It is important to understand that if a company purchases meta data access and/or integration tools, those tools define a significant portion of the meta data architecture. Companies should, therefore, consider these essential characteristics when evaluating tools and their implementation of the technology.

Integrated

Anyone who has worked on a decision support project understands that the biggest challenge in building a data warehouse is integrating all of the disparate sources of data and transforming the data into meaningful information. The same is true for a meta data repository. A meta data repository typically needs to be able to integrate a variety of types and sources of meta data and turn the resulting stew into meaningful, accessible business and technical meta data. For example, a company may have a meta data requirement to show its business users the business definition of a field that appears on a data warehouse report. The company probably used a data modeling tool to construct the physical data models to store the data presented in the report's field. Let's say the business definition for the field originates from an outside source (i.e., it is external meta data) that arrives in a spreadsheet report. The meta data integration process must create a link from the meta data on the table's field in the report to the business definition for that field in the spreadsheet. When we look at the process in this way, it's easy to see why integration is no easy feat. (Just consider creating the necessary links to all of the various types and sources of data and the myriad delivery forms that they involve.) In fact, integrating the data is probably the most complex task in the meta data repository implementation effort.

Scalable

If integration is the most difficult of the meta data architecture characteristics to achieve, scalability is the most important characteristic. A meta data repository that is not built to grow, and grow substantially over time, will soon become obsolete. Three factors are driving the current proliferation of meta data repositories:

Continuing growth of decision support systems.   As we discussed in Chapter 1, businesses are constantly demanding greater and greater functionality from their decision support systems. It is not unusual for both the size of a data warehouse database and the number of users accessing it to double in the first year of operation. As these decision support initiatives continue to grow, the meta data repository must be able to expand to address the increasing functional requirements.

Recognition of the value of enterprise-wide meta data. During the past three or four years, companies have begun to recognize the value that a meta data repository can bring to their decision support initiatives. Companies are now beginning to expand their repository efforts to include all of their information systems, not just decision support. I am aware of two Fortune 100 firms that are looking to initiate an enterprise-wide meta data solution. As soon as one of these major companies builds a repository to support all of its information systems, many others are likely to follow suit. Chapter 11, The Future of Meta Data, addresses the value of applying enterprise-wide meta data to corporate information systems.

Increasing reliance on knowledge management. Knowledge management is a discipline that promotes the application of technology to identifying, capturing, and sharing all of a company's information assets (e.g., documents, policies, procedures, databases, and the inherent knowledge of the company's workforce). The concept of knowledge management is a good one: Capture the information assets and make them available throughout the enterprise. However, knowledge management is generating mixed reviews in the real world. Companies are just now beginning to understand that a meta data repository is the technical backbone that is necessary to implement a knowledge management effort. Software vendors and corporations alike are now expanding their meta data solutions to provide a real-world approach to knowledge management. (Once again, Chapter 11, The Future of Meta Data, offers a detailed discussion of this topic.)

META DATA: IT'S NOT JUST FOR DECISION SUPPORT

A number of years ago I was speaking at a conference in Chicago about the value that meta data can bring to a decision support system. After the talk, a member of the audience approached me and asked why I limited my meta data discussion to only those topics under decision support, since meta data can support all of a company's IT systems. I agreed that meta data can significantly aid a corporation's IT systems, but explained that I did not address it during the talk because it was difficult enough to convince people that meta data can help a decision support system, let alone provide value to every information system in the company.

My stance on this topic and my presentations have changed dramatically in the past few years. Now that people understand the value, they're looking for the specifics of how to use enterprise-wide data most effectively and leverage it to their information systems.

Robust

As with any system, a meta data repository must have sufficient functionality and performance to meet the needs of the organization that it serves. The repository's architecture must be able to support both business and technical user reports and views of the meta data, as well as providing acceptable user access to these views. Some of the other functionality required from the meta data architecture includes:

- Ability to handle time- or activity-generated events
- Import/export capability
- Support for data lineage
- Security setup and authorization facilities
- Archival and backup facilities
- Ability to produce business and technical reports

Customizable

If the meta data processes are home-grown (i.e., built without the use of meta data integration or access tools), then customization is not a problem since the entire application is tailored for the specific business environment. If, however, a company uses meta data tools to implement the repository architecture (as most do), the tools need to be customized to meet the specific current and future needs of the meta data initiative.

Customization is a major issue for companies that purchase prepackaged meta data solutions from software vendors. These solutions are generally so rigid in their architecture that they cannot fill the specific needs of any company. In the case of a meta data solution, one size definitely *does not* fit all! To be truly effective, these prepackaged solutions require a significant amount of customization to tailor them for each business environment.

Open

The technology used for the meta data integration and access processes must be open and flexible. For example, the database used to store the meta data is generally relational, but the meta data architecture should be sufficiently flexible to allow a company to switch from one relational database to another without massive architectural changes.

Also, an open meta data repository enables a company to share meta data externally, and most important, make it accessible to all users. If, for example, a company decides to Web-enable all of its meta data reports, the processes for providing access to these reports should be able to use any standard Web browser.

Key Elements of Meta Data Architecture

In addition to the general characteristics of good architecture, all good data repositories share a set of key elements that are essential for success, regardless of the architectural approach used to build the repository. In short, all good repositories:

- Are based on clear, well-defined management direction
- Use the same front end as the data warehouse
- Use the same entity and attribute naming standards throughout
- Incorporate multiple sources of meta data
- Include automated and reusable processes
- Use a standardized integration process
- Use a flexible meta model
- Manage multiple versions of meta data
- Incorporate update facilities
- Use a component-based multitier architecture
- Incorporate a security management scheme
- Incorporate cross-tool meta data dependency and lineage

Clear Management Direction

A set of clear, well-defined repository requirements are critical to the success of the meta data project. While this may not seem like an architectural issue, it is. I have seen more than one repository effort in which management changes in direction caused severe changes in the repository architecture.

Probably the most extreme case of misdirection that I dealt with involved a company that, for many years, depended on UNIX-based hardware and a Sybase database. When we began to evaluate meta data tools, therefore, we focused on tools that would be compatible with UNIX and Sybase. After we had selected the tools and finished designing the repository architecture, the company hired a new CIO, who quickly decided to replace Sybase and the

UNIX boxes with IBM DB2 running on a mainframe. This edict absolutely devastated our repository project and threw the IT department into general disarray since the staff was configured to support Sybase and UNIX. The tools we had selected would have worked well with a UNIX box, but were likely to be far less satisfactory on a mainframe. This change in management direction made the tools that we had selected far less than optimal for the company's environment, but the new CIO was reluctant to allow us to go through the tool selection process a second time. As a result, we had to implement using tools that were not well suited for the environment. See Chapter 6, Building the Meta Data Project Plan, for details on how to clearly define the project scope.

The Same Front End

Whenever possible, the meta data repository should use the same front end as the data warehouse. Business users do not like to learn new tools, so it's always best to limit the number of tools that they need to use.

There is a caveat to this, however. If the decision support system's front end cannot meet the needs of the meta data repository, it is far better to select or build a new one than to try to make do just to eliminate the need for users to learn a new tool. Using an inappropriate front end can severely limit the functionality of the data repository and is sure to cause more user dissatisfaction than learning a new tool.

Entity and Attribute Naming Standards

The vast majority of most companies' data is stored in relational databases of some sort. The physical names used to represent the entities (i.e., tables) and attributes (i.e., fields) in these databases should be standardized. For example, policy number is a common attribute in an insurance company database. Policy number may be physically named Policy_Num, Policy_Nbr, or Policy_No. If an insurance company is not consistent is its naming standards, that is, if it uses more than one of these names to refer to the attribute policy number, problems arise when we use a meta data integration tool to prepare the company's data for a repository. Meta data integration tools compare entity and attribute names across transformation programs to see if they represent the same data element. Most tools would interpret Policy_Num, Policy_Nbr, and Policy_No as three different data elements, thereby causing the meta data in the repository to look "cluttered" and difficult to use.

Ideally, businesses should standardize their database naming conventions throughout the enterprise, but, after many years of consulting, I've yet to find a Global 2000 company that has done this across all systems. At a minimum, though, companies should standardize their database and file naming standards across their data warehousing projects—and many manage to do this.

Multiple Sources of Meta Data

Business and technical meta data is stored at numerous locations throughout an organization and exists in a wide variety of formats, including diverse software applications and tools. Table 7.1 lists some typical locations for the most common types of meta data.

These sources of meta data should flow directly into the repository and be integrated through the meta data repository build process, as Figure 7.1 illustrates.

Table 7.1 Meta Data Locations and Types

COMMON META DATA LOCATIONS	TYPES OF META DATA
ETL tool/process	Data transformation rules Program job dependencies Data warehouse balancing statistics Data warehouse load statistics Data lineage
Data modeling tools	Logical and physical data models Technical entity definitions Technical attribute definitions Domain values
Documents	Business policies
Employees	Business policies Business entity definitions Business attribute definitions Data stewardship Data lineage
Reporting and OLAP tools	User access patterns Report execution time
Vendor applications	Logical and physical data models Data dictionary
Data quality tools	Audit controls

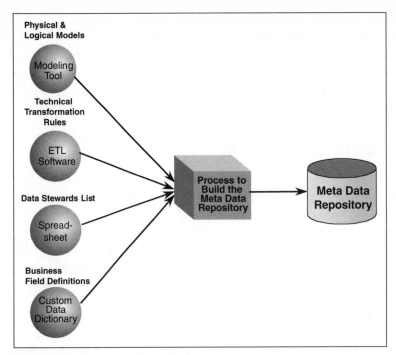

Figure 7.1 Meta data source flow.

Automated and Reusable Processes

I can't say this often enough! The process for loading and maintaining the meta data repository should be as automated as possible. Many of the less-than-successful meta data implementations contain far too many manual processes in their integration architectures. The task of manually keying in meta data becomes much too time consuming for the meta data repository team to perform, and over time usually capsizes the repository initiative. With careful analysis and some development effort, the vast majority of these manual processes can be automated.

Typically, a significant amount of the business meta data needs some type of manual activity to initially capture it. Unfortunately, this activity is usually unavoidable and requires a good deal of time. In these situations, it is usually best to create a front end for the business users and let them become the data stewards and create and maintain their own business meta data. Although the users may be reluctant to create meta data, at least until the repository is built and functioning, a good front end and lots of encouragement and assistance from the meta data implementation team go a long way toward convincing users to create and/or modify their own meta data. The two key elements here are: a *good* front end and a clear understanding on the part of the users that they are responsible for their own meta data. The project manager needs to make this clear to the business users. Don't make the mistake of forcing them to attain approval from the meta data repository team to change the meta data. Requiring such approval sends a very clear message to the users that the repository team, not the users, are responsible for the meta data.

Standardized Integration Process

The architectural process for integrating sources of meta data is based on the same concepts as the ETL (extraction, transformation, and load) process of a data warehouse. In the next several pages, we'll walk through each layer of the process and discuss the architectural reasons for each. Keep in mind, however, there is no absolute formula for the physical architecture of a meta data repository (or for any other IT system, for that matter). The physical architecture depends entirely on, and is unique to, the individual environment. It is, however, crucial to understand and enforce the sound architectural concepts for each layer. When this architecture is implemented, it is highly flexible and easily distributed as the need arises. Figure 7.2 illustrates the entire ETL process.

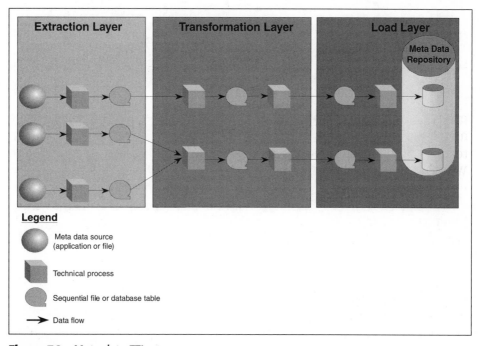

Figure 7.2 Meta data ETL process.

Extraction (Data Acquisition) Layer

The primary activity of the extraction layer (sometimes referred to as the data acquisition layer) in the meta data architecture is getting the data out of the various sources with minimal impact on those sources. Figure 7.3 illustrates this layer.

The resulting extraction file or table closely resembles the source of the meta data. No meta data integration or cleansing should take place at this level; those functions properly belong in the next layer, the transformation layer. In fact, only two changes should occur to the data in the extraction layer. The repository architect must decide if record selection should be used in this layer or in the transformation layer. I generally try to avoid record selection criteria at this step unless the data in the meta data source is rather voluminous and the amount of data we will ultimately load into the repository is a significantly smaller subset. Second, the developer can add the specific fields to be used in the repository at this point. These fields typically include: *From Date*, *To Date*, and *Load Parameter*.

Although there is some additional storage overhead in creating a copy of the meta data source, this overhead tends to be quite minimal since data in the meta data source files is rarely very large. On the other hand, there are

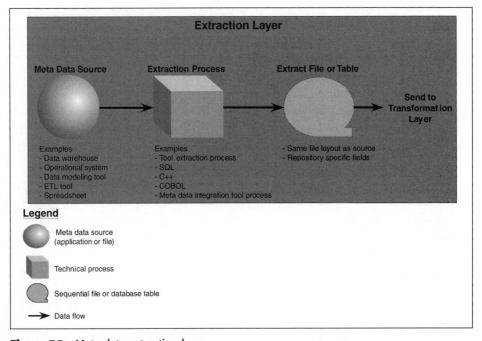

Figure 7.3 Meta data extraction layer.

three distinct advantages to separating the extraction layer from the transformation layer:

Timeliness.   The extraction layer is critical for keeping the meta data in the repository in sync. To illustrate this point, let's suppose that we have three meta data repository tables that need data from the same meta data source. If we construct a process to build each of the three meta data tables directly from the same meta data source, the data in the meta data source may have changed by the time we execute the process to build the table. This is especially probable if the source for the meta data is highly dynamic (i.e., constantly changing) and occurs because the direct reads on the meta data sources files occur at different points in time. As a result, the information in the meta data repository will not be in sync. By creating an extract file once in the integration process, all of the meta data tables can be built from that extract file, which eliminates any possible timeliness problem.

Scalability.   Because we are creating an extraction file that very closely resembles the meta data source file or table, we only need to read from the meta data source one time. Without the extraction file or table, each table in the meta data repository would have to have separate reads into the meta data source itself, which may not be desirable.

Backup.   Creating an extraction file provides a natural backup copy of the source meta data. Therefore, if a situation occurs that causes us to have to stop the meta data integration process, we can easily roll back our changes and rerun the process without affecting the meta data sources again.

Transformation (Cleansing) Layer

The transformation or cleansing layer is the backbone of the repository's architecture. The most significant activity in the meta data repository effort occurs at this level: integrating and cleansing the meta data sources. After these activities are complete, the meta data is ready to be loaded into the repository.

Figure 7.4 illustrates the transformation layer. As the figure shows, the transformation and cleansing activities should occur on the same physical platform as the meta data repository. With this arrangement, as the requirements for the repository increase over time, all of the meta data sources can be integrated in the same physical area, thereby minimizing future changes to the extraction layer and reducing the changes requested in the meta data source environments.

The transformation and cleansing functions may occur in the same program or process or may occur across several processes, but the files that result from the transformation processes should always exactly mirror the meta data

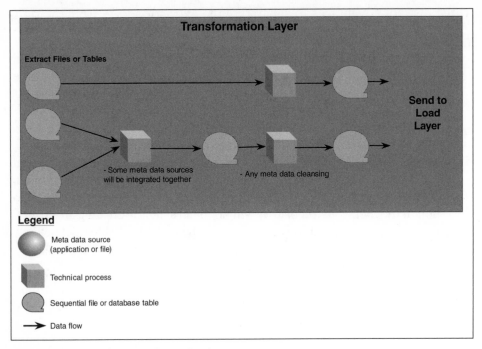

Figure 7.4 Meta data transformation layer.

tables that they will be loaded into. Any errors that may prevent the meta data repository from being loaded usually occur in this layer. It is, therefore, important to create sound rollback procedures in case the load run has to be halted.

Load Layer

The load layer takes the files that are generated in the transformation layer and loads them into the repository. Rollback procedures are also critical in the layer in case problems arise during the load process. I usually use the bulk loading mechanism that is standard in all open relational database systems. If the need arises in the future to switch relational databases, the processes in the extraction and transformation layers are not affected, but the processes in this layer need to be modified. Fortunately, because minimal processing occurs here, the modifications are likely to be relatively easy. Figure 7.5 illustrates this layer.

Flexible Meta Model

Meta models usually use an entity-relationship schema to store a repository's meta data content and organization. (Chapter 9, Building the Meta Model, offers a step-by-step approach to constructing a meta model.)

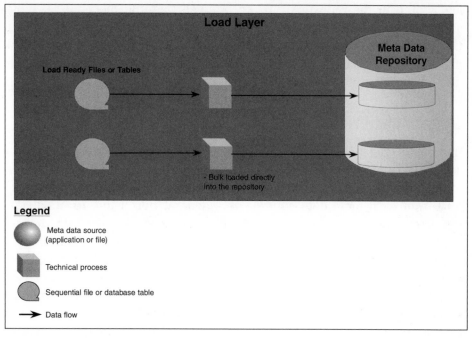

Figure 7.5   Meta data load layer.

A meta model provides the framework for establishing a protocol for meta data access, administration, and interchange among various teams and software that access the repository. The meta model must be able to capture the various meta data abstractions that are of interest to the applications that use that meta data repository. For example, in a data warehousing or decision support environment, abstractions such as relational and nonrelational data objects, multidimensional concepts, transformation logic, business rules, and job scheduling parameters are key meta data content that must be handled by the repository architecture. The meta modeling methodology must be able to accommodate various types of relationships, such as one-to-one, one-to-many, many-to-many, aggregation, and inheritance. Last, compatibility with the emerging model standards being developed by the Meta Data Coalition and Object Management Group is a key requirement for any meta data repository architecture.

Multiple Versions of Meta Data

Because meta data provides a context for interpreting the meaning of information, the meta data repository must manage the structure of the data in the data warehouse over a broad spectrum of time. For that reason, it is necessary to know the period of time that the meta data covers as it is extracted and stored in the repository. To accomplish this, the meta model tables should be captured with a *From* and *To* date on each column. (Refer to Chapter 9 for more details on building a meta model.) These dates enable users to easily trace back through the repository to past versions of the meta data (data lineage).

Update Facilities

Inevitably, changes will occur in the applications that support the various sources of meta data after the repository is initially loaded. The repository implementation team needs to decide when to update the meta data repository from each meta data source. As a general rule, I like to update the repository on a monthly basis with those sources of meta data that are highly static. For most meta data sources, there is no need to update the repository every time a change occurs. For example, if an additional index is added to one of the data warehouse tables, it probably isn't necessary to update the meta data repository. If, however, a major data warehouse enhancement occurs, the meta data repository should be updated to incorporate the new data models, business definitions, and so forth. Of course, some meta data types, such as data warehouse load statistics and user access patterns, are continually updated in the repository. Table 7.2 summarizes the most common meta data updating frequencies.

Some companies are expanding the use of their repositories to have changes to the meta data in the repository sweep backward through the originating applications and/or tools. Because the repository serves as a

---

VERSION NUMBERS VERSUS DATES

Some meta data integration tools use version numbers rather than *From* and *To* dates to accomplish data lineage. By version number, I mean a numeric value that represents a specific release of the decision support system.

In my opinion, version numbers are not the best way to control meta data versions. I say this because I've yet to meet a business user who cared what version of the data warehouse software he or she was looking at. Instead, users want real information. They want to see any changes in the way that we calculate sales dollars on their domestic sales report between 1995 and 1998. If your integration tool utilizes version numbers, it is a simple matter to add an additional table to the meta model to cross-reference the version numbers to the actual period of time they represent. The key lesson to remember here is that business users understand time, not warehouse version numbers.

Table 7.2 Meta Data Update Frequency

META DATA LOCATIONS	TYPES OF META DATA	UPDATE FREQUENCY
ETL tool/process	Data transformation rules	As changes occur
	Program job dependencies	As changes occur
	Data warehouse balancing statistics	As changes occur
	Data warehouse load statistics	As changes occur
	Data lineage	As changes occur
Data modeling tools	Logical data models	With major system enhancement
	Physical data models	As changes occur
	Technical entity definitions	As changes occur
	Technical attribute definitions	As changes occur
	Domain values	As changes occur
Documents	Business policies	As changes occur
Employees	Business policies	As changes occur
	Business entity definitions	As changes occur
	Business attribute definitions	As changes occur
	Data stewardship	As changes occur
	Data lineage	As changes occur
Reporting and OLAP tools	User access patterns	As changes occur
	Report execution time	As changes occur
Vendor applications	Logical data models	With major system enhancement
	Physical data models	As changes occur
	Data dictionary	With major system enhancement
Data quality tools	Audit controls	As changes occur

central hub for storing all of a company's information, this trend is likely to continue. We address the advantages of bidirectional meta data architecture later in this chapter.

Component-Based Multitier Architecture

Most existing meta data repository architectures are based on a two-tier client/server foundation, such that the repository runs on a database server, which in turn is accessed by a number of client applications. However, a multitier, component-based architecture provides a more open and extensible architecture for inputting, extracting, and modifying the repository meta data. This architecture includes a repository server that encapsulates the underlying physical database management system (either relational or object-oriented) and provides several component-based tiers to handle the various interoperability interfaces (e.g., XML, COM, CORBA, or OLE-DB). A component-based architecture must also provide mechanisms for accessing and managing the meta data through local area networks (LANs) and wide area networks (WANs) to effectively accommodate various distributed computing environments. With the rapid emergence and adoption of Web-based applications, such as those used for electronic commerce, a component-based multitier architecture is an important requirement for an advanced meta data repository.

Security Management Scheme

It is important to remember that meta data is a priceless asset of an organization, given that it represents a knowledge-base that has been created over time by many individuals. Access to meta data must be carefully controlled to protect the enterprise's intellectual assets and ensure the validity and integrity of the meta data for all of its users for all time.

The security management scheme for a meta data repository is similar to that of many database management systems; however, it must be tailored for the specific needs of the meta data creators, users, and administrators. Furthermore, it may restrict access to meta data according to type, or by the operations that users and administrators of that meta data intend to perform. A robust security management scheme is a critical requirements for a meta data repository architecture.

Cross-Tool Meta Data Dependency and Lineage

Given that most enterprises deploy multiple tools in their data warehousing and decision support environments, it is important for them to be able to track the meta data dependencies and lineage across the various tools. It is also important to be able to capture and store the mappings between related meta data as it flows among the various modeling, ETL, and analysis tools used in the lifecycle of a project.

Meta data content should also be able to incorporate critical information about itself, such as when and from what source it was created, how and when it was updated, what business rules were used in creating it, and what dependencies exist. This self-awareness pays off in meta data integrity in that it gives the user a tool for checking the likelihood of validity. Lineage awareness also permits the meta data architects to perform impact analysis, evaluating the enterprise-wide impact that may result from a change such as a modification to a business rule. Cross-tool meta data dependency and lineage awareness are important requirements for any meta data repository architecture.

A Real-World Architecture Example

Figure 7.6 illustrates an actual integration architecture that was implemented by one of the companies my firm works with. This company purchased a meta data integration tool to integrate its various sources of meta data. As you can see, the company has an array of meta data sources (which are listed in Table 7.3), but the process for integrating all of these sources thoroughly amazed us.

Because we used a data integration tool, we needed to understand which meta data sources were generic or not supported by the tool. (Chapter 4, Understanding and Evaluating Meta Data Tools, describes how meta data integration tools function.) It is vital to identify these sources and their integration requirements early in the project because they may require modifications to the base meta model supported by the meta data integration tool. On the positive side, we made sure that the repository tool was certified with the current version of the data modeling tool and on the version of the

Table 7.3   Meta Data Sources

META DATA SOURCES	META DATA DESCRIPTION	SOURCE TYPE	META MODEL EXTENSION
Data modeling tool	Physical and logical models, domain values, technicalentity definitions, and technical attribute definitions.	Certified	No
ETL tool	Technical transformation rules. Job dependencies.	Certified	No
Custom Data Dictionary	Business attribute and entity definitions.	Nonsupported	No
MS Excel	Data steward's list.	Generic	Yes
Reporting tool	Database and report access patterns and frequency of use statistics.	Generic	Yes

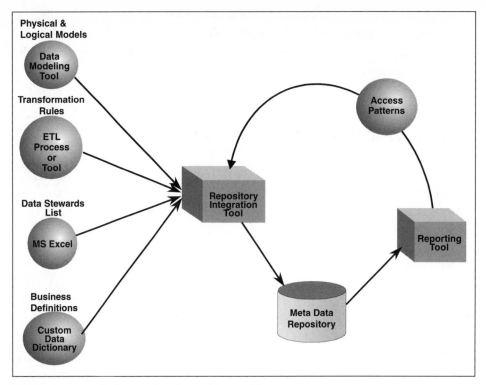

Figure 7.6   Detailed meta data integration architecture.

ETL tool that the company was using. It is always critical to make sure that the meta data integration tool supports the same version of the tool that holds the meta data.

Integrating the data dictionary, however, was not quite as easy. The data dictionary was located in a third-party application in a proprietary database format. The answer to this problem was to design and write a complex program to manipulate the data dictionary into a format that could be integrated by the repository tool. This process took a dedicated programmer one full month to accomplish. Fortunately, the base meta model supported by the meta data integration tool had the fields necessary to support this meta data.

The data steward's list was the next source of meta data to tackle. Because this information did not initially exist as a spreadsheet, we had to create it manually, then modify the base meta model to hold the data. Luckily, we only needed to add one field to the meta model, so the time for this modification was negligible.

On a final note, we used an OLAP tool to access the information in the meta data repository. This tool captured access patterns and frequency. We fed the final pieces of meta data back into the repository and provided the decision support staff with access to it. The staff used this information to guide them on their future data warehouse development phases. We did need to add two additional tables to our meta model and modify three others to accommodate this change. It is extremely important to document any and all changes to the base meta model that the meta data integration tool supports to facilitate the upgrade to the new meta model when the next version of the meta data integration tool is released. Of course this expansion will not contain the changes that you have made to the model.

Structuring the Meta Data Architecture

Now that we've discussed the basic characteristics of meta data architecture and the fundamental elements of good repositories, we need to talk about the various ways that we can assemble those elements. Essentially, there are two basic approaches to meta data repository architecture:

- Centralized
- Decentralized

All of our discussions in this chapter, to this point, have focused on a centralized approach to meta data architecture. This is because the concepts that govern the centralized approach also apply to the decentralized approach.

A meta data repository is the logical place for uniformly retaining and managing corporate knowledge within or across different organizations. For most small to medium-sized organizations, a single meta data repository (centralized approach) is sufficient for handling all of the meta data required by the various groups in the organization. This architecture, in turn, offers a single and centralized approach for administering and sharing meta data by various teams. However, in most large enterprises that deploy multiple information management applications (e.g., for data warehousing and decision support), several meta data repositories (decentralized approach) are often necessary to handle all of the company's various types of meta data content and applications.

Centralized Meta Data Repository Architecture

The underlying concept of a centralized meta data architecture (like the one illustrated in Figure 7.7) is a uniform and consistent meta model that mandates that the schema for defining and organizing the various meta data be stored in a global meta data repository, along with the meta data itself. In a

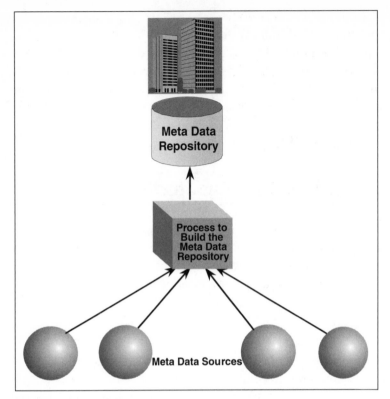

Figure 7.7 Centralized meta data architecture.

typical repository installation, the meta data repository shares a hardware platform (e.g., mainframe, AS400, UNIX, etc.) with the DSS or some other application(s). This is because the repository database usually requires only about 5 gigabytes (GB) to 15 GB of raw, physical database storage, with perhaps another 5 to 15 GB for data staging areas, indexes, and so forth.

Decentralized Meta Data Repository Architecture

The objective of a decentralized architecture, like the one illustrated in Figure 7.8, is to create a uniform and consistent meta model that mandates the schema for defining and organizing the various meta data be stored in a global meta data repository *and* in the shared meta data elements that appear in the local repositories. All meta data that is shared and reused among the various repositories must first go through the central global repository, but sharing and access to the local meta data are independent of the central repository.

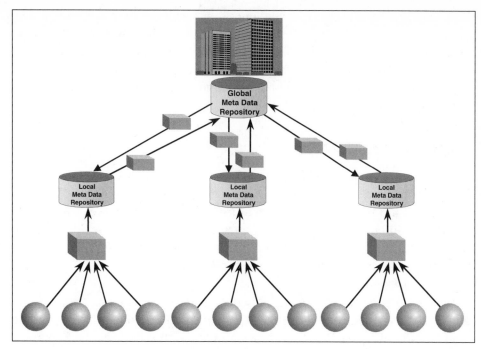

Figure 7.8   Decentralized meta data architecture.

Keep in mind that the global repository is a subset of the meta data stored in the local repositories. The reason for this is that if all meta was stored globally, there wouldn't be the need to have local repositories. This architecture is highly desirable for those companies that have very distinct and nonrelated lines of business.

While this architecture provides the means for centrally managing the administration and sharing of meta data across multiple meta data repositories, it also allows each local repository to be autonomous for its own content and administration requirements. This architecture is similar to a federated management in that its central governing architecture provides the guidelines that are common to all of its members, and each of its members can also create localized guidelines for their specific needs.

Looking Ahead: Advanced Architectural Techniques

In the earlier sections of this chapter we discussed the architectural elements that are applicable to all successful meta data repository efforts. In this section, we address the challenges of implementing some advanced meta data repository requirements. While most repository efforts do not attempt to implement these features, sophisticated users are beginning to demand the type of functionality that these features offer. It is also important to note these features can be implemented separately or in conjunction with one another.

Bidirectional Meta Data

A bidirectional meta data architecture, like the one illustrated in Figure 7.9, allows meta data to be changed in the repository, then fed back from the repository into the original source. For example, if a user goes through the repository and changes the name of an attribute for one of the decision support system's data marts, if the repository has a bidirectional architecture, the change is fed back into the data modeling tool to update the physical model for that specific data mart.

Bidirectional architecture is highly desirable for two key reasons. First, it allows tools to share meta data, which is particularly desirable in the data warehousing market. Because most companies that built decision support systems did so with best-of-breed tools rather than integrated tool sets, the tools are not integrated with one another and do not communicate easily.

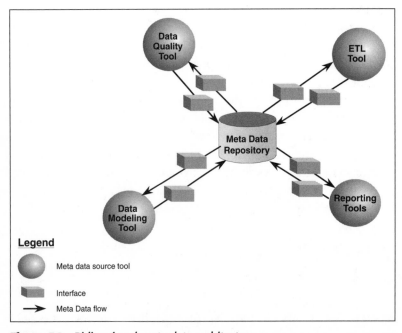

Figure 7.9 Bidirectional meta data architecture.

Bidirectional meta data resolves this lack of integration and communication by letting the tools share meta data. Second, because bidirectional meta data enables companies to sweep meta data changes throughout the enterprise, it is extremely attractive for organizations that want to implement a meta data repository on an enterprise-wide level. (See Chapter 11, The Future of Meta Data, for a detailed discussion on enterprise-wide meta data.) This would allow a corporation to make global changes in the meta data repository and have them sweep throughout the enterprise.

There are three obvious challenges to implementing bidirectional meta data: (1) it forces the meta data repository to contain the latest version of the meta data source that it will feed back into; (2) changes need to be systematically trapped and resolved because one user may be changing the meta data in the repository at the same time that another user is changing the same meta data at its source; and (3) additional sets of process interfaces need to be built to tie the meta data repository back to the meta data source.

Closed-Loop Meta Data

A closed-loop meta data architecture allows the repository to feed its meta data back into a company's operational systems. (Figure 7.10 illustrates this

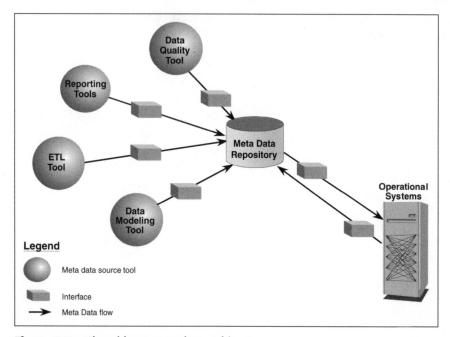

Figure 7.10 Closed-loop meta data architecture.

type of architecture.) This concept is similar to bidirectional meta data architecture, but in this case the meta data repository is feeding its information into operational systems rather than into other applications. Closed-loop meta data architecture is gaining popularity among organizations that want to implement an enterprise-wide data repository because it allows them to make global changes in the meta data repository and have those changes sweep throughout the operational systems of the enterprise.

Closed-loop meta data architecture adds some of the same complexities to the meta data repository initiative as does bidirectional meta data architecture. If the meta data that will be fed from the repository to the operational system can also be maintained in the operational system, the meta data repository must contain the latest version of that meta data. If the repository does not contain the latest version, there is no assurance that the repository user is updating the latest copy of the meta data. Also, one user may make changes to the meta data in the repository at the same time that another user is changing the operational system. These conflicts must be systematically trapped and program interfaces built to tie the meta data repository back to operational systems. Although relatively few companies are using closed-loop architecture at this time, it is a natural progression in the architecture of meta data repositories.

Now that we have explored the fundamental elements of a sound meta data repository architecture, in the next chapter we'll address the question of how to best implement data quality standards through the meta data repository initiative.

## CHAPTER 8

Implementing Data Quality through Meta Data

Few data warehouse implementations fully exploit the advantages of incorporating specialized technical meta data into their decision support data model and ETL processes. This missed opportunity often leads to a reduction in the flexibility of the data warehouse architecture, which leads to additional time and expense for maintenance, data acquisition design, and reconciliation and auditing of information. It can also cause business users to incorrectly interpret the information stored in the warehouse. In this type of situation, it is advisable to revisit the meta data repository and look for opportunities to improve the data identification and quality before information is merged into the data warehouse.

This chapter focuses on the use of meta data to control the quality of information stored in the data warehouse. The topics I cover in this chapter include the use of *specialized technical meta data* (sometimes referred to as *operational meta data*) in the decision support data model and extraction, transformation and load processes. The meta data operators enable administrators to precisely control what and how data is added to the warehouse based on the business rules stored in the meta data repository. They also provide the technical administrators a means for measuring the content quality of the data warehouse. Using these technical meta data operators can also help to identify process improvement opportunities in the ETL procedures used to load the warehouse. Regardless of whether you have developed your own home-grown meta data repository solution or purchased a commercial product, you can use these techniques to improve data quality in your data warehouse.

This chapter is primarily directed toward the repository architect, data acquisition developer, and data modeler responsible for implementing the meta data repository. If these individuals apply these quality controls correctly during the repository implementation, the business and technical users involved with the data warehouse will be able to use the technical meta data components in their various functions.

Expanding the Use of Technical Meta Data

As I explained in Chapter 1, many companies use a meta data repository with their data warehouses to access information for business and technical requirements. In this respect, the meta data repository serves as the information card catalog for the decision support environment, providing a guide to the information stored in the warehouse. While this is an important function of the environment, the functionality of the repository can be expanded beyond this passive role of information identification and collection to that of an active participant in data processing.

The meta data repository maintains information on the decision support data model, operational source systems, ETL processes, and load statistics that populate the data warehouse. Integration between these components in the repository is at a fairly high level. For example, I can use the repository information to determine that a particular order management operational system is the source that feeds a specific target table in the warehouse. By reviewing load statistics from the repository, I can determine when and how often the data warehouse is updated. This information enables users of the warehouse to maintain a macro-level view of the decision support environment, but this level of information is insufficient when a technical or business user needs a more detailed view of the data content in the warehouse.

To achieve a micro-level view of the information content in the data warehouse, the repository architect, data modeler, and data acquisition developer use extended technical meta data as a method to forge a tighter relationship between the repository and the decision support database. This is accomplished by incorporating technical meta data into the data warehouse design. This technique is used to extend the design and architecture of the data warehouse to provide increased processing optimizations for data acquisitions, maintenance activities, and data quality measurement opportunities.

Tagging Technical Meta Data

In order to facilitate the use of technical meta data as a bridge between the repository and data warehouse data model, the repository architect must select operators to be incorporated into the physical data model design. This technical meta data, unlike information stored in the repository, is referenced at a row level of granularity in the data warehouse. These meta data tags provide a detailed, micro-level explanation of the information content in the data warehouse. This direct association of meta data to each row of information in the data warehouse is a key distinction of extended meta data.

To select operators, each row of data is tagged from the operational source systems during ETL processing with extended technical meta data. The technical meta data tags on each row in the warehouse provide a clearer semantic meaning to the data by placing the information in context with the repository. Take, for example, the case of a customer dimension table that derives its information from two operational sources. The customer information is extracted either from a sales force automation application or an enterprise resource planning application, depending on availability. Without extended technical meta data in the dimension table, you can only use the information as it is, without consideration of the operational system that provides it. Technical meta data tagging allows you to determine which rows of information were derived from the two sources. Answers to business questions that relate to possible customer prospects or where to focus customer relationship management attention is easily identifiable due to the use of the operators.

The repository architect, data modeler, and data acquisition developer need to carefully consider the planned use of technical meta tags in the decision support model. The technical and business users of the data warehouse must identify and agree on a clear, consistent method of tagging the data originating from the operational systems. Any technical meta data tied to the row must be applicable to the entire row, not just the majority of columns in the table.

I like to keep technical meta data tagging to a minimum in simple dimensional data model designs, such as those in which there are only one or two fact tables, or where a single source system feeds the warehouse. I prefer to increase its use in very complex schema designs that use multiple fact tables with several conformed dimension tables, or when numerous operational source systems need to be integrated to load a decision support table. These intricate schemas make tracing the origin of meta data from the source operational systems more challenging.

The data warehouse staff is responsible for evaluating the design and maintenance impact caused by the use of meta data tagging to the repository, ETL processes, data model design, DBMS sizing, and front-end data access tools. For example, some front-end OLAP tools require a very strict adherence in the design of the decision support data model in order to function properly or fully. This may preclude the use of some or all technical meta data tags on certain tables such as the time dimension in the warehouse. Certain types of extended technical meta data can require substantial additional ETL processing to occur, which may interfere with restrictive processing window time frames. For example, you need to carefully consider ETL processing times in cases where rows in the warehouse are flagged to indicate whether they are still active in the operational source system.

Can your repository tool manage the incorporation of extended technical meta data into the warehouse design? If your repository is developed in-house, the answer should be a resounding *yes*, depending on the flexibility built into the design. The repository architect is responsible for evaluating the extensibility of a meta data repository in the case of a purchased vendor or in-house developed solution.

Extended Technical Meta Data

A variety of technical meta data tags can be incorporated into the design of the decision support data model in order to increase the micro-level knowledge of the warehouse information. Depending on the business requirements of the application, the number of operational source systems feeding the warehouse, or the complexity of the decision support model, inclusion of certain technical meta data tags may make more or less sense. For example, adding a column into a dimension table of the warehouse to identify the operational system, where only a single source of information exists to populate the table, may seem counterproductive and to provide little value. But you need to carefully consider the possible effects of not incorporating this meta data tag. First, just because the data warehouse has only one source today does not ensure that will be the case later. Second, it is difficult to change a large warehouse table schema once it has been loaded. Finally, having the operational system tag on all tables, regardless of the number of sources, provides consistency to all your decision support models and promotes discipline in your methodology implementation.

Incorporating technical meta data into the design of the data warehouse model occurs during the transformation of the business logical data model.

During this modeling exercise, the physical columns are added to the appropriate tables as determined by the business requirements and technical evaluation previously completed. Technical meta data is incorporated into the physical model based on the type of table being addressed. Certain tags that make sense for use with a dimension or entry point table do not necessarily make sense for a fact or associative join table. For example, placing an update date on a fact row typically provides little value since these type of rows are never updated in a standard decision support architecture design. In contrast, a load date provides enormous value, particularly for ensuring report consistency.

The following sections describe technical meta data columns that I have found useful in implementing decision support systems. Depending on the business requirements of your own project, these columns may provide an additional semantic layer of knowledge about information in your warehouse. The extended technical meta data columns I am going to discuss include:

- Load date
- Update date
- Load cycle identifier
- Current flag indicator
- Operational system identifier
- Active in operational system flag
- Confidence level indicator

Load Date

One of the most fundamental differences between a third-normal form operational system data model and a data warehouse model is the addition of time to all data in the database. The most commonly used and understood extended technical meta data field in data warehouse designs is the *load date* column. It denotes when (i.e., date and/or time) a row of information was loaded into the data warehouse. This snapshot date is used to maintain temporal integrity of the data in the warehouse as new information is added during each refresh cycle. This column is usually added to the data model during transformation of the business logical model into the physical data warehouse model. The column can be referenced by warehouse administrators to identify candidate rows for archival or purge processing. End users can also use this column to reconcile and audit information in the data warehouse with the operational source systems.

Some of the warehouse projects I've been involved with have used a variation in this technique. In these cases, the date that the data was loaded to the warehouse had little relevance to the business scenario. The effective date of the data extracted from the operational system was more important. This is an important distinction to keep in mind when determining what technical meta data tags to add to your data model. First, you can capture the effective date of the data from the operational system. This is typically a column in the source system. For example, benefits enrollment data extracted from human resources application may not be effective until the beginning of a new fiscal year. Second, you can capture the date when the data was extracted from the operational system. This can be important where data is extracted and stored in a staging area for some period of time prior to being ETL processed to the warehouse. Third, you can capture the date the data was actually loaded into the warehouse. Administrators can often use all three of these date columns to measure the quality of the content of the data warehouse.

Update Date

Another common technical meta data column is the *update date*. This column indicates when a row was last updated in the warehouse during a refresh cycle. This column, like load date, is used to maintain the temporal integrity of information in the data warehouse. It is routinely used in dimension table designs that implement slowly changing dimensions (SCD) type 1 or 3 processing methods, to identify when the row was refreshed or updated. For those not familiar with the implementation of SCD, type 1 maintains a single row per production key(s) in the dimension table which is updated as required over writing any history about the row. Type 3 also maintains one row per production key(s) but doubles the number of columns to keep both a current and previous view of the information. The column, like load date, is used in administrative activities such as archival/purge processing or reconciliation/audit by end users.

Load Cycle Identifier

One of the technical meta data columns a data warehouse development team can incorporate is the *load cycle identifier*. This column is a sequential identifier assigned during each load cycle to the data warehouse regardless of the refresh frequency. As a sequential identifier, it can be used to easily remove data from a particular load cycle run if data corruption or other data quality issues arise. The load cycle identifier is typically used in conjunction with a look-up or meta data repository table that describes other operational statistics about the load cycle. Using the meta data repository alone you can determine how many load cycles have occurred against the warehouse, and when they occurred. Then, by tying the repository statistics to the actual warehouse content, you know exactly which rows were loaded and when. Figure 8.1 illustrates an example of load cycle identifier statistics collected in a meta data repository table.

Current Flag Indicator

The *current flag indicator* column identifies the latest version of a row in a table. It facilitates quick identification of the latest version of a row as compared to performing date comparisons. This flag is especially useful for managing the processing of SCD, type 2, where history of a production record is maintained. This tag is also very useful in nonstar-like schema, data model designs such as an atomic data warehouse where structures tend to conform closer to third-normal form. Instead of querying a table for the latest date field, the ETL process assigns a *Y* to the latest record loaded for a particular production key field while setting any previously loaded record to a *N*. This provides an efficient means for users to get at the latest information loaded into the warehouse. The challenge here for the data acquisition developer, particularly using a SCD method, is to identify the previous or old row that the new data supercedes.

Operational System Identifier

One of the most useful technical meta data fields for both the warehouse administrators and the end user is the *operational system identifier*. This column is used to track the originating source or sources of a data row in the data warehouse. In cases where your ETL process is required to extract and

Load Cycle Indicator	Load Date	User ID	Status
5	02-Apr-1999	25652	Complete
4	03-Mar-1999	25652	Complete
3	01-Feb-1999	25652	Complete
2	03-Jan-1999	25652	Complete
1	01-Dec-1999	25652	Complete

Figure 8.1 Load cycle identifier example.

integrate data from more than one source, this column uses an integration designator to denote which operational systems were used. This field allows you to individually identify, for each row in a warehouse table, what sources were used in its construction. This provides the business user, repository architect, and data acquisition developer with a powerful tool for identifying and measuring the quality of the data received from an operational source.

For example, in cases where a row of data is integrated from more than one operational source system, a column value denoting the combination of these systems can be assigned. It can be used by business users that are questioning the quality and/or validity of data in the warehouse to trace back information to the operational source system that furnished the information. The suspect data can then be corrected by the operational system or easily tagged with a lower reliability factor in the warehouse for measurement purposes.

In certain cases, administrators can use this column to identify and remove corrupt data from a particular operational source system(s). I have had situations where, during an overnight ETL process, the data loaded into the warehouse became corrupted due to operating system or database errors. The corruption errors found in the data required me to remove the previous night's load and repeat the ETL process once the source of the problem was rectified. Fortunately, I was able to easily identify and quickly remove the corrupted data using this technical meta data tag feature in the database. Figure 8.2 illustrates an example of operational system identifiers collected in a meta data repository table.

Active Operational System Flag

This flag is used to indicate whether the production keys in a warehouse table are still active in the originating operational system or systems. The

Operational System(s) Identifier	Operational System(s) Description
1	Order System 1
2	Billing System 1
3	Customer System 1
4	Customer System 2
5	Integration of Customer Systems 1 & 2
6	Atomic Data Warehouse
7	External Client Extract 6
8	Internet/Web

Figure 8.2   Operational system identifier example.

active operational system flag provides an intriguing analysis alternative to queries posed to the data warehouse. This column can be used effectively in a variety of analysis activities to identify dormant data or data that should be constrained in reporting.

For example, let's imagine that you are performing a churn analysis of former customers to identify potential candidates for a new marketing campaign. Running a query against the customer table using the active operational system flag would easily identify previous clients. Another example is when an operational system flag is used to identify and filter out products that are no longer supported by the manufacturer. Yet another example is when the tag is used in a query to identify items that have not been ordered by any customer in the past 90 days. I am continually amazed by the innovative ways that business users employ this column in their analysis efforts.

Confidence Level Indicator

One of the more controversial technical meta data fields is the *confidence level indicator*. This column is used to indicate how business rules or assumptions were applied during the ETL processes for a particular row of data. This field provides a means for the end user to measure the credibility level of a data row based on the transformation processing performed.

Confidence level indicators are often used to identify potential problems with data quality from operational source systems and to facilitate correcting these issues. Each decision support organization and/or project differs in how it ranks this particular technical meta data field. Figure 8.3 illustrates an example of confidence level indicators collected in a meta data repository table.

I use the confidence level indicator column to clearly identify rows of information where information has had to be integrated or derived during

Confidence Level Indicator	Confidence Level Description
6	Directly sourced from an operational system
5	Integrated from multiple operational systems
4	Derived
3	Estimate
2	Missing or Null Value Surrogate Key
1	Unknown

Figure 8.3 Confidence level indicator example.

transformation. I also use this column to identify data that has had to be estimated, forecasted, or trended. If the business requirements dictate that all operational system data is to be loaded into a fact table, I use this column to identify rows that have "not available" surrogate keys due to missing information in dimension tables.

On one decision support project I was involved in, this technical meta data tag was used to identify the various data loaded into the warehouse based on stability. Data from a relatively stable source like customer and product were loaded at the highest level. Data that was considered more volatile, easy to clean, or relatively moderate to define, was loaded at the second level. The third level consisted of data that was considered more problematic to define, such as planning or forecasting data. The fourth level consisted of data that did not originate from one of the corporate operational systems but was provided by management, usually in the form of a spreadsheet. The last, or fifth, level was used to tag the data from external sources such as news services or commercial sources. I have found this tagging schema to be particularly useful on telecommunications and human resource decision support engagements.

Technical Meta Data Column Assignment

Now that you have a better understanding of the importance and measurement potential of using technical meta data in your decision support data model, I will describe how to derive these columns. In the next phase of development, the repository architect, data modeler, and data acquisition developer move forward by incorporating these technical meta data columns into the design of the data warehouse data model, meta data repository, and ETL processes. This is not as easy a task as it may first appear. If you have purchased a meta data repository product or ETL tool, it may have unique requirements for integration with other warehouse components in order to allow you to add these columns to the model. ETL processes may need extensive work in order to be able to properly tag data that is being collected or derived from the various operational systems.

There are several ways to assign value to these columns. Some examples of the methods used to assign the various technical meta data columns include:

Load cycle identifier.   The value for this column is assigned by inserting a new row in a meta data or look-up table that is created within the data model to capture operational statistics. The primary key on the table consists of a serial or sequence data type. Regardless of the completion status, the value to the data warehouse is incremented during each refresh cycle.

Current flag indicator.   The value of this column is assigned by comparing data that is currently in the data warehouse to data in a new load cycle. The two data files are sorted and then consecutively read to determine the current record. The current record has a *Y* value assigned to it, while historical records are assigned an *N*.

Load date.   The value of this column is determined at the beginning of the load cycle. If a load cycle or ETL statistics table is available in the meta data repository or has been added to the model, the value for this column can be extracted for this source. In many cases, this column value can be derived one time at the beginning of the ETL load cycle. In some cases, depending on business requirements, the value assigned may be the extraction or effective date from the operational system rather than the actual date the information was loaded into the data warehouse.

Update date.   The value of this column, like that of load date, is determined at the beginning of the load cycle, but is applied only to historical rows.

Operational system identifier.   The value of this column is assigned according to the operational system or systems that provided the information to the data warehouse. If two or more sources are integrated to construct a single row in a data warehouse table, the assigned value should represent the multiple operational systems.

Active operational system flag.   The value of this column is determined by comparing the natural or production keys of the operational system to data rows in the data warehouse table. A value of *Y* is assigned to a record that currently exists in the operational system.

Confidence level indicator.   The value of this column is assigned during ETL processing based on conformance to the business rules associated with the data warehouse target table. If business rule validation indicates that transformation occurred correctly without any unknown or missing information, the confidence level can be set high. If derived or estimated data is inserted during ETL processing, the confidence level may need to be set lower.

Strategies for Using Technical Meta Data Tags

Incorporating technical meta data tags into the architecture makes it possible to perform a variety of processing optimizations in data acquisition design, maintenance activities, quality measurements, and end user reconciliation and information auditing against the data warehouse. In this section of the chapter, I will walk through the following examples of using this technique:

- Extracting current dimension table data
- Identifying rows for archive/purge processing
- Rolling back the load cycle
- ETL processing of slowly changing dimensions type 2 records
- Slowly changing fact table ETL processing
- Performing current and history-dimension ETL processing

These are not the only tasks that can benefit from the use of technical meta data columns in your decision support data model, but these examples demonstrate a good starting set for your review. Chapter 10, Meta Data Delivery, provides several repository report examples that use these technical meta data columns; pay special attention to the ETL statistics repository report for further ideas on how to use this type of information.

Extracting Current Dimension Table Data

The typical data warehouse data model requires the use of the load date column in order to maintain a unique perspective of history for a row of data in a table. Although this column maintains referential integrity, it causes a high degree of processing overhead when a user attempts to determine which row in a dimension table is most current. The DBMS must determine, by sequentially reading each row of data in the table, which row has the most current load date. Figure 8.4 illustrates an example of a employee dimension table that uses the current indicator technical meta data tag to extract data.

An alternative to this brute-force method is the use of the current flag indicator column. Through ETL processing and comparison of natural or production keys, this column helps business users to quickly identify which row of information from the operational systems is most current. The last

Employee Surrogate Key	Employee ID	Employee Name	City	Region	Country	Postal Code	Current Flag Indicator	Load Cycle Indicator	Load Date	Operational System Identifier
33500	25652	Mary Johnson	Lincolnshire	Illinois	USA	60069	Y	5	02-Apr-1999	3
22100	25652	Mary Smith	Lincolnshire	Illinois	USA	60069	N	2	03-Jan-1999	3
11100	25652	Mary Smith	Kenosha	Wisconsin	USA	45652	N	1	01-Dec-1998	3

Figure 8.4 Extraction of current dimension table data example.

row added to a data warehouse table for a particular production key is given an assignment of *Y* for the current indicator flag, while historical records are set to *N* or null. Business users can use this column in their queries as a constraint to retrieve only the most up-to-date information. For certain reporting requirements, RDBMS views can be established to constrain the current indicator column, tagging it with a value of *Y*, to automatically avoid the use of *Where* clauses in SQL statements and potential interpretation issues by business users.

Rolling Back the Load Cycle

The implementation of extended meta data columns offers administrators several options for removing corrupt or suspect data from a data warehouse. Let us suppose, for example, that a monthly load cycle occurs against the data warehouse. During ETL processing of the load cycle, an error is detected in the RDBMS, or data from an operational source system is suspected of being corrupt, or some other data quality measurement issue is discovered in the data. Before technical meta data columns were incorporated into the data model design, the infrastructure developer and data acquisition developer had limited options for isolating and removing such corrupt or suspect information. Technical meta data tags allow developers to be selective in their methods for removing the erroneous data from the database.

One rollback option is to use the load cycle indicator to completely remove the last refresh cycle to the data warehouse. This can be accomplished simply by constraining the value of the load cycle in question and removing the affected rows in each table from the data warehouse. This same method can be tailored, in certain circumstances, to remove rows from a particular load cycle for a specific operational system by further constraining the operational system indicator in question. Figure 8.5 illustrates an example of an employee dimension table that uses the load cycle indicator technical meta data tag to remove data.

Employee Surrogate Key	Employee ID	Employee Name	City	Region	Country	Postal Code	Current Flag Indicator	Load Cycle Indicator	Load Date	Operational System Identifier
33500	25652	Mary Johnson	Lincolnshire	Illinois	USA	60069	Y	5	02-Apr-1999	3
22100	25652	Mary Smith	Lincolnshire	Illinois	USA	60069	N	2	03-Jan-1999	3
11100	25652	Mary Smith	Kenosha	Wisconsin	USA	45652	N	1	01-Dec-1998	3

Figure 8.5 Load cycle rollback example.

Regardless of the method used, once the suspect rows are removed from the data warehouse, the rollback process needs to accommodate the reassignment of the current indicator for rows that were flagged with a *Y* prior to the last load cycle.

Archiving and Purging

Let us imagine that our data warehouse has been up and running for some period of time, and monthly load cycles are being processed successfully. Our business users or our database monitoring tool alerts us to data that has become dormant over time or which is inactive for some other reason. Because we are not currently using this data on any type of regular basis, we must decide to either archive it to a near-line storage device or purge it from the data warehouse for size and performance reasons.

Once again, if we are using technical meta data columns, we (or actually, our data warehouse administrator) have a variety of options for isolating and flagging candidate rows for archiving or purging. First, the load date can be interrogated to isolate rows of data from a particular period. This method again requires additional overhead on the part of the RDBMS to analyze the load date. The second option is to constrain rows of data from a particular set of load cycles. This method provides a more efficient means of flagging candidate rows and avoids tokenizing a date column to identify a particular period. Figure 8.6 illustrates an example of an employee dimension table that uses the load date or load cycle indicator technical meta data tag to purge and archive data.

Slowly Changing Dimensions (Type 2)

Data warehouses or marts that employ some variant of a star schema data model design can use the current flag indicator to aid in SCD type 2 processing for dimension table loads.

The established method for processing of SCD type 2 records is to sort both sources of information, operational system versus data warehouse/mart,

Employee Surrogate Key	Employee ID	Employee Name	City	Region	Country	Postal Code	Current Flag Indicator	Load Cycle Indicator	Load Date	Operational System Identifier
33500	25652	Mary Johnson	Lincolnshire	Illinois	USA	60069	Y	5	02-Apr-1999	3
22100	25652	Mary Smith	Lincolnshire	Illinois	USA	60069	N	2	03-Jan-1999	3
11100	25652	Mary Smith	Kenosha	Wisconsin	USA	45652	N	1	01-Dec-1998	3

Figure 8.6 Archiving and purging example.

based on the production or natural key of the dimension table. The current flag indicator can be used to constrain those records from the dimension table that will be compared to the current load cycle data being processed to the warehouse. Only dimension records containing a *Y* in the current indicator column need to be compared to the load cycle data since they contain the most updated information for the specific production key(s).

A consecutive comparison is made between the two data files based on these key column(s). Current load cycle records with production key values not found in the dimension table are loaded as new rows. These rows receive new surrogate keys for the dimension and have their current indicator flag set to *Y.* The current flag setting is due to the fact that no other occurrence of the production key(s) combination exists in the dimension table to date. Figure 8.7 illustrates the initial steps for ETL processing of a slowly changing dimension type 2 using technical meta data.

Production key(s) found in both the load cycle data and the dimension table are further interrogated based on columns deemed relevant to track changes by the business users. The two sources (i.e., the load cycle data and the dimension table) are sorted by the key and relevant columns, then a consecutive comparison is made against these files. Current load cycle records that have relevant columns that do not match their corresponding dimension table rows are flagged as new rows. These rows are inserted with new surrogate keys and have the current flag indicator set to *Y* due to an update made to a relevant column since the last load cycle. Figure 8.8 illustrates the final steps for ETL processing of a slowly changing dimension type 2 using technical meta data.

Previously loaded dimension rows that have a matching production key(s) when compared to the current load cycle file but which have differences in relevant columns are assigned a current indicator of *N.* These rows receive this setting due to the fact that new information on relevant columns of the dimension have been received in the most recent load cycle.

This same process of constraining on the current flag indicator and performing a comparison on production keys between the dimension table and load cycle is repeated during each update process to the data warehouse.

Slowly Changing Fact Table ETL Processing

Many data warehouse design teams are faced with the challenge of keeping track of dimension table columns over the course of time while also providing direct access to the latest version of the data. Initial iterations of these dimensional models often use standard data warehouse modeling techniques, such as SCD type 2 or 3, in an attempt to address this business

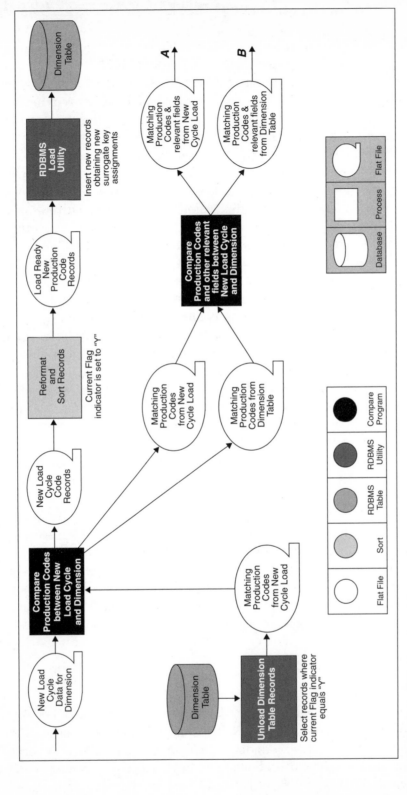

Figure 8.7 SCD type 2, part 1 example.

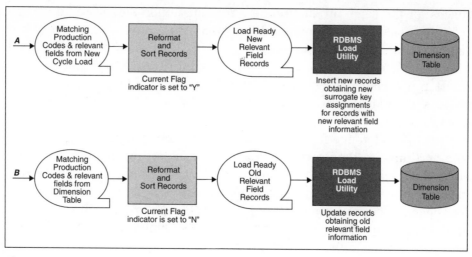

Figure 8.8 SCD type 2, part 2 example.

requirement. An alternative method is to maintain two sets of surrogate keys, one for current and one for history, on the fact tables. However, the front-end tool must be capable of selecting between the alternative sets of surrogate keys on the fact table. This technique allows all dimension tables that require information from either a current or a historical perspective to use the SCD 2 design method. This method also depends heavily on the use of technical meta data columns on the dimension tables to distinguish current versus historical rows. Referential integrity between the dimension and fact tables is maintained through the ETL processing method. Updates to the fact table surrogate keys should use a DSS-optimized DBMS that has a high-speed or parallel load option.

You should complete successful ETL processing of all dimension and fact tables for the current load cycle before beginning this process. Then, you may begin the task of restating history on the previously loaded fact table rows by sorting and splitting the dimension table rows into two groups.

Dimension table rows are separated through use of the current flag indicator (a technical meta data column). Dimension records containing a *Y* are grouped into one set and those with an *N* are grouped into another with the production keys of the dimension table. A consecutive comparison is made between the two dimension table file sets that associates the current surrogate key to all corresponding historical surrogate keys based on the production keys. The current surrogate key for an equally matching production key is appended onto the resulting file set. This output file provides a cross-reference of the current surrogate key to all historical surrogate key occurrences for the same production key. You must build surrogate key cross-reference files for each dimension table that has a current and history surrogate key on the fact table (see Figure 8.9). The dimension table record file, with current indicator set to *Y*, is saved for normal fact table record insert processing later in this method. Figure 8.9 illustrates the initial process of building surrogate key cross-reference table file using technical meta data.

The cross-reference files are then consecutively compared, one dimension at a time, to the previously loaded fact table rows history surrogate keys. When matches are found on a history surrogate key between the two files, the current surrogate key on the fact row is updated from the cross-reference file created from the dimension table. Figure 8.10 illustrates the process of comparing the fact table keys to the dimension cross reference surrogate key file looking for modifications.

Fact rows that have had no updates to their current surrogate keys, after comparison to all dimension cross reference files, are dropped from further processing (see Figure 8.11). Removing these rows reduces overall update processing because only fact rows that have new current surrogate keys assigned during this particular load cycle are updated.

The resulting file set is formatted for use with the DBMS high-speed parallel load function and updates to the current surrogate key are applied to the affected fact rows. The fact rows now have the latest surrogate key values for a dimension in their current surrogate key set. Figure 8.11 illustrates the process of updating the fact table current surrogate keys to match the latest value found in the corresponding dimension table.

ETL processing of the new load cycle fact table records is initiated by consecutively comparing production codes between the current load cycle fact records, from the operational system, to each dimension table that has an associated current surrogate key (see Figure 8.12). This comparison appends the current surrogate key of the dimension to the new fact table rows being processed. Before insertion into the fact table, these new fact rows have the history surrogate key set to match the current surrogate key. These records are then formatted to match the target fact table and inserted into the fact table using the DBMS load facility. Figure 8.12 illustrates the final ETL processing of new fact table records using the technical meta data tags.

This technique does not require as much additional storage space as maintaining both current and history fact tables, the technique that I describe in the next example. However, ETL processing of fact tables is more complex and updates will, in most cases, depend on the availability of a high-speed parallel DBMS load function. I have seen update speeds of bet-

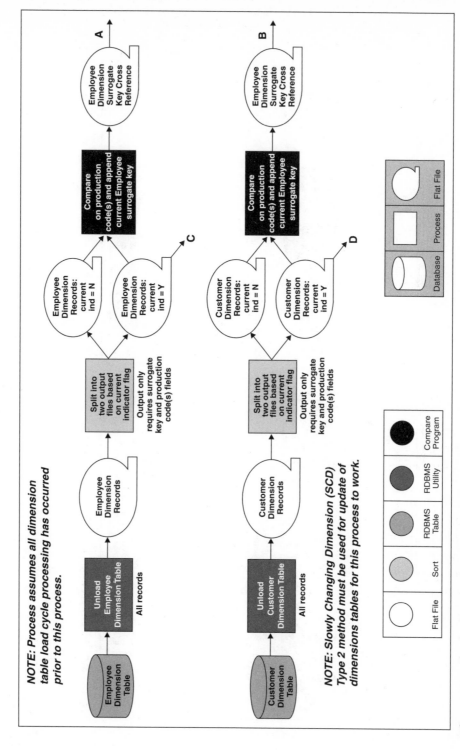

Figure 8.9 Slowly changing facts ETL process, part 1.

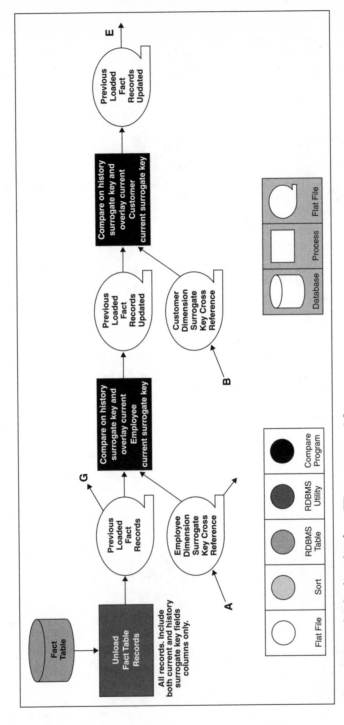

Figure 8.10 Slowly changing facts ETL process, part 2.

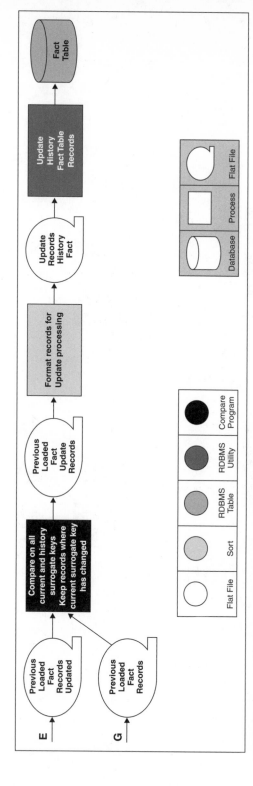

Figure 8.11 Slowly changing facts ETL process, part 3.

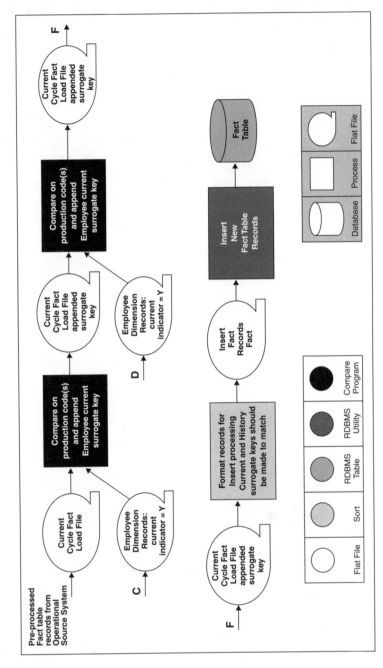

Figure 8.12 Slowly changing facts ETL process, part 4.

ter than a half million rows per minute on a fact table that uses the RDBMS's high speed parallel load function. Insert speed processing is also impressive, running at about 3 million rows per minute. This type of performance measured on a 24-node Symmetrical MultiProcessing (SMP) UNIX box with 6 gigabytes of RAM. The database contained no indexes or referential integrity, which is performed during ETL, but made use of the light scan option available with this particular RDBMS.

Maintaining Current and History Dimension Tables

Another alternative for maintaining current and history fact data is simply maintaining two sets of dimension tables, one for current use and one for historical purposes. This technique requires the front-end tool to easily choose which set of dimension tables to use in a report, based on a selection of either history or current outlook. The two sets of tables share common column names and are distinguished only by the actual table names.

ETLs for the two sets of tables require different processing methods. The history table uses the SCD 2 technique for maintaining a history on production keys and makes extensive use of technical meta data columns to perform processing. New records inserted into the history dimension table, due to new production code(s) or changes to relevant columns from previously loaded production code(s), need to also be inserted into the current dimension table. This is done to maintain balance in surrogate key assignments between the two tables. Figure 8.13 illustrates the ETL processing of current and history dimension tables utilizing SCD type 2 and the technical meta data tags.

The current table's ETL technique uses the updated old relevant fields file from the SCD 2 process (Figure 8.13, reference E) and the newly inserted rows from the history table, with the current indicator flag equal to Y, to build update records for the current table (Figure 8.14, reference D). These two sources are consecutively compared, and the old surrogate key is overlaid to match the newly loaded records where the production code(s) were the same but other relevant field changes occurred (see Figure 8.14). The resulting file can then be used to update the surrogate key on the current dimension table to match the surrogate value of the newly inserted records. Figure 8.14 illustrates the update processing of current dimension tables surrogate using the technical meta data tags.

You must follow the sequence of the ETL processing steps carefully or the two tables' surrogate keys can shift out of balance and cause erroneous results in a report from the current versus the historical dimension table.

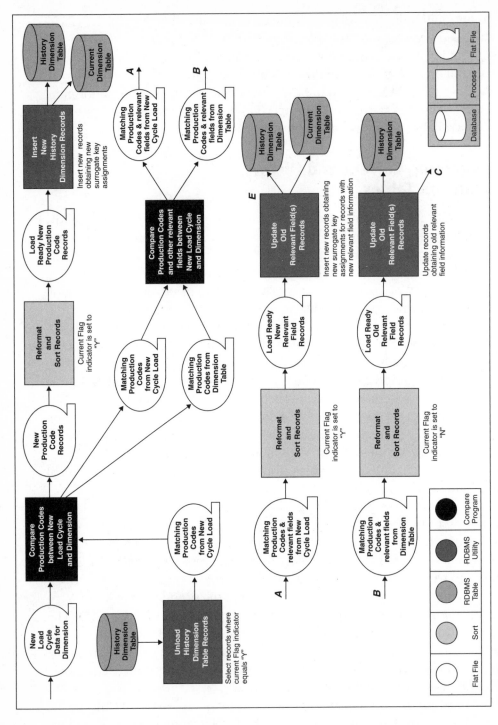

Figure 8.13 Current and history dimension tables ETL processing, part 1.

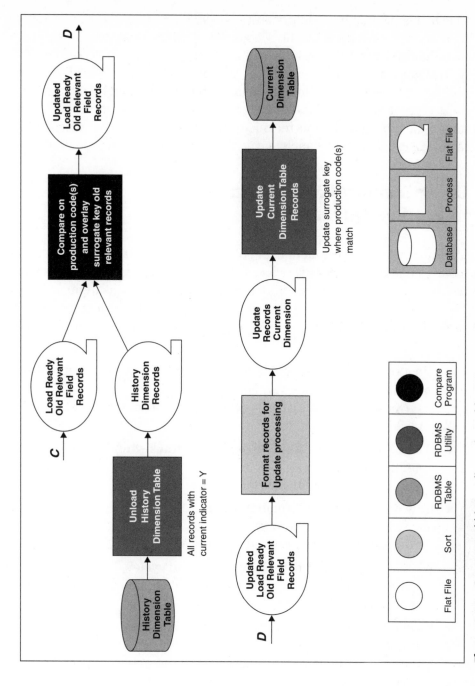

Figure 8.14 Current and history dimension tables ETL processing, part 2.

This technique requires additional storage space and the creation of supplementary ETL processes for the second set of tables. Additionally, this technique goes beyond the SCD 3 method because it allows reporting of all occurrences of history to a production code(s), not just two. It also surpasses the SCD 2 method in that all fact table records can be related to the most current values of a particular production code or natural key from a dimension table. Finally, this technique may affect query development where historical cross-sectors, which may include current data, are required.

Using Technical Meta Data to Resolve Quality Issues

Incorporating technical meta data columns into the data warehouse architecture enables business users and warehouse administrators to efficiently resolve a number of administrative and data quality measurement issues. These issues, many of which would have been difficult or impossible to resolve without the addition of technical meta data columns, include questions like:

- What operational system or systems provided this particular row of information to the data warehouse?

    Purpose: Data quality measurement and publishing of ETL load cycle results.

- When was this particular row of information last refreshed by the operational systems?

    Purpose: Data quality measurement.

- How many rows of information will be affected by an archive to near-line storage or a purge process?

    Purpose: Administrative and maintenance.

- What is the growth rate for a table per load cycle?

    Purpose: Administrative, maintenance, and publishing of ETL load cycle results.

- What effect on growth rate is being experienced from a particular operational system on the data warehouse?

    Purpose: Administrative, maintenance, and publishing of ETL load cycle results.

- What is the relative confidence level of the data currently loaded in the data warehouse?

    Purpose: Data quality measurement.

- What percentage effect on confidence level would be measured if dirty data from an operational system was corrected at the source instead of through ETL processing?

   Purpose: Data quality measurement.

The positive effect that technical meta data fields can have on a data warehouse is readily apparent. The depth and scope of the questions that administrators and data warehouse users can ask is significantly increased through the use of technical meta data fields. Can you answer these questions in your own decision support environment today? Would you need to consult multiple sources of information, then compile the results? Would you like to be able to quickly reference and measure this type of information?

Chapter 10 provides some examples of meta data repository reports for your consideration. You may want to especially note those reports that illustrate some uses of technical meta data tags in reporting information from the repository. In particular, look closely at Figure 10.7, the ETL Statistics Repository Report example on page 292, which uses some examples of technical meta data tags from this chapter.

Too Much of a Good Thing?

Technical meta data columns should not be universally and blindly incorporated throughout all the tables of the data warehouse. The repository architect, data modeler, and data acquisition developer need to work together closely to determine what makes sense to incorporate for a particular project and table. Remember, adding these columns into your decision support data model can affect how some ETL, meta data repository, and front-end access tools function. You should consult with the tool vendors to determine how they support such extensibility in their products. I have yet to see a meta data repository tool that can support this type of expansion in its content. In several scenarios, technical meta data tags contribute little to the design of the data model and ETL processes.

- Consider the case of an aggregation table added to the database to improve the performance of the front-end reporting tool. Using a load cycle identifier, current flag indicator, operational system identifier, load date, or update date would not be beneficial since the context of the technical meta data would be lost after aggregation is performed. It might be possible to maintain some type of reference to their technical meta data origins by keeping the values from the lowest level of granularity of the surrogate dimension key.

- In the case of a fact table, it would not be helpful to use the current flag indicator on a row since the concept of slowly changing dimension does not apply to a fact. This is also true for the *active in operational system flag*, since the fact row points to many dimensions, each of which usually has its own production or natural key.

- In very simple cases, identifying an operational system may provide little value to an end user due to a very limited number of sources with insignificant integration requirements. For example, a data warehouse project that uses an ERP application as its principal source of operational information would not benefit greatly from the addition of a source system identifier tag.

Summary

After reading this chapter, you should have a better understanding of how to tie the meta data repository and decision support data model closer together by using technical meta data to improve overall quality of the data content. Technical meta data tags provide warehouse administrators and business users with a means for measuring the content quality of the data in the warehouse and can also help to identify process improvement opportunities, such as removing dirty data from operational systems.

Adding these types of data tags into the decision support data model and ETL processes can help you to reconcile data quality issues in your environment. Such reconciliation promises an increase in data integrity that can benefit both the data warehouse administration and your business users by increasing the level of confidence in the quality of the information provided through the data warehouse. Additionally, data warehouse developers benefit from the use of technical meta data tags by gaining increased options and flexibility in accomplishing administrative and maintenance tasks.

Numerous ETL processing methods use technical meta data tags to increase capability and efficiency when loading information to the data warehouse. Standard ETL techniques such as SCD 1, 2, and 3 can benefit from use of these operators, as can some less traditional routines. You should be able to use these tags to interrogate your entire infrastructure and data acquisition environment by asking questions that find opportunities for improvement in it. Finally, use the techniques described in this chapter only where it makes sense. If your decision support environment is relatively simple, keep it that way by not overcomplicating the processing requirements it needs to fulfill. These methods provide the most benefit to data warehouse environments where a large number of operational source systems exist or complexity of the decision support model requires this type of organization. Keep the complexity level at a minimum for your environment by doing only what makes sense for your enterprise and project.

The next chapter discusses building the meta data repository model. It examines the basic components that comprise the model and explores the integration among the components. It also discusses a variety of meta data repository elements, including the operational source systems, decision support logical and physical data models, data mappings, subject areas, ETL statistics, and query statistics. The chapter is particularly relevant for repository architects, infrastructure developers, and data modelers.

Building the Meta Model

Building a meta model can be a difficult task at the best of times. There are many factors to consider, such as what types of meta data you need to store, how you are going to store it, who has access to it, and who is going to build it. In this first part of this chapter, I discuss the types of information that you need to identify so you can start designing your meta model, then I examine some of the factors that can influence your choice of a design.

In the second part of the chapter, I describe two approaches to modeling meta data—generic object models and traditional relational models—and discuss the factors that you need to consider when choosing a model type. Then, to help you determine which modeling approach is best for your company, I walk through the differences between object models and traditional models and build a sample model using a theoretical company. (If you are already familiar with basic data modeling concepts, you may wish to briefly skim over these sections.) Last, I explain how to apply the modeling concepts in this chapter to a real-world decision support system environment.

NOTE If you are not familiar with any of the modeling terms and structure names used in this chapter, please refer to the Glossary.

What Is a Meta Model?

Let's begin by examining exactly what the meta model is. A meta model is the physical database model that is used to store all of the meta data. A meta model differs from typical models in that it contains the business functions and rules that govern the data in our systems. Therefore, a meta model is simply a model created at a higher level of abstraction than the thing being modeled. In this case, you make a model of the business functions and rules that form the data you use every day. In a nutshell, this is a model to store information about your information. As with most things, of course, there are some trade-offs involved.

In an object model, the actual model is very atomic and generic in nature. The object model comprises a fixed number of entities that hold the relationships and entity information in their structure. The actual layout of information is stored in the meta model, forming a model within a model, if you like. This allows for great flexibility in storing just about anything because the model does not need to change.

In a traditional model, you have entities that have relationships to other entities. These entities form the basis for the physical design of the database. In the traditional model, the model is very specific and detailed but can only store the specific information that is modeled. Any additions or changes to the meta data require changes to the model as well. Thus, the trade-offs for an object model versus a traditional model are the ability to store anything without having to change the model (object) versus the ability to store only predetermined things and having to change the model (traditional). Figure 9.1 depicts the increase in complexity as you move from a traditional model to an object model.

As you can see, the traditional model starts with a more complex model, but has less complex programs that use it. The object model has a very simple model, but all of the smarts go into the programs that use it. To determine which model is better suited for your needs, you need to examine the specifics of your organization in more detail.

Goals for Your Meta Model

To determine which model is better suited for your project, you need to consider the goals that your repository has to meet. Far too many people want to just jump in and start modeling. How many times have you heard someone say, "We don't have the time to look at requirements," or, "We will get back to it later." Well, guess what? You had better make the time to do it at

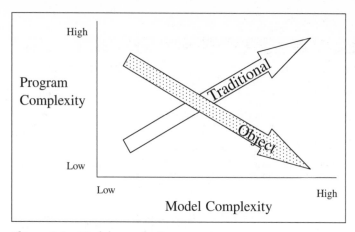

Figure 9.1   Model complexity.

the beginning of the project or you'll spend a lot of time doing rework, or worse yet, produce a final deliverable that is unusable. I remember working with a company that was in such a hurry to get the model done that the project managers couldn't stop long enough to talk to the business users to determine if what they were doing was what the business users wanted. In every meeting, major design issues were decided solely by IT people who didn't really understand what the data was or how it was going to be used. The users were consulted only after the IT team had put its interpretation of what was needed into the design. The end result was a model in which users could not tie together such basic information as orders and invoices. The users could not use the data, and the model was a flop. If the team members had done more analysis, they would have known that linking orders and invoices was critical to the kinds of information that the users need to get out of the model. In the end the project failed, and the model had to be redesigned. This is the type of situation that can be avoided if full requirements are documented and reviewed regularly.

If you examine the goals that you have for the model, you are likely to gain a better understanding of what it is that you are trying to model. Table 9.1 shows some common business goals and the type of model that may be appropriate.

You can see that just looking at the very high level requirements does not yield sufficient information to make a decision about the model type. You need to closely examine what you expect to get out of the repository to answer the question of which model is most appropriate for your project. You will also have to examine other factors that may influence your choice

Table 9.1 Common Business Goals

BUSINESS GOAL	MODEL TYPE
Gather meta data about application ABC	Object or traditional
Empower business users to query the decision support system	Object or traditional
Allow future developers to see what was done and why	Object or traditional
Capture everything in the company	Object
Quickly deploy a small meta data solution	Traditional

of model styles. Table 9.2 lists some of the other factors that you need to consider before you begin the task of modeling the repository. For example, suppose you ask management what the time frame for deployment is and they answer "ASAP." This response might lead you to a traditional model because the access programs and logic are easier (and quicker) to build. After you have examined all of these factors, you can make an informed decision about which model is right for you.

There are many things to consider when building a meta model, such as the personnel, project time lines, current IT infrastructure . . . the list can go on and on. Personally, I believe that if you spend the time up front, and answer as many of the questions as possible, you can design a product that precisely meets your needs. It is important to note that you are unlikely to ever have *all* of the answers that you need. Be wary of ending up in analysis paralysis. There must be a point at which you stop analyzing the model and start building it. Also be wary of scope creep. Be sure that you have defined a deliverable that contains a set of requirements that can be met. Do not attempt to address every request at one time. Enough said about analysis and deliverables; I will now begin to explain the basic differences between the object model and the more traditional entity relationship (ER) model.

Object Model Example

In an *object model*, the relationships and facts that your business is driven by are stored in a series of tables. To better see just what an object model is, let's look at a real-world example. The system catalog tables of your favorite RDBMS are a real-world example of an object model. The system catalog tables are a series of tables that store in their structure the information about the database. The system catalog contains the details of the tables, columns, column data types, indexes, relationships, and all the other information about the database. When you are using the database of your

Table 9.2 Influential Factors in Your Choice of a Model

FACTOR	QUESTION	ANSWER	CONSEQUENCES
Data architect/ modeler experience level	Can the data architect/modeler build an effective model?	No	A model built by an inexperienced staff or without good management supervision is unlikely to be usable for very long and will be difficult to change in the future.
Time frame for deployment	Does this repository need to be built quickly or is the time frame flexible?	Quickly	Trying to build a meta data repository quickly leads to problems in understanding the data inputs and formats, which makes a traditional model hard to design.
Programmer experience level	Can the programmers writing the front end that will access the repository perform the task?	No	The programmers will be unable to extract meaningful information from the repository. Programmers need to have advanced SQL knowledge and query tuning knowledge.
Program complexity versus model complexity	Do you prefer a model that is easy to maintain and access programs that are complex, or a model that is somewhat complex and access programs that are simple?	Simple access programs	An object model allows you to have a predefined set of queries and pass them the parameters for specific meta data elements.
IT infrastructure	Can the current environment support the model being proposed?	No	The infrastructure needs to be in place before you start building the repository; other-wise performance will not be acceptable and the repository will not be used.
Flexibility	Do you want to be able to add anything at anytime to the repository without changing its structure?	Yes	An object model, because of its design, allows for any item to be stored in it without major modifications to the model itself.

favorite RDBMS, the image of the database that you see is really just the representation of the information contained in the system catalog. This is an example of an object model. The object model's strength lies in its ability to capture the objects themselves and the relationships among them. Its weakness is that the programs that use the object model must understand how to piece the information together again so that it makes sense. If you take a look at the system catalog tables of your favorite RDBMS, you might see tables like those illustrated in Figure 9.2.

Can you make much sense out of the tables of model? Can you work with this model? This model requires a good understanding of what is in it, as well as how to get information out of it. You cannot tell by looking at this model what any of the tables, columns, or indexes are in your relational database. With the proper query, you can retrieve the information that will tell you the structure of your database, but you have to understand what is stored in the database first. I remember being at a client site that was just getting used to using relational databases. I was invited to attend a requirements gathering session with the business users, the analysts, and the database administrators. One of the DBAs brought along the system catalog

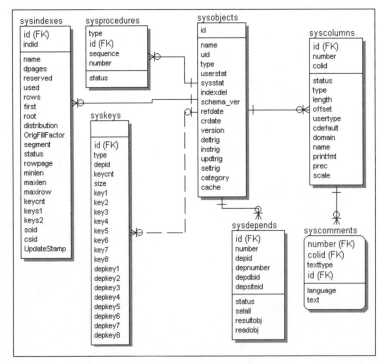

Figure 9.2   Sample object model from a RDBMS.

diagram. (I think he was going to try to impress the business users with it.) He did not get the response he was expecting, because the business users went nuts right away. They said that they could not use this database, and how were they ever going to get anything out of it? What they did not know (and what the ill-fated DBA did not tell them) was that they did not need to worry about using this database. This was the meta model for their databases. My point is that the object model does not easily reveal the secrets that are stored within its structure. You must be very well versed in the contents of the model to make any sense out of it, or have an application that can take care of all the extractions for you.

You are probably asking yourself why you would use an object model. An object model is useful when all the data elements are not known or will be added at a later time. If you think back to the RDBMS system catalog example, you have no idea what databases you are going to design in the future, so the RDBMS's object model (system catalog) allows you to add the databases as you need them without changing the system catalog's structure. Now, let's look at a model that may be more familiar to most of you.

Traditional Model Example

The traditional model is made up of entities, or tables if you prefer, and the relationships among them. This makes the traditional model easier to understand than an object model. A traditional model can be extended by the addition of entities and relationships. Since the traditional model is based on normalization theory, you end up with lots of tables that contain specific data about that table. To stay within the scope of this chapter, I will not go into detail here about the rules of normalization, but you can refer to the Glossary if you want to read up on the rules before proceeding. I believe I heard normalization summed up best as "one fact in one place." By following the rules of normalization, you can successfully build a model that will store your meta data. One thing to be aware of is that some denormalization may occur in the model when the physical design is done. Denormalization is the process of combining entities or objects to speed up access to the data. This occurs because you have fewer joins to perform in a denormalized structure. Let's look at another example of a model from a RDBMS. The model in Figure 9.3 shows you what the tables, columns, primary keys, and foreign keys are for the example.

As you can see, this is much easier to understand than the object model in Figure 9.2. You can quickly see the tables that make up your database. Adding another table is just a matter of adding another entity to the model. It is important to note that this style of model can quickly become unread-

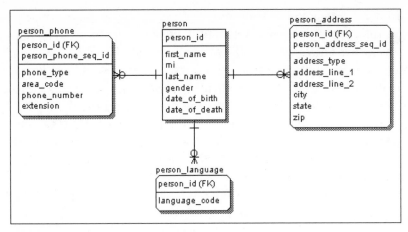

Figure 9.3 Sample entity relationship diagram.

able to the business users if too many entities are modeled in one diagram. Can you imagine users looking at a model with more than 100 entities on it? They would be very confused by the model. This is what can happen to your traditional model when it is used to store meta data. If the requirements for your meta data repository are large, then the model will be very complex because each object of your repository is stored in a separate entity. As you add more and more to the traditional model, it becomes increasingly difficult to scale the database and access requirements to this new larger database.

Summary of Meta Data Models

Clearly, there is no one right answer in choosing a model to store your meta data. Every company has many factors to consider when choosing a model. Table 9.3 compares the major attributes of the two types of models.

The influencing factors differ from company to company, but if you spend sufficient time analyzing the factors and business requirements, you can be pretty sure that you're not overlooking anything. Otherwise, you are likely to end up with a model that does not fulfill your business needs. I remember one client who just wanted to start building the repository without spending any time gathering requirements or talking to the business community. After many months of attempting to model the repository, we had to stop working and meet with the managers to inform them that we did not know what we were building. We had no idea of the data that was available or any of the business rules that would shape the way things were done. The company's management answered this by hiring more people, assuming that more people could solve the problem. Last I heard, that company still had

Table 9.3 Object Model versus Traditional Model

	OBJECT MODEL	TRADITIONAL MODEL
Model Complexity	The object model is very simplistic in its design. The model consists of very generic entities that are capable of storing anything. The actual complexity is in the relationships in the data.	The traditional model has entities for each type of information that you want to store. The model is more complex because of all the relationships and tables that must be defined.
Access Program Complexity	The access programs for the generic object model are complex. The programs must understand the rules that allow the data to be put back into information.	The access programs for the traditional model are quite straightforward. Depending on the information that is required, the access program may simply be a series of joins.
Expandability	The object model is infinitely expandable because of its generic nature. It is designed to allow anything to be added into its structure.	The traditional model is expandable but becomess increasingly complex as the number and types of information required expand. The model could easily grow to incorporate tens or hundreds of tables.
Development Time	The majority of the development time for the object model is in understanding the information required and the rules that define that information.	Most of the development time for the traditional model is spent understanding the information that is required.
Ease of Understanding	The object model is not easy to understand just by looking at it. It reveals none of the information contained within it. To understand the information in an object model, you need to examine the values contained in the model.	The traditional model is much easier to understand. By examining it, you can see the kinds of information contained in it and the relationships among that information.

not successfully created the meta model. This illustrates what can happen if you do not have any idea of the available data or the repository requirements. As we move on to the actual building of the meta model, we'll examine the object and traditional models in more depth and show the strengths and weaknesses of each.

Building the Meta Model

To begin building a sample model, we need to have an example company. The example that I will be using in this chapter is ABC Corporation. ABC is a small consulting and training company looking to capture the meta data about its organization. Let's pretend that we, as IT professionals, have been asked to design a model that will store ABC's meta data. ABC would like to have meta data about all of its employees, projects, and courses that are in progress at client sites as well as those under way at their own offices. To understand the full requirements, we begin by interviewing the managers at the company, then conduct business and technical user interviews. After reviewing all the information from the business users and managers, we produce a diagram showing the hierarchy of business at ABC. Figure 9.4 shows the relationships among the various operations at ABC.

As you can see from Figure 9.4, ABC has two types of employees: consultants and trainers. In this figure you can see that consultants work at client sites and that clients have projects for the consultants to work on, and the projects have requirements that must be met for the client to be happy. Con-

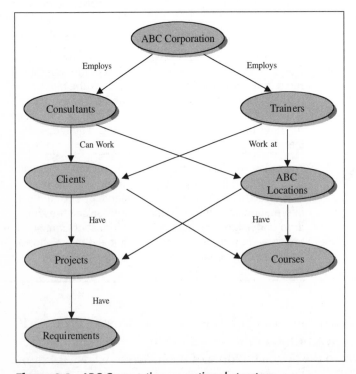

Figure 9.4 ABC Corporation operational structure.

sultants can also work at an ABC office on projects, and those projects also have requirements. The trainers can teach a course at a client site or perform the same duties at an ABC office. We can gather quite a bit of information from the simple diagram in Figure 9.4. This method of examining the people and places in your organization can help you identify the different types of meta data that you need to capture. As you investigate further and break things down more to show the actual relationships among the people, places, systems, and other components of your organization, you are determining the meta data that is available for you to use in your repository. Table 9.4 shows the people, companies, and tasks that are occurring at ABC, based on the information gathered from the interviews and requirements. From this point on in the chapter, I'll use the term *object* to refer to the actual people, companies, and work that is going on at ABC. For example, if I am just talking about the employees at ABC, I'll refer to them as the *employee object.*

The preliminary object list in Table 9.4 is just the starting point from which you can derive other objects and relationships that further expand the meta data available to the repository. Because we've only defined the basic objects, we must determine the details of the relationships among these objects. Figure 9.5 depicts the current assignments and projects that are being worked on by ABC employees. From Figure 9.5 we can see that ABC currently has six employees. Four of them are consultants and two are trainers. The consultants are working on two projects at two different client sites and one project at the ABC office. One trainer is working at a client site and the other is working at the ABC office. As you examine all of the infor-

Table 9.4 Preliminary Object List for ABC

OBJECT
Employees
Consultants
Trainers
Clients
ABC Offices
Projects
Course
Requirements

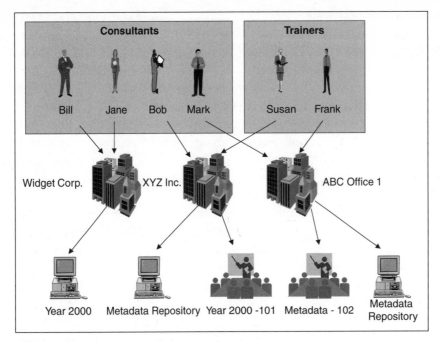

Figure 9.5   Current ABC employee assignments.

mation that is available from the business users and managers, you can determine the types of meta data that is available to be stored in the repository. If you break the information down into objects, as we have done in this example, you can determine the meta data that exists.

Expanding on the object list in Table 9.4, we can further divide the objects and requirements. Table 9.5 lists the object type, subtype, and meta data requirements about those objects that we need based on the preliminary list from Table 9.4. The listing in Table 9.5 is by no means extensive, and has been kept small to keep in line with the scope of this chapter. I am sure that each of you could come up with a different list for ABC. As an exercise, you might want to try to come up with other types of meta data that you would need for your company and use them in our ABC example. This way, you can start thinking about your own situation as you are working along with the example.

The listing in Table 9.5 shows you some of the types of objects that are available to be used in the repository model. From this example, we could have gone even further and broken down subtypes like addresses into their basic elements (e.g., address line one, city, state, and zip). It is up to you to determine the granularity, or smallest detail level, of the meta data that you

Table 9.5 Meta Data Requirements by Object Type

OBJECT	OBJECT SUBTYPE	BUSINESS META DATA DEFINITION
Consultants	Name	Consultant's full name in last-name, first-name format
	Address	Current address for the employee
	Skills	Listing of all current skills
	Pay range	Current pay range or pay classification
Trainers	Name	Trainer's full name in last-name, first-name format
	Address	Current address for the employee
	Certifications	Listing of all current training certifications
	Pay range	Current pay range or pay classification
Client	Address	Client's full address
	Name	Client's name, as well as any aliases
	Business	Business function the client is in (e.g., insurance, finance)
	Contact	Business contact at the client
ABC Corporation Offices	Address	Full office location
	Manager	Office manager's name and information
	Office specifics	Office-specific information (e.g., number of classrooms, number of PCs)
Projects	Definition	Business definition for the project
	Project plan	Location of actual project plan
	Budget	Budgeted amount for the project (this can be for the entire project or just the amount allocated for the consultants)
Courses	Definition	Description of the course and the need it tries to fulfill
	Dates offered	Current course schedule
	Prerequisites	Any previous knowledge that attendee would need to take this course
Requirements	Program specifications	Actual program specifications that the programmer will be working from
	Contacts	Any business contacts at the client

are storing. It is important to understand what is available and what is required, so that the model can accommodate all things. And, going through this process helps you to start thinking about all of the information that is available and helps you to make informed decisions. The ABC example is very small in comparison to today's corporations. The requirements at your company may include hundreds or even thousands of objects that need to be modeled. After you have established the meta data and the objects that exist in the organization, you can proceed to the task of building of the meta model. This way, you have a fairly complete picture from which to build your model. It may be impossible to fully model a whole corporation. One strategy is to model a small part first, then evolve that model by adding new areas incrementally. I have seen many repository projects fail because the developers tried to "swallow the whole whale."

Using the Model

In this section I build on the information from the previous section and apply this information to the models that were discussed earlier. I will begin with the generic object model and walk through the process of incorporating the meta data requirements from ABC into the generic object model. Then I'll walk through the more traditional model and its requirements at ABC and the process of incorporating them into the model. It is important to remember that each model has some advantages and disadvantages, and that there is no wrong choice when building a model. If the model suits the needs of your company, then it cannot be deemed a failure. As we examine how to apply the models to our example, the differences between the two model types (object and traditional) will become more apparent.

Generic Object Model

Using the ABC example, we will look at how you would store the meta data in the generic object model as it is shown in Figure 9.6. Figure 9.6 illustrates a basic, generic object model structure composed of three entities. We'll explain the entities in the object model and their purpose as we work through the section. In the ABC requirements, we identified 7 distinct object types and 23 subtypes from the listing in Table 9.5 that we need to store in the repository. The meta data objects that we need to store are all types of business meta data. The object list could be further expanded to include all of the technical meta data about the systems at ABC, but to keep the scope

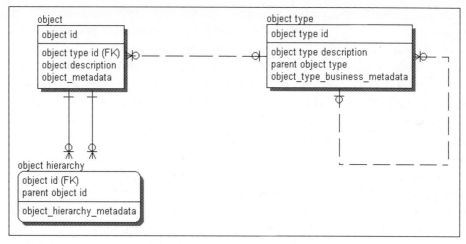

Figure 9.6 Storing meta data in a generic object model.

of the example small, we've left this information out. Earlier sections of the book offer examples of business and technical meta data that you can use to expand the ABC example.

We have already identified the objects for our example so now we can look for the relationships among these objects. Because every object is going to contain some relationship to some other object, it is important to ensure that we identify all of these relationships. Identifying the relationships may also reveal other object types that we need to store. An example of a relationship is that a client cannot be the same as an ABC location and a course does not have project requirements. Table 9.6 lists some of the relationships that we can identify from Figure 9.4.

Table 9.6 ABC Corporation Relationships

RELATIONSHIP
ABC Corporation employs two types of employees: consultants and trainers.
A consultant can work at a client site or an ABC office.
The client can have projects as well as courses.
Each project contains requirements.
A trainer can work at a client site or an ABC office.
A trainer teaches a course.

The object relationships help highlight the business rules that exist in an organization. Our generic object model in Figure 9.6 contains three entities or tables: the OBJECT table, the OBJECT TYPE table, and the OBJECT HIER-ARCHY table. Figure 9.7 illustrates the definition of the columns for the OBJECT TYPE table. The OBJECT TYPE table is used to store the lowest-level objects that we need in our repository; you can think of it as defining the objects' subclasses. Using our ABC example, we have objects for the address, the pay range, the course, the course dates, and so on. This can lead to a very large object type table, but it is helpful for identifying what is really needed.

The first column in our object type table is the OBJECT_TYPE_ID. This is a synthetic identifier that uniquely identifies this object type in our database. It is most often a sequence number that is defined when the row is inserted into the table. It is important to be sure that you do not have duplicate objects in this table. A periodic review of all objects in the table is useful for ensuring that there are no duplicates or widowed or orphaned objects. A *widowed* or *orphaned* object is an object that has no parent and is not a root object. An object that is in this state can cause unpredictable problems when a query is run against the repository.

The second column is the OBJECT_TYPE_DESCRIPTION. This column contains a brief description of the object type that you are storing. It does not need to be lengthy but it must be meaningful to anyone looking at the data. Try to keep it generic because you never know who the intended audience for the meta data repository may be.

The third column is the PARENT_OBJECT_TYPE_ID. This column is used to define the hierarchy of object types that exist. It is useful for avoiding *holes* in your meta data. An example of appropriate use for this column is to ensure that the parent object type for a project is a client. It is impor-

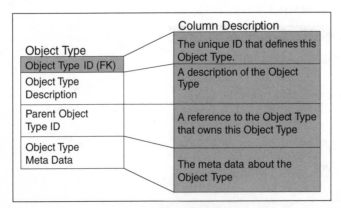

Figure 9.7 Column descriptions of object type table.

tant to note that this column defines the meta data hierarchy. Make sure that this hierarchy is correct; otherwise you will be unable to extract the information you want.

The final column in the table is the OBJECT_TYPE_META DATA. This column can be used to store any business information about the object type that you need. For example, the client object might contain a detailed description of what a client is to ABC.

Table 9.7 lists some sample data for the object type table based on the ABC example.

Because the OBJECT_TYPE table is used to represent the hierarchy of the objects in the model, we can see that an OBJECT_TYPE_ID of 1 indicates that this is an ABC Corporation type. The ROOT_OBJECT in the hierarchy is determined by finding the object that has no PARENT_OBJECT_TYPE_ID. The root object is just as it sounds, the object at the beginning of everything for this hierarchy. It is important to note that a repository that is created in an iterative fashion can have multiple hierarchies or root objects. This allows all the other objects in the hierarchy to be owned by one high-level object. As you look at Table 9.6, you can see a hierarchy of object types being defined. A client company is under the ABC Corporation. An employee is under the ABC Corporation. A consultant is under the employee at ABC Corporation. Constructing a hierarchy like this defines the relationships that exist between our objects and the business rules.

Table 9.7 Sample Content of Object Type Table

OBJECT TYPE ID	OBJECT TYPE DESCRIPTION	PARENT OBJECT TYPE ID	OBJECT TYPE META DATA
1	ABC Corporation	N/A	ABC Corporation information
2	Client company	1	The client company that we deal with directly, cross-referenced into the company table
3	Employee	1	The employee's name
4	Consultant	3	Any specific information about the consultant
5	Trainer	3	Any specific information about the trainer
6	Employee address	3	The employee's address
7	Skills	4	The employee's skills

The next table in our generic object model is the OBJECT table. Figure 9.8 illustrates the definition of the columns for the object table.

The OBJECT table holds all of the meta data about the objects that we need to store. It contains rows for every piece of meta data that we need to store for all of the objects defined in the OBJECT TYPE table.

The first column is the OBJECT_ID. This is a synthetic identifier that uniquely identifies this object type in our database. It is generally a sequence number that is defined when the row is inserted into the table. This identifier serves no purpose except to allow us to join the information together so that we can retrieve it later. The OBJECT_ID is unique in this table and is the primary key for this table and is referenced as a foreign key from the OBJECT_HIERARCHY table.

The second column is the OBJECT_TYPE_ID. This is a reference to the OBJECT_TYPE table's primary key. This is how we know what type of object we are working with. The OBJECT_TYPE_ID must contain a value that is in the OBJECT TYPE table, or we will have a lost piece of meta data. This is known as *referential integrity*. Referential integrity means that the foreign key in any referencing table must always refer to a valid row in the referenced table. Referential integrity ensures that the relationship between two tables remains synchronized during updates and deletes.

The third column is the OBJECT_DESCRIPTION. This column contains a brief description of the object. It can contain things like the company name, employee name, skill name, and so forth. The fourth and final column of the object table is the OBJECT_META DATA. This is where you store the meta data about the object; it contains the business rule or business information that is important to you.

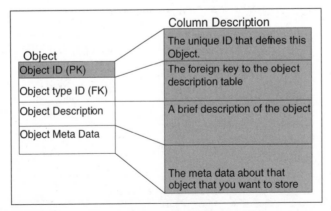

Figure 9.8   Column descriptions of object table.

Table 9.8 lists some sample data for the object table based on the ABC example. Each row in this table contains meta data about a specific instance of an object.

In Table 9.7 we have identified Object 11 as an object type of 1. If we look in the object type table, we see that this is defined as the ABC Corporation object. The meta data for ABC Corporation is listed in the OBJECT_META DATA column for this row. We can also see the definitions for most of the other meta data that we need for our ABC example. We have the employees'

Table 9.8 Sample Contents of Object Table

OBJECT ID	OBJECT TYPE ID	OBJECT DESCRIPTION	OBJECT META DATA
11	1	ABC Corporation description	ABC Corporation is in the business of providing consultants to help in the design of widget systems and to help in the training of business users in the widget systems.
12	2	Widget Corporation	Widget Corporation is in the business of distributing widgets to its many clients around the world.
13	3	Bill	Bill is a systems analyst at ABC corporation.
14	4	Consultant Bill	Bill has been a consultant since 1988.
15	7	Meta data	Six years of meta data experience.
16	7	Oracle	Seven years of Oracle.
17	6	Bill's address	123 Anywhere Street, Lostville, MA 99999-2345
18	3	Susan	Susan is a senior technical trainer at ABC Corporation.
19	5	Trainer Susan	Susan has been a trainer since 1990.
20	8	Lotus Notes	Level 3 notes guru.
21	8	Microsoft Exchange	Level 2 exchange guru.
22	6	Susan's address	999 Partytown Road, Somewhere, CA 66666-9999

information, indicating their skills and certifications, and the clients and projects in process, and so forth.

The last table in our generic object model is the OBJECT HIERARCHY table. Figure 9.9 illustrates the definition of the columns for the OBJECT HIERARCHY table.

The object hierarchy table holds the relationships between specific instances of the objects. It defines the chain that links all the information together. Without this table we would be unable to determine which address object belongs to which employee object or which project belongs to which client.

The first column is the OBJECT_ID. This column is a foreign key back to the main object table. It identifies which object we are currently on. The second column is the PARENT_OBJECT_ID. This is used to identify which instance of the object in the hierarchy is above this one or the parent to this object. The last column is the OBJECT_HIERARCHY_META DATA. This column is used to store any specific information about the relationship between these two objects. In practice, it may not be used very often, but we include it here for completeness.

Table 9.9 lists a sample of the object hierarchy table contents based on the ABC example. Each row in this table contains a relationship between two of the meta data objects.

The OBJECT_HIERARCHY table contains a linked list, which allows us to follow the chain and piece together the information that we need. Let's say that we want to determine the specific skills that employee Bill has. We could follow the chain starting at OBJECT_ID 11 and work our way down until we came across the rows for OBJECT_ID 15 and 16. These identify the skills that Bill has as an employee of ABC. By browsing up and down the chains, we can put together the specific meta data that we are looking for. Taking the data that is stored in the tables and turning it back into useful information can be a difficult task, depending on the levels of complexity in

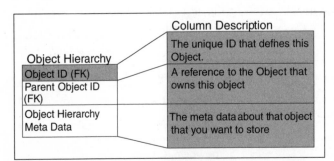

Figure 9.9 Column descriptions of object hierarchy table.

Table 9.9 Sample Contents of the Object Hierarchy Table

OBJECT ID	PARENT OBJECT ID	OBJECT HIERARCHY META DATA
11	N/A	Top-level object.
12	11	Widget Corporation is a client of ABC Corporation.
13	11	Bill is an employee at ABC Corporation.
14	13	The employee Bill is a consultant.
15	14	Bill has meta data skills.
16	14	Bill has Oracle skills.
17	13	Address of employee Bill.
18	11	Susan is an employee at ABC Corporation.
19	18	The employee Susan is a trainer.
20	19	Susan has Lotus Notes certification.
21	19	Susan has MS Exchange certification.
22	18	Address of employee Susan.

the object hierarchy. The last section on the generic object model deals briefly with the possible techniques to extract data from this model.

Extracting Data from a Generic Object Model

Now that we have fully explored the object model, let's investigate how we would extract data from this model. Because this model is extremely generic and abstract, we need to use a more advanced method to get the information out. We can explore this model from many different views to gather information. Let's say that we're interested in finding all the addresses of employees; we would start with the employee objects and proceed to find all of the children objects for the employees. We would then filter all of those objects to select only the address objects. Similarly, if we were interested in seeing if anyone at ABC had experience with Visual Basic, we could query the object table and select only where the object type is equal to the skill VB. We would next select all of the parent objects that were of an employee type. Voila, we have our list! For a final example, we might want to find all the meta data we have on a given employee. We could do this by creating a recursive join on the object hierarchy table. A *recursive join* is a join in which one occurrence of an entity or table is related to one or more occurrences of the same entity or table. We would apply as our first-level filter the employee that we were looking for; then by using the recursive join we could see all the meta data associated with that employee. The following listing is an example of a recursive query to select all of the meta data about the employee Bill. The example has specific Oracle enhancements for performing recursive queries and will only work on Oracle 7.3 and higher.

```
SELECT o.object_id,
       o.object_description
       ot.object_type_id
,      ot.object_type_desc
FROM object o
,    object_type ot
, (SELECT object_id
    FROM object_hierarchy
     START WITH object_id = (SELECT object_id FROM object
WHERE
                      object_description = 'Bill')
     CONNECT BY PRIOR object_id = parent_object_id) b
WHERE o.object_id = b.object_id
AND o.object_type_id = ot.object_type_id
/
```

This query would produce the following output if we were using the example data for ABC. As you can see, it has navigated the hierarchy and returned all of the meta data about Bill.

OBJECT_ID	OBJECT_DESCRIPTION	OBJECT_TYPE_ID	OBJECT_TYPE_DESC
13	Bill	3	Employee
14	Consultant Bill	4	Consultant
15	Meta Data	7	Skills
16	Oracle	7	Skills
17	Bills Address	6	Employee Address

The same example using IBM DB2© would look like this:

```
WITH parent (object_id, parent_object_id) AS
  (SELECT object_id,
          parent_object_id
     FROM object_hierarchy
     WHERE object_id = (SELECT object_id
                     FROM object
                     WHERE object_description =
                'Bill')
```

```
        UNION ALL
        SELECT    c.object_id,
                    c.parent_object_id
        FROM object_hierarchy c,
              parent p
        WHERE p.object_parent_id = c.object_id)
    SELECT      o.object_id,
                o.object_description,
                o.object_type_id,
                ot.object_type_desc
       FROM        parent p
    ,       object o
    ,       object_type ot
        WHERE p.object_id = o.object_id
        AND    o.object_type_id = ot.object_type_id;
```

In another example, if we want to see all of the employees that have a certain skill, we can modify the preceding queries to return the results that we need. The following is an Oracle query that will return all of the parent objects given a child object. In this example, we want to find all of the employees with Oracle experience.

```
SELECT      o1.object_description
FROM            object o
,           object o1
,           object_hierarchy oh
,           object_type ot
,    (SELECT object_id
FROM object_hierarchy
START WITH object_id = 11
CONNECT BY PRIOR object_id = parent_object_id) b
WHERE o.object_id = b.object_id
AND o.object_type_id = ot.object_type_id
AND UPPER(ot.object_type_desc) = 'SKILLS'
AND UPPER(o.object_description) = 'ORACLE'
AND o.object_id = oh.object_id
AND oh.parent_object_id = o1.object_id
/
```

This query would produce the following output if we were using the example data for ABC. As you can see, it has navigated the hierarchy and returned all of the employees that have Oracle experience.

```
OBJECT_DESCRIPTION
------------------
Consultant Bill
Consultant Mark
```

By modifying these sample queries, we can retrieve nearly anything that we need from the repository. You may need to do cursor processing or use recursive stored procedure calls to extract the results that you want for more advanced processing. Please refer to your database documentation for more information about recursive SQL and stored procedures. As you can see from these examples, we can perform some powerful database extracts by modifying these sample queries. By being able to traverse up and down the hierarchy of objects, we can find any of the information that we need. It just takes a little bit of up-front thinking to figure out how to get it. This is why the object model is a more complex model to work with than the traditional model but is much more scalable and flexible.

Traditional Model

The traditional model is based on standard Entity Relationship (ER) diagrams. (We will not go into details about ER diagrams—there are plenty of good books that explain how to develop ER models.) Figure 9.10 illustrates a possible design based on our ABC Corporation requirements. Because modeling is almost as much an art as a science, there are many different ways in which to model this data. Your design could be very different from the example in Figure 9.10 and still perform the same function. As you can see, this model has many more tables and relationships than the object model from the previous section.

The trade-offs that we talked about in the beginning of the chapter are becoming easier to see now that we can compare a traditional model to the generic object model. The traditional model is easy to read, and we can almost instantly determine the kinds of meta data that will be stored in its structure. The price that we pay for this ease of understanding is that the model is not easily expandable and can present maintenance problems if it continues to grow. This type of model may be particularly attractive for the first iteration of the repository, but as the environment expands, you may have no choice but to move to an object model.

In the traditional model, it is relatively easy to see the types of meta data that are going to be stored in the repository. We can look at the entity names like *location* and *employee* and know immediately that these are going to store meta data about locations and employees. The generic object model that we described in the previous section did not give us this luxury. We will not go into great detail about the entities and attributes in the traditional model because they are self-explanatory and are based on the meta data that you need to capture. The attributes can be very specific or very generic, depending on the meta data requirements. The *employee* entity would contain an employee name attribute, date of birth, and any other employee spe-

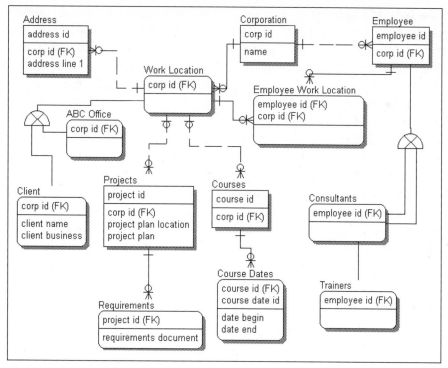

Figure 9.10   Traditional model.

cific data that we need. The *skills* entity would contain the skills that the employee has, and all of the other entities would contain attributes that are specific to that entity.

Some specific modeling techniques allow the traditional model to more easily accommodate change. An example of one such technique is the concept of *subtype* and *supertype*. In a subtype/supertype relationship, the supertype (or parent) contains the specific attributes that are common to all subtypes. The subtype (or children) entities contain the attributes that are specific to that entity. As you can see in Figure 9.10, we have a subtype/supertype relationship with the employee, consultant, and trainer entities. The employee entity is the supertype, which contains all of the specific employee information that is common to all employees at ABC. The children entities contain the specific information about that employee type. In this case, it contains the specific trainer and consultant information. This technique allows for a greater flexibility if other types are needed later and does not greatly disrupt the model.

The use of *associative entities* is another technique that helps the traditional model to accommodate change. An associative entity is one that helps resolve many-to-many relationships in the model. The entity usually contains only the keys from the entities on each side of it. In our sample model, the associative entity (work location) allows an employee's work to be carried out at any location. In this model, each entity contains the specific meta data facts that we need for that part of the business. If you refer back to the generic object example you can see how the meta data requirements could easily be fit into this model. Appendix C contains the detailed DDL to create the full traditional model.

A traditional meta model allows your business users to easily understand the contents of your meta data repository and to answer fairly simple meta data questions without much IT involvement. As the meta data requests become more complex, however, the query required to extract the data also becomes more complex, and performance deteriorates as the query complexity increases. Generous use of indexing can help alleviate some of the performance problems associated with the multiple joins that occur in a traditional model.

Extracting Data from a Traditional Model

To extract the meta data from a traditional model, we need to write queries that join across all of the tables that we're interested in. This is one of the main disadvantages of using a traditional ER model for storing meta data information. If we needed to extract all of the meta data from the ABC example, we would have a very large query that joins all of the tables together. Database performance would be very poor and might not run at all depending on the RDMS. On the other hand, if we are interested in a very specific piece of meta data, we can query just the relevant table without having to worry about anything else. We should also consider using indexes in this type of model in order to speed up our queries as much as possible. (If we join two nonindexed columns together, we may wait a very long time for a response.)

The following are sample queries that extract meta data information from a traditional model. In the first example, we select all the meta data about an employee.

```
Query to extact employee information

SELECT    e1.emp_id,
          e1.emp_name,
          e1.emp_dob,
          e1.emp_classification,
          e3.skill,
          e2.emp_address
FROM employees e1
```

```
,     skills e3
,     address e2
WHERE e1.emp_id = e2.emp_id
AND e1.emp_id = e3.emp_id
```

In the preceding query, we could add filters, or predicates, to restrict which employees we want to see. For example, if we were only interested in seeing the employee named Bill, we could add a filter to the emp_name field to select only those records.

```
SELECT     e1.emp_id,
           e1.emp_name,
           e1.emp_dob,
           e1.emp_classification,
           e3.skill,
           e2.emp_address
FROM employees e1
,     skills e3
,     address e2
WHERE e1.emp_id = e2.emp_id
AND e1.emp_id = e3.emp_id
AND UPPER(e1.emp_name) = 'BILL'
```

For another example, we could:

```
SELECT     e1.emp_id,
           e1.emp_name,
           e1.skill
FROM employees e1
,     skills e2
WHERE upper(e2.skill_name) = 'ORACLE'
AND e2.emp_id = e1.emp_id
```

By modifying these queries, we should be able to retrieve any of the information contained in the repository. There are, however, some important things to remember: The traditional model uses simpler queries, but it requires a number of joins to get the facts that you want. Also, if you need changes or different data, you have to write a whole new query rather than just changing some parameters.

Meta Models and Decision Support Systems

A decision support system is the perfect project for the meta data repository because a DSS generally encompasses all parts of an organization and is typically fed from disparate systems throughout the organization. Applying either of these models to a real-world DSS can, however, be an incredibly large and difficult undertaking because the data that you want is likely to be stored in many computer systems, and the business rules may only be known by the business users, and not documented at all. Implementing a meta data repository for your DSS can have a multitude of benefits, though, letting your users do a lot of the fact-finding that the IT staff normally performs to determine what data exists. Business users can query the repository to find the business definitions of specific columns in the DSS, look into the transformations that the data has gone through, and track a specific data element back to its source system. A sample object list in Table 9.10 shows some of the kinds of information that can be stored in the repository.

Imagine being able to simply give your users access to the repository, along with some predefined queries that would let them determine anything they want about the data warehouse. If, for example, a business user needs a new report that requires some very specific data, he or she could query the meta data repository and find all occurrences of that data without needing the IT department to determine whether the data is available and where it resides. In addition, the user could trace the data back to the source systems and determine which DSS field(s) contains the necessary information. Wouldn't that be great!

Real-World Example of a Meta Model

Now that we have explored both types of models and discussed how to access information from either, let's look at a real-world example of a traditional model that is used to store meta data. This model would allow you to store meta data about the following DSS components:

- Source system data definitions
- Logical DSS model
- Physical DSS model
- Source/target data mapping and semantic resolution
- Business subject areas
- Query statistics
- ETL statistics

Figure 9.11 illustrates a meta model that would allow you to store basic meta data about a DSS environment. It outlines the fundamental components that are necessary to keep track of meta data from the source systems that

Table 9.10 Repository Meta Data Facts

OBJECT DESCRIPTION
Query access patterns, frequency, and execution time
User report name and definitions
Audit controls and balancing information
The structure of data as known to the data administrator
The system of record feeding the decision support system
Identification of source system fields
Mappings and transformations from the system of record to the decision support system
Encoding/reference table conversions
The data model, both physical and logical
Decision support system table names, keys, and indexes
Decision support system tables structures and table attribution
The relationship between the data model and the decision support system
The history of extracts
Decision support system table access patterns
Decision support system archiving
Job dependencies
Program names and descriptions
Version maintenance
Security
Purge criteria
The structure of data as known to the business analyst
Common access routines for the data in the warehouse/mart
Subject areas
Table names and business definitions
Attribute names and definitions in business terms
Decision support system field mappings, transformations, and summarization
Rules for drill-down, drill-up, drill-across, and drill-through

continues

Table 9.10 Repository Meta Data Facts *(Continued)*

OBJECT DESCRIPTION
Domain values
Data owner
Data location
Decision support system refresh dates

feed the DSS systems to the statistics of the queries that the end users run against the DSS tables. I depict this basic model in the traditional ER format and will explain it in this format. After I've fully explained it, you should be able to see, based on the previous sections, how you could take this model and convert it to a generic object model to store the same information.

First, we need to look at the key entities that will store the meta data. The key entities are those that contain data values and are not comprised totally of foreign keys from other entities. Table 9.11 lists the entities (tables) in the model and provides a brief description of the purpose of each. Table 9.12 lists the associative entities from the model.

The associative entities in the model allow for the many-to-many situations to be resolved. This way the same table name can be used in multiple subject areas and can be used more than once in the target tables. The source systems column can be mapped to multiple target tables, and those target tables can have the same name if they are in different databases.

The entities in Table 9.11 are the main entities for the meta model. To fully understand this model, let's examine each of the key entities to understand its purpose in the model. Table 9.13 outlines the SUBJECT_AREA entity and briefly describes the attributes of the entity. The SUBJECT_AREA entity contains the definitions of the subject areas in the DSS environment. The attributes in the primary key are a unique identifier and the date that the subject area became effective. Subject areas like finance, orders, sales, and so forth are contained here, along with the date that they became effective and their status. The SUBJECT_AREA_DESCRIPTION attribute is included to allow for a detailed description of the subject area if it is not readily apparent, or if some definitions about the scope of the subject area are needed.

The next entity that we look at is the TARGET_TABLE. Table 9.14 shows the TARGET_TABLE and its attributes. The TARGET_TABLE entity is used to store information about the tables in the DSS environment. The primary key contains the table's name, the type of table it is (i.e., logical or physical), and the date that the table became effective in the system. The remainder of

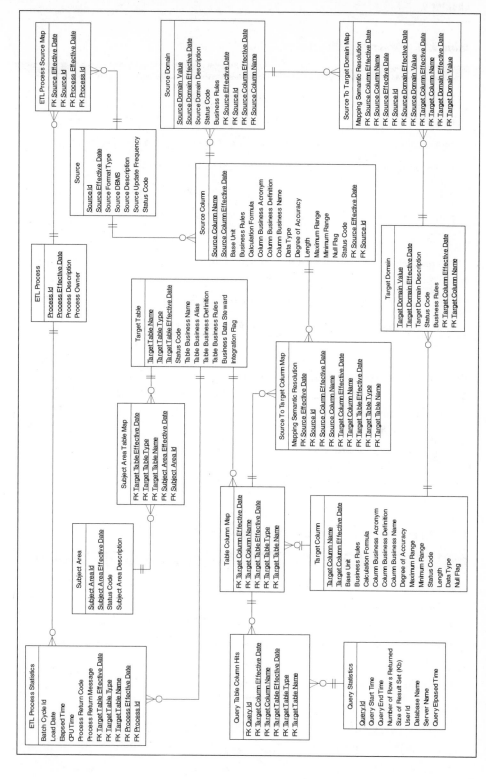

Figure 9.11 Simple meta model.

Table 9.11   Key Entity Listing from Traditional ER Model

ENTITY NAME	PURPOSE
Subject area	Subject area information
Target table	Information about the target table
Target column	Information about the columns in the target table
Target domain	Information about the target domains
Source domain	Information about the source domains
Source column	Information about the source columns
Source	Information about the source systems
ETL process	Information about an extraction, transformation, and load procedure
ETL process statistics	Statistics about the ETL process
Query statistics	Information about end user queries

the attributes store business information about the target table. The first attribute stores information about the TABLE_BUSINESS_NAME for the table. The table name in the system might be SALES, but to the business this means SALES_ORDER table. The TABLE_BUSINESS_ALIAS attribute stores any other business names that this table is known by. If, for example, the sales department refers to it as the money table or the monthly numbers, that information should be stored in the alias.

Table 9.12   Associative Entity Listing from Traditional ER Model

ASSOCIATIVE ENTITIES	PURPOSE
Subject area table map	The same target table can belong to multiple subject areas.
Table column map	Table columns can belong to multiple tables.
Source to target column map	Source columns can belong to multiple target columns.
Source to target domain map	Source domains can belong to multiple target domains.
ETL process source map	Source systems can have multiple ETL processes.
Query table column hits	Allows query statistics to be stored for the same table columns multiple times.

Table 9.13   List of SUBJECT_AREA Attributes and Purpose

ENTITY NAME	ENTITY ATTRIBUTE	ATTRIBUTE PURPOSE
Subject area	Subject area ID (PK)	The subject area unique identifier
	Subject area effective date (PK)	The date the subject area became effective
	Subject area status	The status of the subject area
	Subject area description	A description about the subject area

The TABLE_BUSINESS_DEFINITION attribute is used to store a business definition about the purpose of this table. This should be more than just restating the name of the column. Stating "This table store the sales information" is not very helpful. A definition significantly more helpful to the users would be: "This table stores the monthly sales numbers from the northeast region broken down by region, county, city, and zip. It contains three months of information that is archived to backups." The more business information you include, the easier it becomes for the next person to figure it out.

Table 9.14   List of TARGET_TABLE Attributes and Purpose

ENTITY NAME	ENTITY ATTRIBUTE	ATTRIBUTE PURPOSE
Target table	Target table name (PK)	The target table definitions
	Target table type (PK)	Stores the type of target table (logical, physical)
	Target table effective date (PK)	The date the target table became effective
	Status code	If the table is active or not
	Table business name	Any business name the table is referred to by
	Table business alias	Any other business names or aliases
	Table business definition	The business purpose of this table
	Table business rules	Any business rules about this table or how it is used
	Business data steward	The person or department responsible for this table
	Integration flag	Indicates if two or more rows are used to create the target row

The TABLE_BUSINESS_RULES attribute contains any business rules that apply to the table, such as if the business excluded certain sales information because it has not been paid or if other information is included or excluded for a business reason.

The BUSINESS_DATA_STEWARD attribute is used to track the businessperson responsible for this table. The steward may be the person who initially requested the table, the person most familiar with the data in the table, or the person who uses the data the most. It is up to you to decide who the data steward is and to keep track of the person as the responsibility changes. Of course, you also have to make sure that the data steward knows that he or she is responsible for the data and may be fielding questions from users about it.

The last attribute in this entity is the INTEGRATION_FLAG. The integration flag is used to indicate that two or more source mappings were used to create a target table row.

The TARGET_COLUMN and SOURCE_COLUMN entities store all of the information about the target table and source table columns. Tables 9.15 and 9.16 list the attributes of the target and source column entities. The primary key is comprised of the TARGET or SOURCE_COLUMN_NAME and the date that the column name became effective. The remaining attributes are used to describe the information about the target or source column:

- BASE_UNIT attribute states the basic measure used for the column.
- BUSINESS_UNIT attribute refers to the department or group within your organization that the data comes from.
- BUSINESS_RULES attribute contains any business rules that apply to the column, such as if the business excluded certain information or if other information is included or excluded due to a business reason.
- CALCULATION_FORMULA attribute is any calculation of formula that is used to create the value.
- COLUMN_BUSINESS_ACRONYM attribute is used to store any business buzzword or abbreviation that describes the column. For example, the column may be known as the EPD column, which means *already shipped.*
- COLUMN_BUSINESS_NAME attribute is the name that this column is known by the business. For example, the business may call this the "EPD42 indicator" but in the source system it is known as the *already shipped* column, and in the target table it is known as the *shipment status* column. This also helps to keep track of the various names that different departments use to describe the same thing.

Table 9.15   List of TARGET_COLUMN Attributes and Purposes

ENTITY NAME	ENTITY ATTRIBUTE	ATTRIBUTE PURPOSE
Target column	Target column name (PK)	Target column name
	Target column effective date (PK)	The date the target column became effective
	Base unit	The base unit for the column (dollars, inches, etc.)
	Business unit	The business department of group
	Business rules	Any business rules that apply to this column in the target table
	Calculation formula	Any calculations that are applied to get the column
	Column business acronym	Any business acronym that the column is known by
	Column business name	The business name for the column
	Degree of accuracy	The degree to which this column is assumed to be correct
	Maximum range	The maximum value for the column
	Minimum range	The minimum value for the column
	Status code	If the column is active or not
	Length	The length of the data item
	Data type	The column data type (character, integer, float, etc)
	Null flag	Can this column be null (Y,N)

The DEGREE_OF_ACCURACY attribute is used to indicate just how accurate this data is. The source system may be littered with incorrect data and may have an accuracy rating of only 65 percent. The target table may have been scrubbed of the invalid data and have an accuracy rating of 95 percent. This helps to identify sources of potential problems in the system and indicates if one system is getting better or worse in terms of data quality.

The MAXIMUM_RANGE and MINIMUM_RANGE attributes are used to indicate the range that the values can occupy. If, for example, the column is a salary column, the maximum may be $200,000 and the minimum may be $10,000. This is useful if some values are not appearing in your table and you see that this filter is excluding the records. The STATUS_CODE attribute is

Table 9.16 List of SOURCE_COLUMN Attributes and Purpose

ENTITY NAME	ENTITY ATTRIBUTE	ATTRIBUTE PURPOSE
Source column	Source Column name (PK)	Target column name
	Source column effective date (PK)	The date the target column became effective
	Base unit	The base unit for the column (dollars, inches, etc.)
	Business unit	The business department or group
	Business rules	Any business rules that apply to this column in the target table
	Calculation formula	Any calculations that are applied to get the column
	Column business acronym	Any business acronym that the column is known by
	Column business name	The business name for the column
	Degree of accuracy	The degree to which this column is assumed to be correct
	Maximum range	The maximum value for the column
	Minimum range	The minimum value for the column
	Status code	If the column is active or not
	Length	The length of the data item
	Data type	The column data type (character, integer, float, etc.)
	Null flag	Can this column be null (Y,N)

used to describe the current state of this column: active, inactive, or proposed. The DATA_LENGTH attribute is just the length of the defined column or source value. The last attribute is the NULL_FLAG, which is used to indicate if there has to be a value in this column for every row or source record or if it can be missing.

Tables 9.17 and 9.18 list the TARGET_DOMAIN and SOURCE_DOMAIN entities. The TARGET_DOMAIN and SOURCE_DOMAIN entities are used to list the allowable values for a given column. The primary key for each entity is made up of the DOMAIN_VALUE and the EFFECTIVE_DATE for

Table 9.17 List of TARGET_DOMAIN Attributes and Purpose

ENTITY NAME	ENTITY ATTRIBUTE	ATTRIBUTE PURPOSE
Target domain	Target domain value (PK)	Target domain value
	Target domain effective date (PK)	The effective date for this target domain value
	Target domain description	A description about the target domain
	Status code	Whether the target domain is active or not
	Business rules	The business rules used to build this target domain

that value. The target or source DOMAIN_DESCRIPTION attributes are used to describe the details about the domain. This should be as descriptive as possible so that it is easy to understand the domain value and its intended purpose. The STATUS_CODE attribute is used to describe the current state of this column: active, inactive, or proposed. The BUSINESS_RULES attribute is the final attribute in these entities, and is used to store any business definitions or logic that go into the definition of this domain value.

The SOURCE entity describes the source systems that are used to feed the DSS environment. Table 9.19 lists the source entity and its attributes. The primary key is made up of the SOURCE_ID and the SOURCE_EFFECTIVE_DATE. The SOURCE_ID is a unique identifying number that is usually

Table 9.18 List of SOURCE_DOMAIN Attributes and Purpose

ENTITY NAME	ENTITY ATTRIBUTE	ATTRIBUTE PURPOSE
Source domain	Source domain value (PK)	Source domain value
	Source domain effective date (PK)	The effective date for this source domain value
	Source domain description	A description about the source domain
	Status code	Whether the source domain is active or not
	Business rules	The business rules used to build this source domain

Table 9.19   List of SOURCE Attributes and Purpose

ENTITY NAME	ENTITY ATTRIBUTE	ATTRIBUTE PURPOSE
Source	Source ID (PK)	Unique ID for the source system
	Source effective date (PK)	The date this row became effective
	Source format type	The format of the source system code
	Source DBMS	The source database for this system
	Source description	Description of the source system
	Source update frequency	How often the source system data is updated (monthly, daily, real-time)
	Status Code	Whether it is active or not

system generated. The effective date is the date that this source system became active in the repository.

The remaining attributes are used to describe information about the source system. The SOURCE_FORMAT_TYPE attribute is used to state the format that the source code is in. This could be anything from COBOL, Java, C, or C++ to REXX and PERL. It allows you to determine language the source system is written in, which can be helpful if you need to look at the source code.

The SOURCE_DBMS attribute is used to describe the source database that is used. This can be any form of database that is used in the source programs. Possible values are: ORACLE, DB2, FLAT FILE, VSAM, IDMS, or IMS. The SOURCE_DESCRIPTION is used to store a description about the source system purpose and use. It should not just restate the name of the system. For example, rather than merely stating, "The sales system stores sales information," it could say, "The sales system is the main business system that is used for all incoming sales in the northeast region. The data is pulled from the smaller sales systems and updated nightly to the main sales system."

The UPDATE_FREQUENCY attribute indicates the time frame used to update or refresh the source system data. The update data may be a feed from a third-party company that comes monthly, or a mailing list that comes quarterly, or the real-time order system that you use on a day-to-day basis. The STATUS_CODE attribute describes the current state of this column: active, inactive, or proposed.

The ETL_PROCESS entity describes the extract, transformation, and load procedures that the source data goes through as it is moved to the target areas. Table 9.20 lists the ETL_PROCESS entity and the attributes for it. The

Table 9.20 List of ETL_PROCESS Attributes and Purpose

ENTITY NAME	ENTITY ATTRIBUTE	ATTRIBUTE PURPOSE
ETL process	Process ID (PK)	Unique ID for the ETL process
	Process effective date (PK)	The date the ETL process became active
	Process description	Description about the ETL process and purpose
	Process owner	The person or department responsible for the ETL process

primary keys are the PROCESS_ID and the PROCESS_EFFECTIVE_DATE. The process ID is a unique system ID that is usually generated by the system. The effective date is the date that this row became effective in the repository. The PROCESS_DESCRIPTION attribute describes the ETL process and its purpose, in plain English. Avoid using complex system terms and system specific jargon here, because this type of language is likely to be meaningless to an executive trying to perform a query. The PROCESS_OWNER attribute records the name of the current process owner. This may be the person who wrote the process, the department that requested the process, or the maintenance team at the company. Be sure that whoever is the owner of this process is aware that he or she is listed as the owner and may receive inquires about the process.

Table 9.21 lists the ETL_PROCESS_STATISTICS and the attributes contained in that entity. The ETL_PROCESS_STATISTICS entity is used to store the processing statistics for a specific ETL process. The primary key is defined as the BATCH_CYCLE_ID and the LOAD_DATE. The BATCH_CYCLE_ID is the identifier that the job is known by in the system. The LOAD_DATE is the date that these statistics were loaded into the repository. The ELAPSED_TIME attribute stores the amount of time the ETL process took for this run. This is useful for determining if a certain process is getting extremely long or if some other process is holding it up. The CPU_TIME attribute stores the amount of CPU time that the process uses. This is useful for comparing actual elapsed time to the amount of time the computer was working on the task. The last two attributes, PROCESS_RETURN_CODE and PROCESS_RETURN_MESSAGE, store any information that is returned from the ETL process. This may be a number such as zero, which indicates all went okay, or a message like "System failure," which indicates that something catastrophic occurred.

Table 9.21   List of ETL_PROCESS_STATISTICS Attributes and Purpose

ENTITY NAME	ENTITY ATTRIBUTE	ATTRIBUTE PURPOSE
ETL process statistics	Batch cycle ID (PK)	Unique ID for the ETL process statistics
	Load date (PK)	The date these statistics were loaded
	Elapsed time	The total time the ETL process took to run
	CPU time	The amount of CPU time required by the ETL process
	Process return code	Any return codes the ETL process returns
	Process return message	Any error or completion messages returned

The final entity that we will look at is the QUERY_STATISTICS entity. Table 9.22 lists the attributes of the QUERY_STATISTICS entity and briefly describes them. The primary key for this entity is the QUERY_ID, which is a unique system-generated number. The statistics about the query are stored in the remaining attributes. The QUERY_START_TIME and QUERY_END_TIME attributes keep track of the duration of queries running against the DSS tables. The NUMBER_OF_ROWS_RETURNED attribute shows the number of actual rows that were returned to the business user. If this number is too high, some intervention may be required to reduce the size of the result set. The USER_ID attribute stores the system ID of the person who initiated the query. The DATABASE_NAME and SERVER_NAME attributes store the database that the query is going against and the server that the database resides on. This information lets you see if the query is using the proper server and databases, and also helps in tracking down problems. The CPU_TIME and QUERY_ELAPSED_TIME attributes store the amount of computer time the query took and the total elapsed time the query took.

Now that we have examined all of the key entities in the traditional meta model, we see that it can contain quite a bit of information about the DSS environment. You can use this model and build on it, or use it as a starting point to design your own object list to build a repository that can accommodate all of your organization's needs. Remember, however, that this model is only a guide to assist you in identifying the components that are necessary to keep your DSS environment humming along. Your meta data needs may require more specific attributes in some of the entities or

Table 9.22   List of QUERY_STATISTICS Attributes and Purpose

ENTITY NAME	ENTITY ATTRIBUTE	ATTRIBUTE PURPOSE
Query statistics	Query ID (PK)	Unique ID for the query statistics table
	Query start time	The system time the query started
	Query end time	The system time the query ended
	Number of rows returned	The total rows returned by the query
	Size of result set (Kb)	The estimated size of the returned result set
	User ID	The user ID of the person who submitted the query
	Database name	The database that the query was going against
	Server name	The server the query was going against
	CPU time	The amount of CPU time the query took to run
	Query elapsed time	The wall clock time that the query took

entirely different entities. When you complete your analysis, you should have a better idea of just what is needed for your repository.

Summary

The choice of an appropriate model type depends on your particular environment and requirements for the meta data and requires careful research on your part to make an informed decision. Choosing the model type is, however, only the first step in the development process. After that decision is made, you must identify the various objects and subobjects that are required to define the model. This is a complex and time-consuming process, but one that is absolutely necessary for building a meta model that meets your users' current needs and is flexible enough to grow as those needs increase or change.

Clearly, putting these models to use in your DSS environment requires lots of up-front analysis to ensure that you've considered all of the complexities of your company's information requirements. To determine precisely what types of information are required in your meta model and how best to store it, you must identify the attributes of the entities that compose the model, as we did in our ABC example. Finally, you'll need to cleanse the data and load it into your model. We cannot overstate the importance of the data quality. This issue, like those of determining appropriate model type and building a model that fits your particular data requirements, is key to a successful meta data project.

In the next chapter, I address the issue of meta data delivery, describing the various options available for providing user access to the repository and examining some of the factors that you need to consider when selecting a delivery method.

## CHAPTER 10

Meta Data Delivery

Okay, you understand the importance of maintaining a meta data repository in your decision support solution. Now comes the question of how business users and the IT staff are going to access it.

This chapter focuses on choosing a meta data delivery solution. It explores the various options for integrating meta data information in the repository, the data warehouse, and the World Wide Web, and suggests some questions you should ask to help determine your meta data delivery needs before you select a particular delivery method. The answers to these questions should help you to review the available options and provide you with criteria for selecting the best method for your business needs. This chapter provides information that is particularly relevant for the meta data repository architect, infrastructure developer, and tool architect, but it should also benefit the data acquisition and data delivery developers.

Evaluating Delivery Requirements

Before you dive into the process of selecting a meta data delivery method, I suggest that you review the following series of questions, then use your answers to help guide you through the process. In some cases the answers will help you select the appropriate delivery method for your needs, but in most cases they will serve as comparison factors to support your selection process. I have often seen political and budgetary constraints within an organization sway the selection process more than any group of business requirements. The initial questions you should be asking yourself are:

- Who are the users of the meta data repository?
- What level of integration does the repository have to other data warehouse components?
- What information do the repository users need?
- Does the repository tool have a data delivery component?
- How many users are going to use the repository tool?
- Where are the repository users geographically located?

Who Are the Users?

You will need to review each type of data warehouse user to determine if they plan to access information from the repository. This type of analysis often shows that certain user groups contribute information to the repository but do not (yet) use it. This provides you with an opportunity to do some marketing within the organization on the value of using an enterprise-wide open source for meta data. During your review, you will need to determine if the various users and the tools they are responsible for will be accessing the repository. Use by the technical users usually depends on the level of integration between the repository and other components, an issue that is weighed in our second question.

The first group of users to consider is the business users (as discussed in Chapter 2, Meta Data Fundamentals). These are the primary users of the data warehouse. They are your clients and can make or break a data warehouse project by simply not trusting, or worse, not using the information in the data warehouse and meta data repository. This user group includes your end users, subject matter experts, sponsors, project champions, and executive management. These users need insulation from the various components that make up the data warehouse environment through a seamless single point of access to the information. They do not want to have to learn how to use more than one access method for the data warehouse. Business users don't care if they are accessing information from the data warehouse or from the meta data repository, and they do not even need to know. If your user analysis reveals that business users require information from the meta data repository, providing a single, common interface should become a priority.

The second group of repository users are technical users and power users (see Chapter 2, Meta Data Fundamentals). These individuals are the primary creators of the data warehouse environment and information. They are also potential secondary users of the information stored in the data warehouse, depending on the level of integration with other components. This user group includes the repository architect, middleware developer, data delivery developer, data modeler, tool architect, infrastructure developer, and data acquisition developer. The data warehouse components that these individuals are responsible for form the bulk of the information that is stored in the repository.

What Is the Repository's Level of Integration?

The ever-increasing number of data warehousing tools include tools for data integrity and cleansing, data modeling, extraction transformation, data movement, decision support, and administration. Despite the numerous tools that address the data warehousing environment, the foremost obstacle to the full potential of a meta data repository is the lack of tool integration.

Tool users are wary of committing to a single vendor for all of their data warehousing tool support. Because of the rapid changes in technology, users are concerned that by locking into a single tool they may be unable to take advantage of new advances offered by other vendors. Tool vendors typically do not have the resources or funding to provide a complete tool suite that fully encompasses all of the development needs for a data warehouse environment. However, as I discussed in previous chapters, vendors are now beginning to embrace standards for tool integration in order to remain competitive. Figure 10.1 illustrates the interaction between data warehouse tools.

The first level of integration to consider is in the presentation of information by the tools and the repository. One of the most fundamental issues of integrating tools is the availability of a common user interface. The cost that an organization incurs in selecting the appropriate tool(s) is far greater than the purchase price of the tool(s). The cost of the time spent for training and support must also be factored into the expense equation. Fortunately, standardized user interfaces, such as the Web, help to control these costs and provide greater flexibility for the users. If business users have to learn one interface method to access the data warehouse information and another to access information in the meta data repository, you will need to consider the training and support costs for both interfaces when you select your specific delivery tool(s).

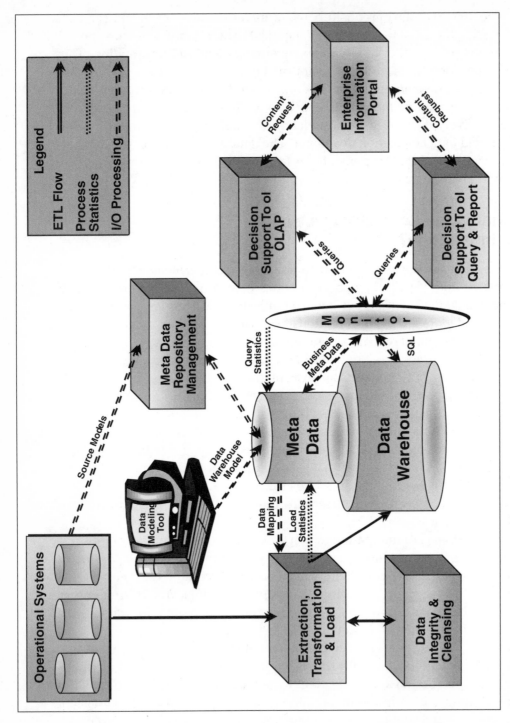

Figure 10.1 Data warehouse tool interaction.

The second level of integration to consider is that of moving data between the tools. This type of integration refers to the transfer of information between the various data warehouse tools and the repository. This integration is usually accomplished by transferring information through an agreed-upon data interface between the tools. The approach is relatively easy to accomplish, but it is often impeded by the lack of standards among data warehouse components. This data transfer method supports data exchange but does not establish a link between the tools or maintain the semantic context of the data. Recent advances in standardization for meta data repositories offer the chance of integration through a shared repository model, which will eventually allow all of the data warehouse tools to store and share their information. The repository maintains a common semantic definition of the information as well as a tool-specific view that allows all of the warehouse tools to work together through the single data store.

I also like to analyze the level of tool integration available between a meta data repository tool and the other warehouse components. This type of analysis allows you to weigh the reality of the technical use of the repository. If integration is complex or manual between the repository and another component, technical users are likely to make only minimal use of the repository's meta data delivery method. If the presentation interface between the repository tool and another data warehouse component is not intuitive or does not exist, technical users may resort to SQL queries between the two data sources to meet their information needs.

What Information Do Users Need?

The answer to this question involves reviewing the information requirements of the various users of the repository. This analysis should allow you to determine which components of the repository need to fulfill information reporting requirements for the organization. The meta data repository can be broken down into six major areas as depicted in Figure 10.2.

The first repository area is the *source system area*, which contains the physical content of the operational applications that feed the data warehouse. Business analysts and subject matter experts can access this area to document source system table and column designs or extract file layout definitions. Changes made to this area can be used to report upcoming source system modification impacts to extraction, transformation, and load processes. This provides the data acquisition developer with an opportunity to prepare for future changes from source systems before those changes take effect. The introduction of new source systems or major changes to existing operational systems can be communicated to the data modelers to

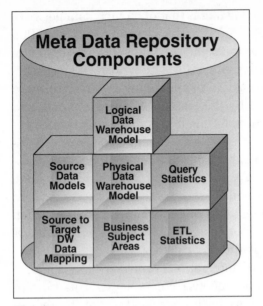

Figure 10.2   Meta data repository components.

alert them of potential design changes to the warehouse model. See Figure 10.3 for examples of repository reports from this section.

The second repository area, the *data warehouse model,* contains the logical and physical content of the target decision support database. The data modeler uses this area of the repository to document changes in the warehouse design. Data acquisition and data delivery developers monitor changes made in the warehouse design by the modeler before implementing modifications to the data schema or ETL processes. Business meta data is also stored in this area. The business analyst in this area documents changes in business definitions. The data delivery developer monitors business rule and calculation changes made to the warehouse to assess their impact on reports. See Figure 10.4 for examples of repository reports from this section.

The third repository area, the *source to target data map,* contains the cross-reference and semantic resolution criteria for transforming the data warehouse information. Data acquisition developers use this area to document the results of their analysis between the source systems and the target warehouse model. Information reports from this section of the repository provide the business analyst and users with the necessary information for auditing and reconciling data warehouse data. One project that I am familiar with uses the source target data map information stored in the meta data repository in ETL processing to convert data and avoid hard coding in programs. See Figure 10.5 for examples of repository reports from this section.

The fourth repository area, the *business subject* area, contains the logical groupings or business views of information. This area provides business users with an intuitive means of navigating the content of the data warehouse and gives a business-oriented view of the warehouse information. See Figure 10.6 for examples of repository reports from this section.

The fifth repository area, the *extraction, transformation, and load* statistics area, contains the record counts, load timings, and other processing results from each load cycle to the data warehouse. The ETL statistics stored in this repository database are used by data acquisition developers and database administrators to highlight issues related to database sizing, index usage, and performance tuning. See Figure 10.7 for examples of repository reports from this section.

The sixth and final repository area, the *report query statistics* area, contains the timings, SQL, and database usage results from each query run against the data warehouse. The query statistics stored in this repository database are used by database administrators and data delivery developers to measure activity and to flag potential issues related to index usage, aggregation strategies, or data fragmentation designs. Correlation of query statistics across various constraints such as user, organization unit, and time is useful for indicating areas for improvements. See Figure 10.8 for examples of repository reports from this section.

It is important to note that these information reporting examples are only fully applicable if the meta data repository project team has managed to create an open and integrated environment for all warehousing meta data. The warehouse architecture needs to be structured such that the information in the repository drives the implementation process. Your data delivery solution should consider the reporting requirements of all the business and technical users throughout the entire lifecycle of the data warehouse. As such, your information reporting needs should include not only the information content of the data warehouse but also the context of the knowledge stored in the repository. This narrow view often limits the success of the data warehouse project.

Does the Repository Tool Have a Data Delivery Component?

If your meta data repository tool is from a vendor, chances are that it incorporates some type of data delivery component. Of course, you will need to examine the data delivery component to determine if it is suitable for your

Source System	Table/Extract File	Table/Extract File Description	Column	Column Description
ERP	Customer	Information on a client of the company	CUSTOMER	A customer who has a direct business relation-ship with this business
ERP	Customer	Information on a client of the company	CUSTOMER	A customer who has a direct business relation-ship with this firm or is a subsidiary or affiliate of a client
Order Processing	GS ORDER P0.1D WEXTRACT(0)	Extract of active customers	CUSTOMER	A customer who has a contractual relationship with the firm
Order Processing	GS ORDER 0.2D WEXTRACT(0)	Extract of active catalog products	PRODUCT	An active product listed in the firm's published catalog
Order Processing	GS ORDER 0.2D WEXTRACT(0)	Extract of active catalog products	PRODUCT PRICE	An active product's list price in the firm's published product catalog
Sales Force	Product	The firm's active published product catalog	PRODUCT PRICE	Listed price in the firm's published product catalog
Sales Force	Product	The firm's active published product catalog	PRODUCT PRICE	Listed price in the firm's published product catalog
Sales Force	Product	The firm's active published product catalog	PRODUCT PRICE CURRENCY	The currency for the listed price in the firm's published product catalog

Figure 10.3   Source system repository report examples.

Data Type	Length	Unit	Domain	Creation Date	Update Date	Status
char	100	N/A	N/A	March 22, 1999	March 22, 1999	Approved
char	100	N/A	N/A	March 22, 1999	January 17, 2000	Pending approval
char	50	N/A	N/A	January 3, 2000	January 3, 2000	Approved
char	50	N/A	N/A	January 3, 2000	January 3, 2000	Approved
real	12	USD currency type in Dollars	N/A	January 3, 2000	January 3, 2000	Approved
real	18	N/A	N/A	November 17, 1999	January 3, 2000	Approved
real	12	USD currency type in Dollars	N/A	November 17, 1999	January 2, 2000	*Cancelled*
char	3	N/A	N/A	January 3, 2000	January 3, 2000	Approved

Data Model Repository Report

Table	Table Description	Column	Column Description	Data Type	Length & Accuracy
Customer	Information on a client of the company	CUSTOMER NAME	A customer who has a direct business relationship with this firm or is a subsidiary or affiliate of a client	char	100.6
Customer	Information on a client of the company	CUSTOMER NAME	A customer who has a direct business relationship with this firm	char	50
Customer	Information on a client of the company	CUSTOMER TYPE	Customer types associated with the firm	char	1
Customer	Information on a client of the company	CUSTOMER TYPE	Customer types associated with the firm	char	1
Product	Information on the firm's catalog products	PRODUCT NAME	An active product listed in the firm's published catalog	char	100
Product	Information on the firm's catalog products	PRODUCT PRICE	An active product list price in the firm's published product catalog	real	18.6
Invoice	Information on the charges billed to a customer of the firm	INVOICE NUMBER	The firm generated number associated with the itemized recurring an nonrecurring charges billed to a customer	char	20

Figure 10.4 Data model repository report examples.

environment. Be particularly careful in examining any tool that has recently been Web-enabled; simply adding a middle tier to Web enable access to the repository does not ensure adequate scalability, maintenance, or security capabilities.

Also, be sure to consider interface differences between the data delivery products for the repository and the front end. Do both have intuitive user interfaces that can be easily maintained and supported in the future? Even if

Domain	Domain Description	Unit	Creation Date	Update Date	Status
N/A	N/A	N/A	March 22, 1999	January 3, 2000	Approved
N/A	N/A	N/A	March 22, 1999	January 2, 2000	*Cancelled*
D	Direct customer	N/A	January 3, 2000	January 3, 2000	Approved
I	Indirect customer	N/A	January 17, 2000	January 17, 2000	Approved
N/A	N/A	N/A	January 3, 2000	January 3, 2000	Approved
N/A	N/A	USD, dollars	January 3, 2000	January 3, 2000	Approved
N/A	N/A	USD, dollars	January 3, 2000	January 3, 2000	Approved

the two delivery products have a common user interface, such as the Web, you will need to consider the architecture, infrastructure, operating system, and RDBMS requirements of each. Depending on your project's needs and enterprise requirements, it may make sense to use the data delivery component from a purchased repository product. Most of the data warehouse projects I have been involved with use a front-end query or online analytical processing tool for the warehouse to access the relational database of the repository.

	Source Data Model Extract File Format						Target	
Source System	Table Name	Column Name	Data Type	Length	Domain(s)	Table Name	Column Name
ERP	Customer	CUSTOMER	char	100	N/A	Customer	CUSTOMER NAME
Order processing	GS ORDER PO 1.DW EXTRACT (0)	CUSTOMER	char	50	N/A		
Sales force	Client	CLIENT DESCRIPTION	char	30	N/A		
Order processing	GS ORDER 02. DW EXTRACT (0)	PRODUCT	char	50	N/A	Product	PRODUCT NAME
Sales force	Product	PRODUCT DESCRIPTION	char	30	N/A		
Order processing	GS ORDER PO 1. DW EXTRACT (0)	CUSTOMER CODE	char	2	AC (Active Customer)	Customer	CUSTOMER TYPE
Order processing	GS ORDER PO 1.DW EXTRACT (0)	CUSTOMER CODE	char	2	AA (Active Affiliate)		
Order processing	GS ORDER PO 1.DW EXTRACT (0)	CUSTOMER CODE	char	2	AS (Active Subsidiary)		
Sales force	Client	CLIENT PRIORITY CODE	char	1	I (Indirect)		
Sales force	Client	CLIENT PRIORITY CODE	char	1	D (Direct)		

Figure 10.5 Source/target data map repository report examples.

Data Model

Data Type	Length & Accuracy	Domain(s)	Semantic Resolution	Creation Date	Update Date
char	100	N/A	Business requirement has the ERP source system as primary source	March 22, 1999	January 3, 2000
char	50	N/A	Business requirement has the Order Processing source system as primary source	January 3, 2000	January 3, 2000
char	1	D (Direct)	Business requirement has the Sales Force source system as primary source	January 3, 2000	January 3, 2000
		I (Indirect)			
		I (Indirect)			
		I (Indirect)			
		D (Direct)			

Business Subject Area Report

January 17, 2000

Subject Area Groups	Subject Area Group Description	Subject Area Sections	Creation Date	Update Date
Customer	A customer who has a direct business relationship with this firm or is a subsidiary or affiliate of a client	Organization	January 3, 2000	January 3, 2000
Customer	A customer who has a direct business relationship with this firm or is a subsidiary or affiliate of a client	Organization Hierarchy	January 3, 2000	January 3, 2000
Customer	A customer who has a direct business relationship with this firm or is a subsidiary or affiliate of a client	Location	January 3, 2000	January 3, 2000
Product	An active product listed in the firm's published catalog	Product Hierarchy	January 3, 2000	January 3, 2000
Product	An active product listed in the firm's published catalog	Product Type	January 3, 2000	January 3, 2000

Figure 10.6 Subject area repository report examples.

How Many Repository Tool Users Are There?

To answer this question, you will need to determine how many users plan to use the meta data delivery system. Your users are more likely to accept the learning curve associated with two or more data delivery products (i.e., for the warehouse and the repository) if you have a relatively small project such as a departmental data mart. However, using two or more delivery tools is not advisable for large, enterprise-wide implementations with hundreds or thousands of users accessing the warehouse and repository.

Where Are Users Geographically Located?

This question considers the geographic location of the repository users. If all of your meta data repository users are located at a single geographic location, technical issues such as network bandwidth and software distribution are probably not an issue. However, if your users are distributed globally or across a continent, the issues related to network bandwidth, software distribution, technical support, and maintenance can be considerable. A globally accessed meta data repository may dictate a larger support window to accommodate the variety of user time zones. A 5 days-a-week, 12 hours-a-day technical support window that works fine in the United States is inadequate if you have users in Europe and Asia, because your window for updates and maintenance will be significantly smaller in those locations. If your users are widely dispersed, you will need to seriously consider your support requirements for the repository.

I know of one situation in which a group of remote users only had dial-up access to the corporate LAN because network connectivity was unavailability in their particular country. The dial-up connection to the LAN was only 14.4 kB through an X.25 connection. Understandably, these users were never very happy accessing the repository or data warehouse for their reporting needs. An investigation into the problem revealed that the cost to provide adequate connection speed was prohibitively high due to the small number of employees at this location. As a last resort, the company agreed to provide these remote users with the information they needed to do their jobs in a series of scheduled reports that are generated through the data warehouse.

ETL Statistics Report

Target Table	ETL Process	Target Table Type	Source System(s)	Processing Time	Load Cycle
Customer	cs0001	Dimension	ERP	0:43:12	3
Customer	cs0002	Dimension	Order Processing	0:27:39	3
Customer	cs0003	Dimension	Sales Force	0:18:45	3
Product	pd001	Dimension	Order Processing	0:29:28	3
Employee	ee001	Dimension	ERP	0:37:55	3
Time	tm001	Dimension	External Source	0:05:41	3
Sales	sl001	Fact	Order Processing	2:35:30	3
Customer	cs0001	Dimension	ERP	0:41:45	2
Customer	cs0002	Dimension	Order Processing	0:25:32	2
Customer	cs0003	Dimension	Sales Force	0:16:48	2
Product	pd001	Dimension	Order Processing	0:28:34	2
Employee	ee001	Dimension	ERP	0:34:59	2
Time	tm001	Dimension	External Source	0:04:13	2
Sales	sl001	Fact	Order Processing	1:04:47	2
Customer	cs0001	Dimension	ERP	0:49:42	1
Customer	cs0002	Dimension	Order Processing	0:28:21	1
Customer	cs0003	Dimension	Sales Force	0:31:09	1
Product	pd001	Dimension	Order Processing	0:45:33	1
Employee	ee001	Dimension	ERP	0:50:18	1
Time	tm001	Dimension	External Source	0:02:21	1
Sales	sl001	Fact	Order Processing	0:20:11	1

Figure 10.7   ETL statistics repository report examples.

Selecting the Delivery Architecture

After you have identified the delivery requirements for your meta data repository, you are ready to select the delivery architecture. In this section, assume that the delivery method available through your meta data repository product is insufficient for your needs and that you want to use the same

January 17, 2000

Number of Records Inserted	Number of Records Updated	Total Number of Records	Load Date	Load Time
223	196	1,194	March 2, 2000	5:18:10
22	5	1,194	March 2, 2000	5:18:10
51	17	1,194	March 2, 2000	5:18:10
41	28	112	March 2, 2000	5:18:10
23	15	276	March 2, 2000	5:18:10
1	0	3	March 2, 2000	5:18:10
36,908,928	0	58,095,382	March 2, 2000	5:18:10
287	201	898	February 1, 2000	3:36:38
15	1	898	February 1, 2000	3:36:38
78	24	898	February 1, 2000	3:36:38
31	24	71	February 1, 2000	3:36:38
9	2	253	February 1, 2000	3:36:38
1	0	2	February 1, 2000	3:36:38
16,130,774	0	21,186,454	February 1, 2000	3:36:38
334	0	518	January 3, 2000	3:47:35
37	0	518	January 3, 2000	3:47:35
147	0	518	January 3, 2000	3:47:35
40	0	40	January 3, 2000	3:47:35
244	0	244	January 3, 2000	3:47:35
1	0	1	January 3, 2000	3:47:35
5,055,680	0	5,055,680	January 3, 2000	3:47:35

delivery method as the data warehouse front end. If, however, the delivery method of the meta data repository product meets your users' needs, the question of your architecture solution is resolved for you.

If your company purchased an off-the-shelf repository tool, the repository architect should be asking some questions to ensure sufficient functionality:

Query Statistics Report

Month	User	Number of Queries	Average Time per Query	Maximum Time of a Query	Average Number of Rows Returned per Query
March	John Smith	30	0:03:32	0:23:17	304,280
	Mary Brown	14	0:10:51	0:14:21	1,676,368
	James Jones	58	0:02:06	0:03:33	275,237
	Jane McDoyle	9	0:13:15	0:14:15	15,629,295
February	John Smith	26	0:03:01	0:19:54	260,596
	Mary Brown	12	0:09:16	0:12:16	1,432,794
	James Jones	50	0:01:48	0:03:02	235,246
	Jane McDoyle	8	0:11:19	0:12:10	13,358,372
January	John Smith	23	02:43:0	17:56:0	234,296
	Mary Brown	11	08:21:0	11:03:0	1,290,805
	James Jones	45	01:37:0	02:44:0	211,933
	Jane McDoyle	7	10:12:0	10:58:0	12,034,569

Figure 10.8   Query statistics repository report examples.

- What types of import capabilities does the repository tool have to capture source system information (e.g., copylibs)?

- Can data mapping between the source and target data models be documented? Can this information be imported/exported to a common media (e.g., MS Excel, Lotus 123)?

- Can the target data warehouse model be documented in the repository tool? Does the product accept imports from popular data modeling tools (e.g., Erwin, Silverrun, Designer 2000, CDIF)? Can the product reverse-engineer any existing data warehouse database schema?

- Can the repository tool capture statistics from off-the-shelf ETL products? Can the capture process be augmented for in-house-developed ETL processes?

- Can the repository tool capture or access operational statistics about queries made to the data warehouse from query monitoring tools or OLAP products?

- If you select an OLAP product that has its own business meta data layer, can the repository tool populate it?

January 17, 2000

Maximum Number of Rows Returned by a Query	Tables Accessed
1,136,639	Customer, Product, Employee, Time, Sales
8,277,267	Customer, Product, Employee, Time, Sales
571,277	Customer, Product, Time, Sales
15,629,295	Customer, Product, Employee, Time, Sales, Receivables
971,486	Customer, Product, Employee, Time, Sales
7,074,587	Customer, Product, Employee, Time, Sales
488,271	Customer, Product, Time, Sales
13,358,372	Customer, Product, Employee, Time, Sales, Receivables
875,213	Customer, Product, Employee, Time, Sales
6,373,502	Customer, Product, Employee, Time, Sales
439,884	Customer, Product, Time, Sales
12,034,569	Customer, Product, Employee, Time, Sales, Receivables

- Is the repository tool's underlying storage method an open relational database management system? If your organization does not currently support this RDBMS, how will database administrator functions be performed? Is the DBMS link native, ODBC, or Java Database Connectivity (JDBC)?

- Which Web browsers does the product support (e.g., Netscape, Internet Explorer)? On which operating systems (e.g., Windows 9x, NT, UNIX, Macintosh)?

- Which Web server products does the tool support (e.g., Apache, Netscape MS IIS)? On which hardware platforms (e.g., Sun, HP, etc.)?

- Are there any requirements for MS ActiveX and/or Java applets on the client PC to support full functionality of the products? If yes, can downloading of these plug-ins be controlled through the administrative facilities?

- How is security controlled? Is administration and security of the repository product done through a Web browser or through a client GUI interface? Is security access based on user IDs, workgroups, projects, or some other means? How is user sign-in authentication performed? Does the product interact with other directory services to provide single sign-on across products (e.g., Novell NDS/LDAP)?

- How is migration handled between major releases? Between development, test, and production environments?

- What reporting capabilities does the repository product provide? Is reporting based on interfaces to another third-party product? Can reports be exported to other third-party products (e.g., spreadsheets)?

- Does the product provide any persistent agents, alert, or trigger mechanisms to notify users of critical changes to the repository data content? If so, can these notifications be made through common e-mail channels (e.g., SMTP)? Where in the architecture does this mechanism reside?

- What types of change management and versioning capabilities does the product support?

In some cases, the reporting capabilities of the Web-enabled repository tool may be insufficient to meet the needs of your organization. In this case, you may decide to implement the same front-end Web reporting tool used to access the data warehouse to access the meta data repository.

Most of the data warehouse projects that I have worked on have used their front-end reporting tool for delivery of meta data reports from the repository. This mechanism simplifies the issues related to the data warehouse project by requiring only one decision support product to be used for both meta and warehouse applications. This type of arrangement can have several benefits, including:

- Single decision support reporting product introduced into the enterprise

- Lower training costs

- Lower cost for administration and maintenance

- Lower cost for hardware and support environments

The decision support product may consist of either a query reporting tool or an OLAP tool, depending on the complexity of the front-end reporting needs of the warehouse. You should make a careful review of any OLAP tool for use against a meta data repository. While these tools work with relational databases in general, some require specialized schema designs, additional types of tables, or alterations made to columns, in order to function accurately. On the other hand, I have found with the products I have used that query and reporting tools work with any type of relational database design.

Architectural Types to Consider

In this section, I examine three type of architecture and discuss some future trends on the horizon. These architecture types encompass most of the various front-end decision support tools that are on the market today. They include query reporting and OLAP decision support tools for the desktop as well as for the Web. I am also going to look at recent trends for providing information to users using enterprise information portals. The tools that I discuss in this section should not be confused with the data mining tools that apply artificial intelligence techniques (i.e., neural networks, fuzzy logic, and genetic algorithms) to data warehouse databases to discover patterns in the information.

The three types of architectures that I will discuss are:

- Fat client
- Thin client or Web-enabled
- Enterprise information portal

Fat Client

The popularity of client-server computing and the proliferation of PCs in the 1980s brought decision support users an unforeseen wealth of capabilities. A decision support product loaded onto a PC (or client) lets the user of that PC access information residing in corporate decision support databases, even those on remote servers. This arrangement reduces the processing load at the source as well as the user's reliance on support from an information services department. This type of architecture is referred to as *fat client*. The programs loaded on the PCs are often very large and require a significant percentage of the machines' resources to function properly, thus the emphasis on *fat*.

The client tools on the PC are capable of managing connections to various decision support databases and generating SQL requests. In addition, the DSS tools can apply prompting, calculations, and filters to reports and control report formatting, including graphical presentation of result sets. Last, these tools handle administration and security functions.

Fat client architecture typically consists of a client PC running a popular operating system such as Microsoft Windows. The PC is equipped with client software for a decision support tool, which provides the primary user interface. The client PC is also equipped with a network hardware card that provides local- or wide-area network (i.e., LAN or WAN) access to a remote server. The remote server, which contains the decision support database, includes a relational database management system. Depending on the level of functionality of the decision support application, the remote server may also have an application component to manage requests from multiple client PCs. Figure 10.9 illustrates fat client architecture.

While fat client architecture offers vast improvements over previous architectures, it also involves some drawbacks. The decision support desktop applications often have to download large volumes of information from the remote server repository database, forcing users with a complex array of large queries to wait until the download operation is complete before they can access their own PCs again. This results in slow response times for the users and saturation of corporate networks. In response to these processing issues, vendors have moved some query functionality onto the remote server to help free up resources on the desktop.

Further issues arise when it is necessary to deliver new or updated decision support applications to the desktop clients. All of the DSS users must have an updated copy of the software installed on their PCs whenever the server software is changed. Many users experience conflicts with other application resources on their PCs during these update procedures due to insufficient memory or hard disk space. In addition, companies that do not have a standardized operating system environment encounter difficulties dealing with a variety of operating systems and/or versions on the users' desktop PCs. These administrative issues are compounded when dealing with remote sites, which involve distributing new or upgraded versions of the decision support software, then installing it on the client PCs and troubleshooting any installation errors.

While the fat client architecture provides improvements in data access, it also introduces new issues related to administration, security, and performance across the enterprise. Deploying a decision support tool across a corporate enterprise to access the meta data repository is an expensive and

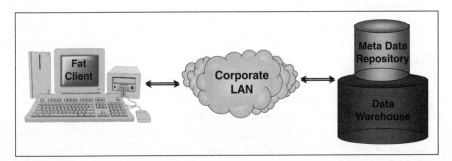

Figure 10.9 Fat client architecture.

labor-intensive exercise. Despite these problems, however, fat client architecture remained largely unchallenged until the mid-1990s, when the World Wide Web and the Internet became the dominant forces for architectural design.

As companies struggle to make use of the Web, many still use fat client architecture for much of their decision support reporting requirements. This type of architecture is still feasible for projects or corporate environments that involve a small number of users accessing reports from a central repository and where network capacity is not at a premium. For some users, the functionality found in a client application on the desktop PC has yet to be matched by a Web-enabled version running within a browser. One of the first questions I like to ask a vendor supplying a Web-enabled decision support reporting tool is: What are the differences between your client product and your Web tool with regard to meta data repository access capabilities?

Web-Enabled or Thin Client

The Web browser on your users' desktops offers the most effective means today for providing them with information from the meta data repository. The Web is recognized as the most effective corporate delivery mechanism for information in the world, and the Internet, with its extensive information resources, is considered the largest data warehouse in the world. Its popularity has flourished in recent years due primarily to the intuitive nature of the World Wide Web application.

The Web allows companies to deploy and manage enterprise information based on its open and superior architecture. The implementation design allows corporate IT departments to be responsive to the fast-paced global business environment. Web-enabled applications with inherent hardware independence are providing the catalyst to replace the old fat client application model design. The Web browser is becoming the single entry point or portal to all internal corporate operational and decision support knowledge.

The Web paradigm and data warehousing share a common implementation goal of providing easy, intuitive access to data. Web-enabled access to the decision support environment allows for consistent presentation of meta data across the enterprise. In the fat client, distribution of meta data was cost-prohibitive and limited to a relatively small number of decision support users. The Web provides a unique and unmatched distribution channel for all repository users, efficiently providing access to the data at a fraction of the cost per user of fat client solutions. Additionally, the Web allows the repository architect to provide meta data access to all areas of the enterprise, including remote sites.

Unlike the fat client architecture, the Web-enabled decision support application uses a thin client, usually a desktop browser, to provide information from the meta data repository. Thin client architecture requires fewer resources from the desktop PC, but uses standard network file service and interfaces. It also supports centralized development through a Web server application and realizes labor and cost savings by reducing administration and distribution efforts.

Thin client architecture involves installing a standard desktop application (i.e., the browser) on the client PCs. The client PC communicates with the corporate Intranet or Internet through standard TCP/IP and HTTP protocol services. The Web server receives a request from the desktop PC and routes it to the decision support application or query engine. This application or engine may reside on the same server as the Web server application or on a separate hardware platform. The decision support application takes the request from the Web server and sends a query request to the meta data repository database. The query results are received and formatted back to the user through the desktop browser. Figure 10.10 illustrates a thin client Web-enabled architecture.

The Web architecture for distributing meta data repository information has continually evolved from its early days in the mid-1990s. First-generation designs consisted primarily of a Web browser and Web server providing static, prepublished HTML reports to users. Functionality could be extended through the use of plug-ins incorporated into the Web browser to duplicate the capabilities provided by the client version of the decision support reporting tool. (Plug-ins are browser extension programs that provide capabilities

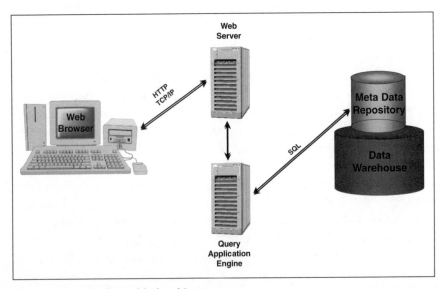

Figure 10.10 Web-enabled architecture.

not possible through HTML and a Web browser.) Second-generation designs were capable of dynamically accessing the meta data repository database through an applications server or query engine. Further functionality is made available in this design by providing prompting, calculations, and filters to the HTML reports. Third-generation Web architecture designs use ActiveX objects or Java applets to improve query capabilities and enhance the user interface through the browser. Some vendors use native Web server interfaces to address performance and scalability problems associated with the Common Gateway Interface, which is used to link Web servers to external programs. The most recent, or fourth-generation designs, use Java to develop the application server. This design can typically produce query results from the repository in either a proprietary or HTML format. A Java server application running Java applets on the client and accessing the meta data repository database through native Java drivers comprise this design.

It is important to note, however, that the Web is by no means a perfect application design environment. The repository architect needs to consider several issues related to Web access to the meta data repository, including:

- Network bandwidth requirements on the corporate wide area network (WAN) and Intranet.

- Ability to provide alerts or triggers, which are limited without the use of downloaded programs.

- Remote site access to the corporate Intranet. For example, if business users in the Middle East have to access the corporate Intranet through a dial-up X.25 line running at 14.4 kB, they will never be happy with the DSS solution.

- Inability of HyperText Transfer Protocol (HTTP), one of the most common methods of transferring documents across the Web, to maintain a persistent connection with the server (stateless connection). This limitation makes HTTP somewhat unsatisfactory for client/server applications. Every request to a server must contain state information, which leads to performance degradation in response to user requests. Cookies, a method of addressing the stateless nature of the Web developed by Netscape, can maintain state information but requires downloading to the client.

- Limited Java performance and reliability. When executed in a Web browser, Java is limited by its interpretive nature. Vendors of Web-enabled applications have had to resort to providing dedicated client plug-ins to execute various application functions. This solution weakens the basic, open environment philosophy of the Web model and leads to additional maintenance considerations during the application's lifecycle. Plug-ins generally work only with one specific browser and/or hardware platform. Additionally, many companies have policies that prohibit downloading and using plug-ins within the security of the corporate WAN or Intranet. This is due to security concerns; viruses and other risks can occur when connecting to external sources such as the Web, or to business partners, vendors, or customers that have been granted access to the warehouse environment.

- Lack of existing standard for emerging Web components such as Dynamic Hypertext Markup Language (DHTML), resulting in requirements for specific browsers and versions in order to fully exploit the component functionality.

- Performance degradation in the text character-based communication channel between the client browser and the Web server. Because of parsing requirements, the problem is particularly troublesome when significant quantities of data are being transferred.

With the recent surge in Web-enabled business solutions, all of the major vendors of decision support reporting products have spent the past year adapting their products for use over the Web, with varying results. Some have simply added a middle tier to their architectures to quickly Web-enable their product, in order to maintain market share. Several new entries to the market have developed products from the ground up that are specifically designed and optimized for use on the Web.

The architecture implementations of these relatively new Web-enabled decision support products vary greatly. You will need to carefully examine the various architecture components that define and support each product. Some areas of particular importance to meta data repository access are:

- How does the product solution support a three-tier thin client solution? Is any information or code stored on the client? Can all design security, administration, and query access be performed through a Web browser?

- How do the product components promote the use of open systems architecture components (e.g., CORBA, COM, Java)?

- What DBMS products do the product components support? Do the product components use common, open DBMSs?

- Can the decision support reporting product access information in the meta data repository for use in standard or ad hoc reports? Can the decision support reporting product use the business meta data stored in the repository for query presentation in the browser? Does the product allow for drill-downs through the data warehouse content database across to the repository database for use in reconciliation and auditing?

- Can the decision support reporting product perform standard or ad hoc reporting against the repository database without any additional and/or modified tables or columns? Are there any restrictions to the number of tables or to the database schema design?

- What existing mechanisms are currently incorporated in the general release version of the product to control security access by individuals or groups to sensitive areas of the repository (e.g., bonus formulas in business rule calculations)? If available, how is row-level security implemented through the product?

- What types of push and/or pull reporting capabilities does the product support? What report scheduling capabilities are available?

In addition, you should thoroughly analyze any client decision support tools that have recently been migrated to be Web-enabled. Review closely the architecture design and technical limitations of the solution from the standpoint of administration, scalability, performance, maintenance, and troubleshooting. I have seen tools that, from a business user perspective, were very flashy and offered impressive presentation capabilities, but were very difficult to administratively support. I also suggest reviewing your corporate policy on the use of ActiveX objects or Java applets, since some organizations have issues with their use. Finally, look very closely at how software migration is performed for new software releases.

Enterprise Information Portal

The popularity of consumer portal paradigms like My Yahoo and My Excite on the Web has led to a highly customizable category of Web products called Enterprise Information Portals (EIP), which can be used to access information in the DSS environment. (New York–based Merrill Lynch & Company coined the term EIP in a November 1998 report entitled "Enterprise Information Portals" by Christopher Shilakes and Julie Tylman.) Enterprise Information Portals are applications that enable companies to unlock internally and externally stored information, and provide users a single gateway to personalized information required to make informed business decisions. According to Shilakes and Tylman, EIPs are: "an amalgamation of software applications that consolidate, manage, analyze, and distribute information across and outside of an enterprise (including Business Intelligence, Content Management, Data Warehouse & Mart and Data Management applications.)"

Merrill Lynch believes the EIP market will eventually reach or exceed that of the Enterprise Resource Planning market. In its 1998 estimates, Merrill Lynch put the total EIP market at $4.4 billion, and forecasted that "revenues could top $14.8 billion by 2002."

EIPs allow an organization to share its business knowledge across the enterprise beyond just the data that is available in the data warehouse and meta data repository. EIPs categorize and group information from multiple sources into a value-added, personalized view of knowledge for the decision support user. Ranking and filtering of information content occurs through the portal to meet the specific needs of the business users, or of the roles they perform in the organization. The portal presents decision support users with information that is relevant to their business needs and ensures that they have authority to access it. Most EIPs allow users to perform searches against the corporate knowledge base to gather not only structured data from databases but also such unstructured data as documents. The combined use of a search engine and the hyperlink paradigm allows users to easily filter large quantities of data, which is perfect for meta data repositories. The portal is integrated with the decision support reporting environment (i.e., query reporting and/or OLAP) and used for meta data delivery. Most EIP products incorporate publish and presentation components for distributing information.

Companies are not limiting portals to business intelligence applications; they are also using them for knowledge management, competitive advantage, field and sales support applications, and for best practices dissemination. EIPs are helping companies to further capitalize on investments made over the past few years in enterprise resource planning applications, data warehouses, and corporate intranets.

The current array of portal products falls into one of two categories: *business intelligence* and *collaborative*. Business intelligence EIPs focus primarily on access to structured corporate information to help users make strategic business decisions. This type of portal often supports access to, or integrates with, decision support query reporting and OLAP products. Collaborative EIPs focus primarily on organizing and sharing workgroup information such as e-mail, memorandums, and other business documents. The two types of EIPs are expected to merge as the market for these products matures and becomes more competitive.

EIP products typically incorporate six components. The first is a *taxonomy* or *category* component that contains a directory of the corporation's business information. The category component allows a company to not only capture its business information, but also to organize its content into channels and workgroups. Maintenance of the directory is through the *publishing* component, the second portion of the EIP. The third component is the *integration* component, which allows the *meta data* component, the fourth piece, sometimes called *meta data crawlers*, to scan the corporate information servers for new business content and to update the directory. The integration component allows third-party vendors to interface with the portal to maintain directory information or run program objects to produce business intelligence information such as decision support query applications or OLAP reports on demand. The *presentation* component, the fifth piece, controls how the information is presented to the user, adhering to the business rules that affect the particular individual or role. The final portal component, the sixth piece, is a *search engine* that is used to process user requests for business information. The search engine uses the category component to find content in the directory. The search engine can generally perform full text searches and can identify content through meta data descriptions of items that are published on the portal. Figure 10.11 illustrates a EIP architecture.

Second-generation portal products are beginning to support automated importing and exporting of meta data across the enterprise through the interoperability of eXtensible Markup Language, which is becoming a widely sanctioned technology standard for meta data interchange among

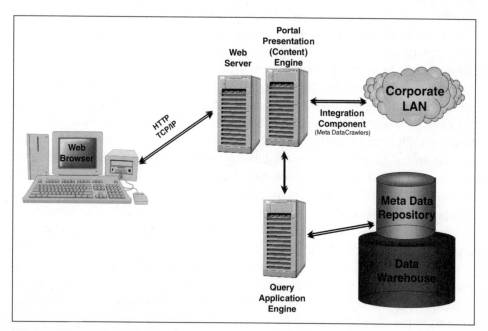

Figure 10.11 EIP architecture.

databases, meta data repositories, business intelligence, and knowledge management products. As I discussed in Chapter 3, Meta Data Standards, XML uses tags to identify, label, and format textual information. The tags in XML describe what the information is, and promote reuse between applications by combining both data and meta data. The popularity of XML is apparent with its recent incorporation in the latest versions of the Microsoft and Netscape Web browsers.

Future portal products are also looking into adoption of the XML Meta Data Interchange (XMI) standard, which allows exchange of software development repository information (sponsored by the Object Management Group). XMI can be used for meta data management in distributed component-based applications, data warehousing, and application integration environments. XMI unifies three industry standards for repositories and meta data management: (1) OMG's Meta Object Facility standard for distributed repositories, (2) Unified Modeling Language for object analysis/design, and (3) W3C XML for Web-based meta data management.

There are several factors to consider before deciding to deploy an EIP in your enterprise. Because the primary focus here is to provide reporting capabilities for the meta data repository, you are already constrained to look at portal products that emphasize business intelligence. The EIP's interface component needs to be able to interact with a decision support reporting tool to present information from the data warehouse or repository. Next, the portal product should be capable of defining the user, individually or by workgroups, through profiling. An EIP administrator uses this profile to control the business information content that the portal presents to the particular group or user. The publishing component needs to support the variety of information types required by your organization, such as relational databases, multidimensional databases, HTML, XML, program objects, documents, spreadsheets, and other pertinent data. The interface component needs to be capable of supporting interfaces to and from external products targeting support of XML. This interface component should also facilitate the support of profile changes for large numbers of users in the organization due to recurring business changes, such as interfacing with a human resources ERP package. The security functionality of the portal requires thorough analysis to determine what features are available to control user access to company-sensitive or proprietary information. In some implementations, individual user-level authentication through the portal is required to ensure that sensitive information is not disseminated throughout the organization or to competitors. Finally, the repository and/or infrastructure architects need to conduct a careful review of the administration and software migration processing steps to avoid future maintenance nightmares.

Summary

After reading this chapter, you should have a better understanding of the decision-making process for selecting a meta data delivery method. You will need to evaluate and weigh several factors in order to select the optimal solution for repository reporting. Understanding your users' business requirements, your meta data repository architecture, your users' reporting requirements, and the number of users and their locations will provide you with valuable information to move forward on the selection process. Be sure to carefully review purchased repository products for information delivery and architecture. A simple delivery solution now may mean maintenance headaches down the line. The additional effort of deploying a decision support reporting tool to access your meta data repository may offer greater benefits in supportability, scalability, and performance in the long run and provide your users with the benefits of a single interface.

If you decide to use your data warehouse front-end reporting tool, as a majority of implementations do, spend the necessary time to understand the tool's architecture. Each of the major architecture types (i.e., fat client, Web-enabled thin client, and enterprise information portals) involve advantages and disadvantages, depending on your organizational and technical environment. Your selection should consider support for emerging standards like XML, XMI, Java servers, and others that are still on the horizon.

Remember, you are about to make a serious investment in a company and it is product vision; be sure you are comfortable that it shares your vision. Nothing is more detrimental to one's career than choosing a decision support product that cannot be supported months after implementation. On the other hand, choosing a technology that offers substantial benefits to the entire organization by offering new ways of looking at information delivery can make you a hero. The technology that works around these decision support reporting tools and meta data repositories is changing every day, continually offering new capabilities and challenges for the repository architect.

In the concluding chapter, I discuss the future trends in meta data and data administration and examine how meta data is being adopted in the knowledge management sector. In addition, the chapter explores the continuing trend toward better integration of decision support tools with the meta data repository and considers the increased visibility that meta data repositories are receiving in the enterprise.

## CHAPTER 11

The Future of Meta Data

Any company embarking on a meta data repository project needs to stay abreast of the technological and political forces that are driving the market. This chapter discusses the trends in the meta data industry that can be discerned from the current market direction. First, I describe the evolution of the current meta data architectures into more advanced architectures. I then show how the knowledge management and meta data arenas are coming together, and how meta data is rapidly moving beyond decision support to span all of the information systems across an enterprise. Last, I examine the growth of XML and meta model standards and discuss how they will enable meta data to help control a company's information systems in the future.

Looking Ahead

Companies involved in meta data development today must be able to anticipate how the meta data market is likely to evolve in the next several years, or risk having to revisit (and possibly redo) their meta data development efforts. It is important to recognize these trends and build meta data repositories that are capable of adapting to them. I see several significant trends occurring in the meta data industry right now:

- Evolution of meta data architecture
- Acceptance of enterprise-wide meta data
- Convergence of meta data and knowledge management
- Evolution of XML and meta model standards
- Development of meta data–controlled systems

Evolution of Meta Data Architecture

The architecture of a meta data repository is critical for efficiently integrating all of the various types and sources of meta data that exist in a company and for providing user access to that meta data for all of the business and technical users. Two key trends are driving the evolution of meta data architecture:

- Simplified meta data integration architectures
- Proliferation of advanced meta data architectures

Although, at first glance, these trends may seem to be diametrically opposed, they are actually complementary. As the meta model standards evolve, the architecture used to integrate the various sources of meta data is likely to become much simpler than it is today. On the other hand, as integration becomes easier, businesses will demand a higher-level of functionality from their repositories. As a result, more advanced meta data repository architectures will be required to support these high-end requirements.

Simplified Meta Data Integration Architectures

As I discussed in Chapter 7, Constructing a Meta Data Architecture, meta data integration architecture is very challenging because of the wide variety of meta data types and sources that need to be brought together in the repository. Companies need to build program interfaces to gather much of this meta data from the various sources, interpret it, and integrate it into the meta data repository—all of which contributes to the complexity of the integration architecture. Meta data integration architectures will become significantly simpler and easier to implement when the dominant modeling groups (i.e., the OMG and MDC) define a model standard, but until that happens, companies must rely on a variety of nonstandard integration tools and custom interfaces to bring their meta data types and sources together.

A global model standard will enable tool vendors to build program interfaces to integrate most—but not all—types and sources of meta data and load it into a repository. Realistically, even after the tool vendors adopt standard interfaces, we can't expect the tools to automatically load more than 80 to 90 percent of a company's existing meta data into the repository. While this is certainly an improvement over the current tool capabilities, integration architectures will still involve a significant amount of custom interfaces.

Proliferation of Advanced Meta Data Architectures

Of course, once the task of integrating meta data becomes easier, companies are likely to want to add more functionality to their meta data repositories and implement their repositories on an enterprise-wide scale. This activity will, in turn, spur the development of even more advanced meta data architectures. The desire for greater functionality is a basic human trait. It is something that all IT professionals understand. Has your executive sponsor ever come to you and said: "I see that you estimate that it will take five months to build the meta data repository. Don't overwork yourself. Eliminate a few features and feel free to take six months for the build"? Of course not! Our users want more and more functionality delivered in less time and at a lower cost. When I was consulting at a global consumer electronics firm, a key person from one of the business units asked me how long it was going to take to make a major enhancement to the company's decision support system. I remember giving him a ballpark estimate of two months, explaining all of the tasks that we needed to complete before the enhancement could be put into place. After listening to my explanation, he turned to me and said, "I understand that we really need to make a lot of changes and bring in a new tool to add the functionality that we need, but is there any way to reduce the development time to . . . say a week?" My first impulse, which I managed to stifle, was to tell him not without an act of God.

End users' demands continually increase as you deliver more features and functionality. This desire will fuel the need for more bidirectional and closed-loop meta data architectures. (See Chapter 7, Constructing a Meta Data Architecture, for an additional discussion of these two architectures.)

Bidirectional Meta Data

In a bidirectional meta data architecture, meta data is changed in the meta data repository and then fed back into the meta data's original source (as illustrated in Figure 11.1).

Bidirectional meta data will become a reality when a meta model standard emerges and the various software vendors modify their applications to work with this standard. Standardization will enable these applications to

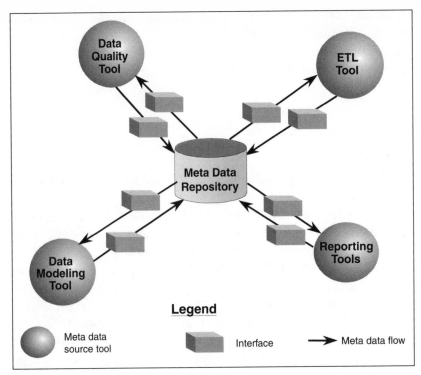

Figure 11.1 Bidirectional meta data architecture.

share data, thereby creating tool interoperability. Keep in mind, however, that even after we have a global meta model standard for decision support, the tool vendors will need at least six months from that point to adapt their tools to the new standard.

The key benefit of bidirectional meta data is that it allows vendor tools to reuse each other's meta data. It will help businesses to reduce their system development life cycles and thereby realize significant savings in their IT spending. Let's suppose, for example, that a company needs to change the valid domain value for a key attribute in one of its systems. Bidirectional meta data would allow the company to make the change once in the meta data repository, then flow the change back to all of the tools that interact with the repository. Without bidirectional meta data, the company would have to change all of the tools manually.

Closed-Loop Meta Data

A closed-loop meta data architecture allows the meta data repository to feed its meta data back into a company's operational systems. This concept is gaining a great deal of momentum at the corporate level as businesses demand the ability to integrate all of their information systems and have each system feed into the other corporate systems (as illustrated in Figure 11.2).

Closed-loop meta data will enable companies to integrate their customer relationship management systems, decision support systems, and e-business solutions with their operational systems, providing a single, integrated business intelligence system. This type of integration will, in turn, enable the entire organization to share information. This capability is particularly useful for sharing customer and product information because it can help companies to provide new, and significantly better, customer services. Similarly, service intensive industries such as banks, brokerages, and retail institutions can use closed-loop meta data to delegate many routine decision-making functions to their information systems, thereby streamlining the decision process and freeing administrative personnel for other activities.

Let's imagine, for example, that a consumer electronics retailer establishes an e-business system with an Internet Web site to allow customers to search for and order whatever components they want. When a customer selects one or more components, a program interface fires off to the customer relationship management system to trigger a message back to the cus-

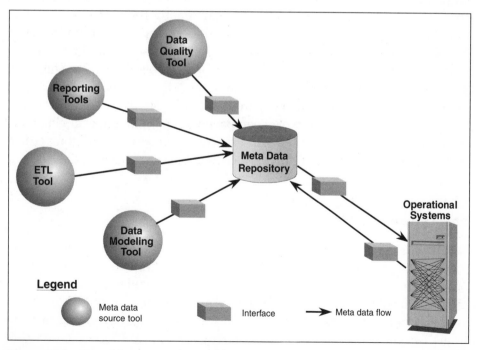

Figure 11.2 Closed-loop meta data architecture.

tomer offering additional, related products. If the customer management system indicates that the customer hasn't placed an order in a prespecified amount of time, the system may offer a discounted price or free delivery as an incentive for the customer to order additional items. When the customer places an order and completes the shopping session, another interface sends a message to the corporate DSS to update the customer file and check the credit rating, then returns this information to the e-business system. Theoretically, this entire transaction can take place without operator intervention and all information is automatically captured and shared with all associated information systems. The applications for closed-loop meta data are limited only by companies' imaginations, and we can all expect to see some innovative uses for this technology in the not-too-distant future.

Meta Data Moves Enterprise-Wide

As business continues to change at an ever-increasing rate, corporate IT departments will be hard-pressed to keep pace with the evolving needs for information. In Chapter 1, Introducing Meta Data and Its Return on Investment, I discussed the need for businesses to run impact analysis reports throughout all of the organization's information systems, thereby enabling corporate IT departments to efficiently adapt their systems to ever-changing requirements. A meta data repository significantly reduces the costs and time for development by allowing the IT development staff to run technical impact analysis reports across all corporate systems stored in the meta data repository. These impact analysis reports help IT developers to recognize the impact of proposed changes on their systems. This type of functionality is critical for any company looking to provide its IT systems with the necessary flexibility and maintainability to keep pace with continually changing business requirements. Forward-thinking companies understand the competitive advantage that meta data offers for their total business, not just their DSS.

Convergence of Meta Data and Knowledge Management

Benjamin Franklin once said, "An investment in knowledge pays the best interest." Something tells me that Ben didn't have knowledge management on his mind . . . but then again maybe he did. Companies are beginning to understand what Ben Franklin knew all those years ago; knowledge is their most valuable asset. Much of the push for knowledge is coming directly from the senior executives. In a 1998 survey of *Fortune 1000* executives, 97 percent of the respondents said that some critical business processes would improve if more employees knew about them. In the same survey, 87 percent of respondents said that costly mistakes are occurring because employees lack the right knowledge at the right time. This tremendous desire to improve and maintain a company's intellectual capital has triggered the field of study and vendor applications that we know as knowledge management.

Knowledge management is the gathering and sharing of intellectual capital (i.e., data, information, and knowledge) to generate a competitive advantage in the market. Knowledge management can benefit a company in a number of ways, including:

- Leverage lessons learned to lower expenses

- Share information to generate new ideas and increase revenues or decrease expenses

- Improve the company's ability to adapt to change and opportunities in the market

- Foster innovation by sharing previous solutions and collective ideas

I remember the first time I read about knowledge management. My first impression was, "This sounds a lot like what I do with meta data." I view a meta data repository as the backbone of a knowledge management solution, and don't see how a true enterprise-wide knowledge management solution can exist without one. The objectives of knowledge management are much the same as those of a meta data repository. After all, a meta data repository is a means for implementing a technical solution that captures, manages, and provides access to our corporate knowledge.

Knowledge Pyramid

As shown in Figure 11.3, the knowledge pyramid is at the heart of knowledge management. As a company's IT systems mature, they progress from collecting and managing data to collecting and managing knowledge.

Of course, data is the basic building block of our IT systems. You capture a great deal of data each time a customer calls your business to place an order, including, at a minimum, the name and address of the customer, the product(s) that is being ordered, and the amount of the order. Unfortunately, this data does not tell us anything about why the customer purchased the product from our company rather than a competitor, or how much the customer was willing to pay, or predict whether the customer is

NOTHING WORTHWHILE IS EASY

Many people wonder if knowledge management is a cure-all or just another fad? I believe that the concept of knowledge management is very sound, but like any other major IT initiative, it takes a lot of discipline, hard work, and a shift in culture to make it happen.

I often like to compare major IT initiatives like knowledge management to a similarly daunting task . . . that of losing weight. The vast majority of us want to lose some amount of weight. We would like to be able to just take a pill and still eat whatever we want while losing all the weight we want. However, there is a proven method for losing weight that works 100 percent of the time. It is called diet and exercise. If we just cut back on all the "bad" stuff that we eat (like ice cream, my personal weakness) and exercise regularly, we can lose weight.

Losing weight takes discipline and hard work; there is no magic bullet, just as there is no magic bullet for implementing a knowledge management solution. We cannot just buy a software program and automatically satisfy our need for knowledge management. While I believe that knowledge management is not likely to go the way of the hula-hoop, I don't think that it's a utopian solution either. But, when we combine knowledge management efforts with the functionality of a meta data repository, we can provide great benefit to business. The meta data repository provides the technical backbone that a sound knowledge management effort requires. Although a meta data repository is not generally recognized as a key component of a knowledge management solution, I believe that for knowledge management to be successful, it must include a meta data repository at its core.

likely to return. Nor do these data facts indicate whether the company is successful or if it is efficiently managed.

In short, data by itself has little purpose and meaning. Information is data that has meaning and purpose—it tells me about my business and how it functions. In the book *Working Knowledge* (Harvard Business School Press, 1999), coauthors Thomas Davenport and Laurence Prusak say that we add value to data in various ways:

- Contextualize: tells us the purpose for which the data was gathered

- Categorize: tells us the units of analysis or key components of the data

- Calculate: tells us if the data was analyzed mathematically or statistically

- Correct: tells us if errors have been removed from the data

- Condense: tells us if the data was summarized in a more concise form

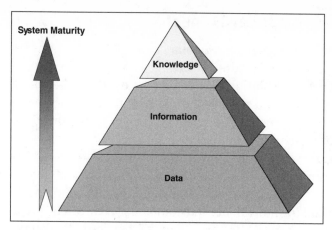

Figure 11.3 Knowledge pyramid.

While this seems a bit theoretical for us technicians, it really relates to the process of making our data have direct meaning to our businesses. For example, when we summarize customer sales amounts, and subtract the expenses for serving those customers, we attain profitability numbers. It we do this for each customer and then compare them, we can see which customers are our most profitable ones. In this way, we're turning data into information.

Knowledge takes us one step beyond information. When I go that extra step to transform information into knowledge, I learn the three "I's" of my business:

- Impacts
- Interacts
- Influences

I understand how my business *impacts* the market in which I compete. I realize how my business *interacts* with the other companies in the same selling space, and last, I understand how my company is *influenced* by the market in which we compete. So knowledge is information about how my business relates to the overall, global picture.

Meta data helps us to bring data, information, and knowledge together in a meaningful way, and a meta data repository enables us to capture and analyze these elements over time to understand them in the context of our evolving business markets. Both meta data and knowledge management provide measurable business value, and I expect interest in both to increase substantially as businesses endeavor to leverage their corporate data, information, and knowledge into a competitive advantage.

XML and Meta Model Standards Meet

Many companies (Sun Microsystems in particular) believe that the network is the database. If this is true, then Internet Web pages comprise the biggest database of all. With e-business solutions expected to grow into a $100+ billion industry by the year 2002, and the number of Web users projected to reach 329 million by 2002 (see Figure 11.4), we can expect to see this database continue to grow at an exponential rate.

Besides being the largest database in the world, the Web is also the world's largest distributed environment. As this heterogeneous environment continues to expand at an ever-escalating rate, it becomes increasingly difficult to manage. Many forward-thinking individuals and companies have already realized that the Web will need a way to make the reams of disparate data on the web homogeneous. Meta data provides the answer to this problem . . . it's called XML. That's right, XML is actually meta data. As I discussed in Chapter 3, Meta Data Standards, XML and its related standards are attempting to resolve the problem of heterogeneous data and enable organizations to share information without designing custom interfaces. XML attaches *data tags* in HTML to describe the data (meta data) on the Web page. The advantage of XML is that the data tag, not the location of the data, describes the data's meaning. Thus, data can be placed on the Web in any order. XML also facilitates the *one off*, customized (ad hoc) exchange of electronic commerce transactions among businesses.

I consider XML to be even more important than the meta model standards being developed by the MDC and OMG, primarily because it is visible to a much larger audience—the Web. XML will enable companies to exchange documents (Web pages) over the Internet without manual intervention or

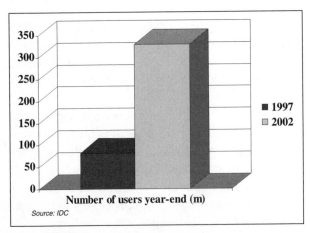

Figure 11.4 Web users worldwide.

the need for custom interfaces. Eventually, XML and the meta model standards will converge, providing businesses with a Holy Grail that will help them to manage the Web.

As the largest decision support system in the world, the Web is actually hindered by its size, which is also it's greatest advantage. The biggest problem with the Web today is finding the information we want. For example, in researching this book I needed to identify any existing books that focus on the subject of meta data. I used various Internet search engines to find books on meta data, firing up one search engine after another looking for "meta data books." My searches returned literally thousands of matches, but none of the matches pointed me to an actual book on meta data. I must admit that I gave up after scrolling through the hundreds of web pages that were returned. XML's goal is to provide the "glue" (meta data) that adds meaning to all of this "stuff" on the web, letting the Internet search engines look at a Web page and differentiate between an actual book on meta data and simply the appearance of the words "meta data book." In my search for books on meta data, the XML data tags would have clearly indicated which sites had information about meta data in the title of the book. Keep in mind that XML, like the meta model standards, is still maturing, but there is a great deal of market pressure to develop a solution quickly. XML is well on its way to becoming the meta data standard for the Web.

Meta Data Controlled Systems

Sharing and exchanging meta data among various repositories and software tools is particularly desirable for global enterprises with dispersed teams trying to solve similar or related data analysis problems using an integrated computing approach. In such enterprises, project coordination relies heavily on network computing and effective use of knowledge and resources developed by the various teams. The ability to share meta data within and across software tools becomes extremely important as these tools' repositories become increasingly interdependent and the various groups using them try to collaborate effectively. Like any other integrated approach to collaboration, information sharing must be managed to minimize duplication of effort while capturing changes to the shared information and propagating those changes efficiently and accurately. Complex software applications, such as data warehousing and decision support, typically involve many types of data obtained from a variety of sources and transformed for various groups with different data analysis needs.

As XML continues to gain popularity as the format of choice for representing Web-based data, XML files are likely to become a distinct source of meta data for many software products. As a result, the ability to interchange the meta data associated with an XML file while validating some or all of that meta data against predefined XML standards is a key requirement for interoperating with the emerging e-commerce and Web-based information systems. The ability to effectively manage the meta data sharing and exchange processes with various software tools and standard protocols is a fundamental requirement of any meta data repository architecture for an enterprise solution.

As the meta models become standardized, the many and various tools that we use for our IT systems will be able to share data, including all of the following:

- Operating systems
- Data modeling tools
- Relational databases
- Access tools (e.g., OLAP, ROLAP, and MOLAP)
- ETL (extraction, transformation, and load) tools
- Meta data integration tools
- Data quality tools
- Corporate information portals
- Data mining tools

Once these tools can share data through standard meta models, organizations will realize that changes to the information in their meta data repository will cascade to all of their supporting tools. This capability will enable businesses to centralize much of their system control processes through the meta data repository, creating a dependent relationship between the decision support system and each application software product. Meta data in this case establishes an interface for the tools, as illustrated in Figure 11.5.

The Meta Data Driven Enterprise

You are nearing the end of your journey into the depths of meta data. As you've learned, meta data has come a long way from its early data dictionary days. With e-business extending the traditional reach of IT systems to the Web, meta data is becoming more important than ever before for managing our legacy system of the future . . . the Web. Without meta data, our information systems are merely modern-day versions of "stovepipe" applications. A meta data repository is vital to a company's ability to prosper in our information-driven business environment, but the repository must be

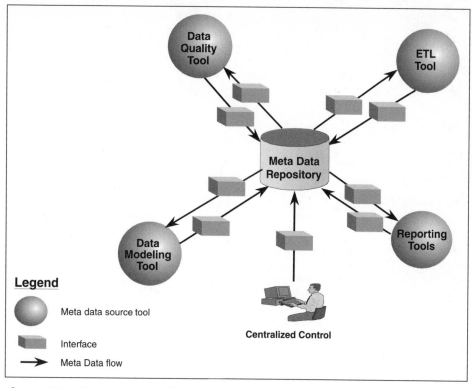

Figure 11.5   Meta data–controlled systems.

built with specific business needs in mind to support business and technical users, and must be built on a technologically sound architecture that will support future growth as applications evolve into true business intelligence solutions.

As with any other major IT undertaking, you will encounter many obstacles in the path to a truly usable and scalable meta data repository. After all, the shortest path between the beginning and ending of a project is rarely a straight one. Just remember that the paybacks are extremely high, so be disciplined, methodical, and work hard, and you will be successful. To accomplish great things we must not only act, but also dream: not only plan, but also believe.

Tool Evaluation Checklist

This appendix presents the Tool Evaluation Checklist introduced in Chapter 4, Understanding and Evaluating Meta Data Tools, in its entirety. You may find it helpful to review this complete checklist and compare it with your organization's tool requirements, then copy and use all or portions of it as a guide when you interview tool vendors. Refer back to Chapter 4 for an explanation of how to apply the Weight, % Met, and Score columns to your own evaluation process.

NO.	SECTION/DESCRIPTION	WEIGHT	% MET	SCORE	COMMENTS
A	**VENDOR BACKGROUND**				
1	Full name and business address of vendor.				
2	Parent company.				
3	Number of years company has been in business.				
4	Company structure. Is it a corporation, partnership, or privately held? List names associated with structure if different from Question #1.				
5	Public or privately held company? If public, which exchange is company traded on, and what is company's market symbol?				
6	When did the company go public, or when is it expected to go public?				
7	Total number of employees worldwide.				
8	Total number of U.S. employees.				
9	Web site URL.				
10	Number of developers supporting proposed product solution.				
11	Company profit/loss for past three years (if available).				

B **PROPOSED SOLUTION OVERVIEW**

12	Provide a summary of the vendor's proposed solution and explain how it meets the needs specified in this document.	
13	What are the names and versions of the product(s) component(s) comprising the vendor's proposed solution?	The repository architect and infrastructure need to carefully review all the components in the proposed solution and compare them with the target technical environment and support structure. How do the components communicate? What hardware platforms, DBMSs, Web servers, and communications protocols do the components require? How is security and migration handled among the various components?
14	Number of worldwide production installations using precisely this proposed solution configuration.	The key word here is *precisely*. Be sure to consider the hardware, DBMS, Web server, etc.
15	Number of U.S. production installations using precisely this proposed solution configuration.	How many other companies are using same configuration? Is vendor going to be the first?
16	What hardware, operating system, DBMS, and Web browser limitations do each of the product(s) component(s) have in the proposed solution on client and server platforms?	Be mindful of any requirements to download Java applets and/or ActiveX controls to the client.
17	What is the release date and version number history of each of the product(s) component(s) over the past 24 months?	

continues

(Continued)

NO.	SECTION/DESCRIPTION	WEIGHT	% MET	SCORE	COMMENTS
18	What is the anticipated release date and new feature list for each of the product(s) component(s) for the next 12 months?				
19	Provide a list of known software bugs, errors or other technical issues associated with each of the product(s) component(s).				
C	**COST OF PROPOSED SOLUTION**				
20	Total cost of proposed solution.				
21	Cost of consulting services required for installation.				Negotiate consulting time up front to complete staff training and get the repository up and running as quickly as possible.
22	Cost of consulting services for initial project setup.				
23	What is the vendor's daily rate for consulting services without expenses?				
24	Annual maintenance cost/fee.				Typically ranges between 14 and 18 percent of solution price.
25	Are all new product component releases/upgrades provided while under an annual maintenance agreement? If not, please explain in detail.				

D **TECHNICAL REQUIREMENT**

26	Are there any database schema design requirements for the DSS data model in order to function with the repository product?	Does the proposed solution require a change in the existing DSS schema design in order to function?
27	How does the tool control the various versions of the meta data (i.e., development, quality assurance, and production) stored in the repository?	
28	How is meta data from multiple DSS projects controlled and separated? How can various projects share meta data?	The answer to this question will determine how you administer the product and provide security.
29	Describe how meta data repository contents are migrated from one system engineering phase to the next (i.e., development, quality assurance, and production). How does this processing sequence differ when dealing with multiple projects on various time lines?	In particular, how is meta data migrated through the various design phases? Can a single project or portion of a project be migrated forward? How?
30	What DBMS privileges does the product support (e.g., roles, accounts, and views)?	
31	Can DBMS-specific SQL statements be incorporated into queries?	Be sure the solution can support the various DBMS techniques required to support the DSS environment. For example, can roles, parallel threads, dirty read, and other unique DBMS features be used through the repository?
32	Describe the security model used with the product.	Can security be centrally controlled or distributed? How can various DSS projects be separated? Is security based on the DBMS, OS, etc.? How is access controlled through the Web?

continues

(Continued)

NO.	SECTION/DESCRIPTION	WEIGHT	% MET	SCORE	COMMENTS
33	Can administration and use privileges be assigned at a user, workgroup, project, and enterprise level? Describe.				
34	How does the product use existing infrastructure security systems?				Can existing access methods be used as pass throughs? Or does the solution require its own database for security?
35	Does the product use any type of single sign-on authentication (e.g., LDAP)?				
36	Are all user IDs and passwords centrally located for all product components? Where?				
37	Where are user security constraints for the product stored?				Does the solution provide row-level security?
38	Can a user have access to the repository tool for one project but no access for another project?				
39	Can a user view the SQL generated by the product?				Also consider controls imposed on SQL generation.
40	Is the product Web-enabled? Describe.				
41	Can the product be fully used through Web browser on the client?				Be sure all desktop client features are available with the Web version of the solution.
42	Can the product be fully administered through a Web browser? Describe.				
43	Which Web browsers does the product support? Which Web server products does the product support?				And, what hardware platforms?

44	What ActiveX controls and/or Java applets are required on the client PC? How large are these controls and/or applets?	
45	What programming requirements are required to support the proposed meta data repository solution (e.g., script, SQL, etc.)?	Consider the training curve.
46	What scalability options are available in the solution to determine where processing is performed for optimization?	
47	What collaborative support comes with the proposed solution (e.g., e-mail, pagers, etc.)?	
48	Describe what processing functions run on the client versus the server.	What options does the solution offer to redistribute processing?
49	Does the product allow multiple meta data developers to work simultaneously with the same DSS project? Describe facilities.	What memory and processing requirements are needed for each user? How does the vendor suggest calculating these needs?
50	What scheduling tools does the product interface with (CA-7, CRON, Control-M, JES/2, etc.)?	
51	Does the product use any middleware components? If so, how do they improve overall performance of the product?	

continues

(Continued)

NO.	SECTION/DESCRIPTION	WEIGHT	% MET	SCORE	COMMENTS
52	Do new upgrades or releases of the product come with automated repository DBMS conversion routines?				
53	What is an average hardware configuration (number of processors, speed of processors, hard disk space, RAM) for the client and server components of the proposed architecture? Please specify assumptions.				Try to obtain configuration examples (even if they do not exactly match your configuration) then extrapolate.
E	**META DATA MANAGEMENT**				
54	Is the meta data repository tool active or passive in controlling the processes of the DSS environment? If active, explain.				What agents and/or triggers can be used to make the repository proactive?
55	Can the meta data repository tool's meta model be extended to include additional tables or columns?				How well does the proposed solution handle the need for customization?
56	What types of source system data can the repository directly read and capture meta data from (e.g., DBMS, flat files, DDL, spreadsheets, copybooks, etc.)?				
57	What CASE tools or data modeling tools can the repository tool directly read and capture?				
58	How are business rules captured and stored in the repository?				

59 How are calculations captured and stored in the repository?

60 What front-end query reporting and/or OLAP tools can access and store meta data directly from the repository?

61 What data monitoring tools can the repository directly access meta data information from?

62 Describe the types of user interfaces that the repository tool has for manual entry of meta data.

63 Can the repository tool read and write CASE Data Interchange Format (CDIF) compliant meta data files?

64 Describe how data mappings between source operational and target decision support data are captured and maintained in the repository tool.

65 What reporting capabilities does the meta data repository tool include as standard? Can data from the repository be exported externally to other applications (e.g., spreadsheets)?

66 Does the tool support predefined and/or ad hoc reporting? Describe.

67 How does the repository share and separate meta data needed for various DSS projects (e.g., atomic data warehouse versus various departmental-specific data marts)?

continues

(Continued)

NO.	SECTION/DESCRIPTION	WEIGHT	% MET	SCORE	COMMENTS
68	What facilities does the repository tool have for analyzing the impact of a change on a source operational system to the DSS environment?				
69	What notification or alert utilities does the tool provide in response to changes to operational systems, data mappings, DSS data model, or reports?				
70	How does the tool support the base components of a meta data repository (i.e., operational source system, logical DSS data model, physical DSS data model, source to target data mapping, ETL load statistics, business subject area views, query statistics)?				
F	**COMPETITIVE ADVANTAGES**				
71	Discuss the extent to which the vendor's proposed solution fits the needs of a meta data repository tool for a decision support environment.				How well does the repository product integrate with existing components (e.g., DBMS, query reporting tool, OLAP, ETL, and data cleansing products)?
72	Discuss the advantages the proposed solution has over other vendor products in this DSS market space.				
73	What is the vendor's market share in this DSS market space? Source of market share?				Use research sources such as Gartner Group, Meta, and Onum.

G   TECHNICAL SUPPORT

74	Discuss in detail the technical support offered in the proposed solution.	
75	Where is the primary technical support center located?	
76	What times and days of the week is the support center available for customer support?	
77	Describe the technical support center's guaranteed response time.	
78	Describe the escalation procedures used to resolve customer problems.	
79	Are technical support costs included in the annual maintenance agreements? If not, how are technical support costs charged backed to the customer?	
80	Are all product components comprising the proposed solution supported out of a single technical support center? If not, explain.	
81	Is an online database(s) of previously closed issues and/or frequently asked questions (FAQs) and their solutions available for customer review?	
82	Describe how upgrades can be installed in parallel with existing versions.	Can two versions of the product be operated on the same platform?

continues

(Continued)

NO.	SECTION/DESCRIPTION	WEIGHT	% MET	SCORE	COMMENTS
H	**DOCUMENTATION**				
83	Discuss the quality and availability of all forms of software documentation (i.e., user, technical, and installation).				
84	What media/format is documentation provided in (e.g., online, CD-ROM, or hard copy)? Are multiple copies or alternative media/formats available at no charge?				
I	**TRAINING**				
85	What training classes are included in the cost of the proposed solution? How many students does the solution include?				
86	What is the training cost for each class?				
87	Where are training classes held?				
88	Are any computer-based training (CBT) courses available? If so, what is the CBT cost?				
89	What training classes are recommended for the repository architect, data administrator, infrastructure developer, and business users, based on the contents of the proposed solution?				

J	**IMPLEMENTATION**	
90	Describe the sequence of events and level of effort recommended for clients to consider in planning their implementation strategy.	Obtain as much implementation documentation as possible from the vendor to use as a planning guide.
91	What is typical duration of implementation cycle?
92	How well does proposed product solution handle the number and types of data sources described in this document?
93	How many DSS database schema dimensions and facts can the proposed product solution handle?
94	Provide a sample project plan for implementing the proposed solution for a single DSS project.
95	What repository implementation reports can the proposed product solution generate?
96	What client resource skill sets need to be in place for installation and implementation?
K	**STRATEGIC PARTNERSHIPS**	
97	Identify and describe the vendor's strategic partnerships with CASE or data modeling tool vendors.

continues

(Continued)

NO.	SECTION/DESCRIPTION	WEIGHT	% MET	SCORE	COMMENTS
98	Identify and describe the vendor's strategic partnerships with DSS extraction, transformation, and loading tool vendors.				
99	Identify and describe the vendor's strategic partnerships with DSS data cleansing tool vendors.				
100	Identify and describe the vendor's strategic partnerships with DSS query reporting and/or OLAP vendors.				
101	Identify and describe the vendor's strategic partnerships with DSS data monitoring tool vendors.				
102	Identify and describe the vendor's strategic partnerships with hardware vendors.				
103	Identify and describe the vendor's strategic partnerships with DBMS vendors.				
104	Identify and describe the vendor's strategic partnerships with VARs.				
105	Identify and describe the vendor's strategic partnerships with integrators.				
106	Identify and describe the vendor's strategic partnerships with consulting implementation providers.				

L **CUSTOMER REFERENCES**

107 Obtain from vendor at least three customer references that may be contacted regarding quality of software, upgrades, proper sizing, implementation, and training.

For each customer reference obtain the following information:

- Company name and address
- Contact name, title, and phone number
- Type of services offered
- Modules installed (names of modules)
- Installation date(s)

Meta Data Project Plan

This appendix presents the Meta Data Project Plan that is walked through in detail in Chapter 6, Building the Meta Data Project Plan. This plan, which uses an iterative development methodology, contains all of the major sections that most meta data repository projects require. Although this project plan focuses on implementing a new repository, the steps for enhancing an existing repository are much the same.

The timelines for a meta data repository project differ widely according to the functionality required and the available staff; however, the timelines presented in this plan are common for a first release of a substantial value-providing meta data repository project.

TASK ID	TASK NAME	DURATION	DEPENDENCY	RESOURCE NAMES
	Meta Data Repository Project Plan	81 days		
1	Orientation phase	15 days		
1.1	Gauge organization's understanding of meta data	1 day		Project manager
1.2	Obtain meta data course instructor	7 days		Project manager[0.25]
1.3	Work with instructor to design customized course	3 days	1.2	Trainer, project manager[0.25]
1.4	Conduct executive training to teach about meta data	1 day	1.3	Project champion, subject matter expert, end user committee, project manager, key executive management, key IT team leaders
1.5	Conduct training for key developers	4 days	1.4	Subject matter expert[0.5], project manager, DBA, data modeler, repository architect, business analyst, data acquisition developers, data delivery developers
2	Feasibility phase	26 days		
2.1	Create project scope document	17 days		
2.1.1	Create interview questions	1 day		Project manager, business analyst
2.1.2	Conduct interviews with key personal	10 days	2.1.1	Project manager[0.5], business analyst, subject matter expert
2.1.3	Evaluate requirements	3 days	2.1.2	Subject matter expert, business analyst, project champion, project manager

2.1.4	Generate project scope document	2 days	2.1.3	Business analyst, project manager
2.1.5	Meet with key personal to approve document	5 days	2.1.4	Business analyst[0.5], project champion[0.5], project manager[0.5], key executive management[0.25], subject matter expert[0.5]
2.1.6	Obtain signoff	1 day	2.1.5	Project champion, project manager, subject matter expert
2.2	High-level planning and funding	9 days		
2.2.1	Develop high-level project plan	3 days	2.1	Project manager
2.2.2	Determine resource requirements	2 days	2.1	Project manager
2.2.3	Approve project plan, resource requirements, and funding	2 days	2.2.2	Project champion, project manager
2.2.4	Obtain resources (internal and external)	5 days	2.2.3	Project manager
2.2.5	Initial project plan and resourcing complete	0	2.2.4	
3	Design phase	36 days	2	
3.1	Meta data tool evaluation and selection	26 days		
3.1.1	Meta data integration tool	26 days		
3.1.1.1	Identify major integration tool vendors	2 days		Data acquisition developers, repository architect[0.25], project manager[0.25], data modeler
3.1.1.2	Create weighted checklist and interview	5 days		Data acquisition developers, repository architect[0.25], project manager[0.25], data modeler

continues

(Continued)

TASK ID	TASK NAME	DURATION	DEPENDENCY	RESOURCE NAMES
3.1.1.3	Send checklist and interview to vendors for completion	0	3.1.1.2	Data acquisition developers, repository architect[0.25], project manager[0.25], data modeler
3.1.1.4	Receive completed vendor checklist and interview	10 days	3.1.1.3	Data acquisition developers, repository architect[0.25], project manager[0.25], data modeler
3.1.1.5	Receive tool demo (check demo to checklist answers)	5 days	3.1.1.4	Data acquisition developers, repository architect[0.25], project manager[0.25], data modeler
3.1.1.6	Check vendor references	1 day	3.1.1.4	Data acquisition developers, repository architect[0.25], project manager[0.25], data modeler
3.1.1.7	Decide upon tool	5 days	3.1.1.6	Data acquisition developers, repository architect[0.25], project manager[0.25], data modeler
3.1.1.8	Create contract and obtain vendor signoff	5 days	3.1.1.7	Project manager[0.25], legal department[0.5], project champion[0.25]
3.1.2	Meta data access tool	26 days		
3.1.2.1	Identify major integration tool vendors	2 days		Business analyst, data delivery developers, repository architect[0.25], project manager[0.25]
3.1.2.2	Create weighted checklist and interview	5 days		Business analyst, data delivery developers, repository architect[0.25], project manager[0.25]

Task	Description	Duration	Pred.	Resources
3.1.2.3	Send checklist and interview to vendors for completion	0	3.1.2.2	Business analyst, data delivery developers, repository architect[0.25], project manager[0.25]
3.1.2.4	Receive completed vendor checklist and interview	10 days	3.1.2.3	Business analyst, data delivery developers, repository architect[0.25], project manager[0.25]
3.1.2.5	Receive tool demo (check demo to checklist answers)	5 days	3.1.2.4	Business analyst, data delivery developers, repository architect[0.25], project manager[0.25]
3.1.2.6	Check vendor references	1 day	3.1.2.4	Business analyst, data delivery developers, repository architect[0.25], project manager[0.25]
3.1.2.7	Decide upon tool	5 days	3.1.2.6	Business analyst, data delivery developers, repository architect[0.25],project manager[0.25]
3.1.2.8	Create contract and obtain vendor signoff	5 days	3.1.2.7	Project champion[0.25], project manager[0.25], legal department[0.5]
3.2	Construct integration architecture document	10 days		
3.2.1	Identify sources of meta data to be integrated	3 days		Repository architect[0.5], project manager[0.5]
3.2.2	Identify meta data needs each source shall provide	2 days	3.2.1	Repository architect[0.5], project manager[0.5]
3.2.3	Detail the specific integration method each source of meta data will need	3 days	3.2.2	Repository architect[0.5], project manager[0.5]

continues

(Continued)

TASK ID	TASK NAME	DURATION	DEPENDENCY	RESOURCE NAMES
3.2.4	Map out hardware/software architecture	2 days	3.2.3	Repository architect[0.5], project manager[0.5]
3.3	Create detailed design document	17 days	2	
3.3.1	Identify business users of the repository	1 day		Subject matter expert, business analyst, data modeler[0.5], project manager[0.25], data delivery developers
3.3.2	Identify technical users of the repository	1 day		Subject matter expert, business analyst, data modeler[0.5], project manager[0.25], data delivery developers
3.3.3	Meet w/users to define specific reporting needs (business and technical)	10 days	3.3.1, 3.3.2	Business analyst, data modeler[0.5], project manager[0.25], data delivery developers, subject matter expert
3.3.4	Review and approve user requirements	1 day	3.3.3	Subject matter expert, business analyst, data modeler, project manager, data delivery developers, project champion, repository architect
3.3.5	Create detailed data delivery specifications	5 days	3.3.4	Subject matter expert, business analyst, data modeler[0.5], project manager[0.25], data delivery developers
3.4	Train development staff (if tool is being used)	10 days	3.1	
3.4.1	Train development staff on meta data integration tool	10 days		Data acquisition developers, repository architect, tool vendor
3.4.2	Train development staff on meta data access tool	10 days		Repository architect, data delivery developers, tool vendor

4	Construction phase	77 days		
4.1	Build meta model	10 days	3.3	
4.1.1	Construct meta model	9 days		DBA[0.25], data modeler
4.1.2	Walk through meta model with team	1 day	4.1.1	DBA[0.25], data modeler
4.2	Design meta data security process	6 days	3.3	
4.2.1	Identify business and tech security permissions	2 days		Repository architect[0.25], subject matter expert[0.25], business analyst[0.25], key IT team leaders
4.2.2	Set up security permissions processes	3 days	4.2.1	Repository architect[0.25], subject matter expert[0.25], business analyst[0.25], key IT team leaders
4.2.3	Gather business users IDs and provide security clearance	1 day	4.2.2	Repository architect[0.25], subject matter expert[0.25], business analyst[0.25], key IT team leaders
4.2.4	Gather technical users IDs and provide security clearance	1 day	4.2.2	Repository architect[0.25], subject matter expert[0.25], business analyst[0.25], key IT team leaders
4.3	Develop meta data integration processes	12 days	3, 3.4, 4.5.3	
4.3.1	Build/unit test meta data integration programs	10 days		DBA[0.25], Data acquisition developers, subject matter expert[0.25], business analyst[0.25], repository architect[0.5], data modeler[0.25]

continues

(Continued)

TASK ID	TASK NAME	DURATION	DEPENDENCY	RESOURCE NAMES
4.3.2	Load meta data repository	2 days	4.3.1	DBA[0.25], data acquisition developers, subject matter expert[0.25], business analyst[0.25], repository architect[0.5], data modeler[0.25]
4.4	Develop meta data reports/access method	10 days	3, 3.4, 4.5.3	
4.4.1	Create business views and reports	5 days		DBA[0.25], subject matter expert[0.5], business analyst, repository architect[0.25], data modeler[0.5], data delivery developers
4.4.2	Create technical views and reports	5 days	4.4.1	DBA[0.25], subject matter expert[0.5], business analyst, repository architect[0.25], architect[0.25], data modeler[0.5], data delivery developers
4.5	Meta data infrastructure	9 days	4.1	
4.5.1	Desktop setup and configuration	9 days	3.1.2	
4.5.1.1	Design desktop configuration	2 days		Project manager[0.25], key IT team leaders
4.5.1.2	Purchase needed desktop hardware	5 days	4.5.1.1	Project manager[0.25], key IT team leaders
4.5.1.3	Purchase needed desktop software	5 days	4.5.1.1	Project manager[0.25], key IT team leaders
4.5.1.4	Install hardware on desktops	2 days	4.5.1.2	Project manager[0.25], key IT team leaders

4.5.1.5	Install software on desktops	2 days	4.5.1.3	Project manager[0.25], key IT team leaders
4.5.2	Select and implement RDBMS	5 days		
4.5.2.1	Implement physical database	5 days		DBA, key IT team leaders
4.5.2.2	Physical database implemented	0	4.5.2.1	DBA, key IT team leaders
4.5.3	Meta data tools setup and configuration	3 days	3.1.2	
4.5.3.1	Install software	3 days		Tool vendor, key IT team leaders
4.5.3.2	Test software connectivity to desktop	3 days		Tool vendor, key IT team leaders
4.5.3.3	Meta data tools are installed and ready for development	0	4.5.3.2	
4.6	User acceptance testing	11 days	4.3, 4.4	
4.6.1	Business user training	6 days		
4.6.1.1	Create meta data access documentation (business)	2 days		Business analyst
4.6.1.2	Prepare training program for business users	2 days	4.6.1.1	Business analyst
4.6.1.3	Conduct training program	2 days	4.6.1.1, 4.6.1.2	Business analyst
4.6.2	Technical user training	6 days		
4.6.2.1	Create meta data access documentation (technical)	2 days		Business analyst
4.6.2.2	Prepare training program for technical users	2 days	4.6.2.1	Business analyst

continues

(Continued)

TASK ID	TASK NAME	DURATION	DEPENDENCY	RESOURCE NAMES
4.6.2.3	Conduct training program	2 days	4.6.2.1, 4.6.2.2	Business analyst
4.6.3	User acceptance testing (UAT)	5 days	4.6.1, 4.6.2	
4.6.3.1	Identify UAT participants	1 day		Project manager, business analyst
4.6.3.2	Plan UAT	1 day	4.6.3.1	Project manager, business analyst
4.6.3.3	Conduct UAT	3 days	4.6.3.2	Project manager, business analyst, data delivery developers[0.5], data acquisition developers[0.5]
4.6.3.4	End user signoff	0	4.6.3.3	
5	Rollout phase	4 days	4.6.3	
5.1	Rollout repository to clients	0		
5.2	Post implementation review	4 days		
5.2.1	Plan review agenda and materials	1 day		Project manager
5.2.2	Conduct review	2 days	5.2.1	Project manager, project champion, subject matter expert, key executive management
5.2.3	Publish results	1 day	5.2.2	Project manager, project champion
5.3	Meta data repository in production	0	5.2	

DDL Sample Model Code

This appendix presents the detailed DDL code required to build the sample models in Chapter 9, Building the Meta Model. You can use this code as a guide to create your own model, but remember that your model must fulfill your organization's unique requirements and is likely to differ significantly from the samples in our chapter.

Object Model Example

The following example illustrates the basic concepts that are required to implement an object model. Although object models can be very complex (as we explained in Chapter 9), we've intentionally kept this SQL code example simple so that you can easily understand the basic concepts.

To use this example as a guide for developing your own object model, first try loading data into the model, then extract that information. This process will help you to grasp the complexities in query design that are associated with object models.

```
DROP TABLE object_hierarchy CASCADE CONSTRAINTS;
□


□
CREATE TABLE object_hierarchy (
```

☐
```
        object_id          INTEGER NOT NULL,
        parent_object_id INTEGER NOT NULL,
        object_hierarchy_metadata LONG VARCHAR NULL
);

DROP INDEX XPKobject_hierarchy;

DROP INDEX XIF1object_hierarchy;

DROP INDEX XIF2object_hierarchy;

CREATE UNIQUE INDEX XPKobject_hierarchy ON object_hierarchy
(
        object_id                         ASC,
        parent_object_id                  ASC
);

CREATE INDEX XIF1object_hierarchy ON object_hierarchy
(
        object_id                         ASC
);

CREATE INDEX XIF2object_hierarchy ON object_hierarchy
(
        object_id                         ASC
);

DROP TABLE object CASCADE CONSTRAINTS;

CREATE TABLE object (
        object_id            INTEGER NOT NULL,
        object_type_id       INTEGER NULL,
        object_description   VARCHAR2 (20) NOT NULL,
        object_business_metadata LONG VARCHAR NULL
);

DROP INDEX XPKobject;

DROP INDEX XIF5object;

CREATE UNIQUE INDEX XPKobject ON object
(
        object_id                         ASC
);

CREATE INDEX XIF5object ON object
(
        object_type_id                    ASC
);
```

```
DROP TABLE object_type CASCADE CONSTRAINTS;

CREATE TABLE object_type (
      object_type_id              INTEGER NOT NULL,
      object_type_description     VARCHAR2 (20) NOT NULL,
      parent_object_type          INTEGER NOT NULL,
      object_type_metadata        LONG VARCHAR NULL
);


DROP INDEX XPKobject_type;

CREATE UNIQUE INDEX XPKobject_type ON object_type
(
      object_type_id                    ASC
);
```

Real-World Model Example

The following model example illustrates the basic components that are
required for capturing meta data for a data warehousing environment. It
should help you to understand the types of information that you need to
capture, and the relationships among items. Use it as a starting point, then
tailor it as necessary to fit your own, specific needs. Again, we've intentionally kept this SQL code example simple to ensure that the basic concepts
are readily apparent.

```
CREATE TABLE Query_Statistics (
☐
      Query_Id                    CHAR (18) NOT NULL,
      Query_Start_Time            DATETIME NOT NULL,
      Query_End_Time              DATETIME NOT NULL,
      Number_of_rows_returned     INTEGER NULL,
      Size_of_result_set          DECIMAL NULL,
      User_Id                     CHARACTER NULL,
      Database_name               CHARACTER NULL,
      Server_name                 CHARACTER NULL,
      Query_elapsed_time          DECIMAL NULL
);


ALTER TABLE Query_Statistics
      ADD   ( PRIMARY KEY (Query_Id) ) ;

CREATE TABLE ETL_Process (
      Process_Id                  SERIAL NOT NULL,
      Process_Effective_Date      DATE NOT NULL,
      Process_Description         CHARACTER NULL,
      Process_Owner               CHARACTER NULL
);
```

```
ALTER TABLE ETL_Process
      ADD  ( PRIMARY KEY (Process_Id, Process_Effective_Date)
) ;

CREATE TABLE Source (
      Source_Id                   SERIAL NOT NULL,
      Source_Effective_Date       DATE NOT NULL,
      Source_Format_Type          CHARACTER NULL,
      Source_DBMS                 CHARACTER NULL,
      Source_Description          CHARACTER NULL,
      Source_Update_Frequency     CHARACTER NULL,
      Status_Code                 CHARACTER NULL
);

ALTER TABLE Source
      ADD  ( PRIMARY KEY (Source_Id, Source_Effective_Date) )
;

CREATE TABLE ETL_Process_Source_Map (
      Source_Effective_Date       DATE NOT NULL,
      Source_Id                   INTEGER NOT NULL,
      Process_Effective_Date      DATE NOT NULL,
      Process_Id                  INTEGER NOT NULL
);

ALTER TABLE ETL_Process_Source_Map
      ADD  ( PRIMARY KEY (Source_Effective_Date, Source_Id,
            Process_Effective_Date, Process_Id) ) ;

CREATE TABLE Target_Table (
      Target_Table_Name           CHARACTER NOT NULL,
      Target_Table_Type           CHARACTER NOT NULL,
      Target_Table_Effective_Date DATE NOT NULL,
      Status_Code                 CHARACTER NULL,
      Table_Business_Name         CHARACTER NULL,
      Table_Business_Alias        CHARACTER NULL,
      Table_Business_Definition   CHARACTER NULL,
      Table_Business_Rules        CHARACTER NULL,
      Business_Data_Steward       CHARACTER NULL,
      Integration_Flag            CHARACTER NULL
);

ALTER TABLE Target_Table
      ADD  ( PRIMARY KEY (Target_Table_Name,
            Target_Table_Type,
            Target_Table_Effective_Date) ) ;

CREATE TABLE ETL_Process_Statistics (
      Batch_Cycle_Id              INTEGER NULL,
      Load_Date                   DATE NULL,
```

```
        Elapsed_Time                    DECIMAL NULL,
        CPU_Time                        DECIMAL NULL,
        Process_Return_Code             CHARACTER NULL,
        Process_Return_Message          CHARACTER NULL,
        Target_Table_Effective_Date     DATE NOT NULL,
        Target_Table_Type               CHARACTER NOT NULL,
        Target_Table_Name               CHARACTER NOT NULL,
        Process_Effective_Date          DATE NOT NULL,
        Process_Id                      INTEGER NOT NULL
);


ALTER TABLE ETL_Process_Statistics
     ADD  ( PRIMARY KEY (Process_Effective_Date, Process_Id,
            Target_Table_Effective_Date, Target_Table_Type,
            Target_Table_Name) ) ;

CREATE TABLE Target_Column (
        Target_Column_Name              CHARACTER NOT NULL,
        Target_Column_Effective_Date    DATE NOT NULL,
        Base_Unit                       CHARACTER NULL,
        Business_Rules                  CHARACTER NULL,
        Calculation_Formula             CHARACTER NULL,
        Column_Business_Acronym         CHARACTER NULL,
        Column_Business_Definition      CHARACTER NULL,
        Column_Business_Name            CHARACTER NULL,
        Degree_of_Accuracy              INTEGER NULL,
        Maximum_Range                   DECIMAL NULL,
        Minimum_Range                   DECIMAL NULL,
        Status_Code                     CHARACTER NULL,
        Length                          DECIMAL NULL,
        Data_Type                       CHARACTER NULL,
        Null_Flag                       CHARACTER NULL
);


ALTER TABLE Target_Column
     ADD  ( PRIMARY KEY (Target_Column_Name,
            Target_Column_Effective_Date) ) ;

CREATE TABLE Table_Column_Map (
        Target_Column_Effective_Date  DATE NOT NULL,
        Target_Column_Name            CHARACTER NOT NULL,
        Target_Table_Effective_Date   DATE NOT NULL,
        Target_Table_Type             CHARACTER NOT NULL,
        Target_Table_Name             CHARACTER NOT NULL
);


ALTER TABLE Table_Column_Map
     ADD  ( PRIMARY KEY (Target_Column_Effective_Date,
            Target_Column_Name, Target_Table_Effective_Date,
            Target_Table_Type, Target_Table_Name) ) ;
```

```
CREATE TABLE Query_Table_Column_Hits (
       Query_Id                         INTEGER NOT NULL,
       Target_Column_Effective_Date     DATE NOT NULL,
       Target_Column_Name               CHARACTER NOT NULL,
       Target_Table_Effective_Date      DATE NOT NULL,
       Target_Table_Type                CHARACTER NOT NULL,
       Target_Table_Name                CHARACTER NOT NULL
);


ALTER TABLE Query_Table_Column_Hits
       ADD   ( PRIMARY KEY (Query_Id,
             Target_Column_Effective_Date,
             Target_Column_Name, Target_Table_Effective_Date,
             Target_Table_Type, Target_Table_Name) ) ;


CREATE TABLE Source_Column (
       Source_Column_Name               CHARACTER NOT NULL,
       Source_Column_Effective_Date     DATE NOT NULL,
       Base_Unit                        CHARACTER NULL,
       Business_Rules                   CHARACTER NULL,
       Calculation_Formula              CHARACTER NULL,
       Column_Business_Acronym          CHARACTER NULL,
       Column_Business_Definition       CHARACTER NULL,
       Column_Business_Name             CHARACTER NULL,
       Data_Type                        CHARACTER NULL,
       Degree_of_Accuracy               INTEGER NULL,
       Length                           DECIMAL NULL,
       Maximum_Range                    DECIMAL NULL,
       Minimum_Range                    DECIMAL NULL,
       Null_Flag                        CHARACTER NULL,
       Status_Code                      CHARACTER NULL,
       Source_Effective_Date            DATE NOT NULL,
       Source_Id                        INTEGER NOT NULL
);


ALTER TABLE Source_Column
       ADD   ( PRIMARY KEY (Source_Column_Name,
             Source_Column_Effective_Date,
             Source_Effective_Date,
             Source_Id) ) ;


CREATE TABLE Source_Domain (
       Source_Domain_Value              CHARACTER NOT NULL,
       Source_Domain_Effective_Date     DATE NOT NULL,
       Source_Domain_Description        CHARACTER NULL,
       Status_Code                      CHARACTER NULL,
       Business_Rules                   CHARACTER NULL,
       Source_Effective_Date            DATE NOT NULL,
       Source_Id                        INTEGER NOT NULL,
       Source_Column_Effective_Date     DATE NOT NULL,
```

```
        Source_Column_Name              CHARACTER NOT NULL
);


ALTER TABLE Source_Domain
     ADD  ( PRIMARY KEY (Source_Effective_Date, Source_Id,
             Source_Column_Effective_Date, Source_Column_Name)
) ;


CREATE TABLE Source_To_Target_Column_Map (
     Mapping_Semantic_Resolution   CHARACTER NULL,
     Source_Effective_Date         DATE NOT NULL,
     Source_Id                     INTEGER NOT NULL,
     Source_Column_Effective_Date  DATE NOT NULL,
     Source_Column_Name            CHARACTER NOT NULL,
     Target_Column_Effective_Date  DATE NOT NULL,
     Target_Column_Name            CHARACTER NOT NULL,
     Target_Table_Effective_Date   DATE NOT NULL,
     Target_Table_Type             CHARACTER NOT NULL,
     Target_Table_Name             CHARACTER NOT NULL
);


ALTER TABLE Source_To_Target_Column_Map
     ADD  ( PRIMARY KEY (Source_Effective_Date, Source_Id,
             Source_Column_Effective_Date, Source_Column_Name,
             Target_Column_Effective_Date, Target_Column_Name,
             Target_Table_Effective_Date, Target_Table_Type,
             Target_Table_Name) ) ;


CREATE TABLE Target_Domain (
     Target_Domain_Value           CHARACTER NOT NULL,
     Target_Domain_Effective_Date  DATE NOT NULL,
     Target_Domain_Description      CHARACTER NULL,
     Status_Code                   CHARACTER NULL,
     Business_Rules                CHARACTER NULL,
     Target_Column_Effective_Date  DATE NOT NULL,
     Target_Column_Name            CHARACTER NOT NULL
);


ALTER TABLE Target_Domain
     ADD  ( PRIMARY KEY (Target_Column_Effective_Date,
             Target_Column_Name) ) ;


CREATE TABLE Source_To_Target_Domain_Map (
     Mapping_Semantic_Resolution   CHARACTER NULL,
     Source_Column_Effective_Date  DATE NOT NULL,
     Source_Column_Name            CHARACTER NOT NULL,
     Source_Effective_Date         DATE NOT NULL,
     Source_Id                     INTEGER NOT NULL,
     Source_Domain_Effective_Date  DATE NOT NULL,
     Source_Domain_Value           CHARACTER NOT NULL,
```

```
           Target_Column_Effective_Date   DATE NOT NULL,
           Target_Column_Name             CHARACTER NOT NULL,
           Target_Domain_Effective_Date   DATE NOT NULL,
           Target_Domain_Value            CHARACTER NOT NULL
);


ALTER TABLE Source_To_Target_Domain_Map
     ADD  ( PRIMARY KEY (Source_Column_Effective_Date,
            Source_Column_Name, Source_Effective_Date,
            Source_Id,
            Target_Column_Effective_Date, Target_Column_Name)
) ;


CREATE TABLE Subject_Area (
      Subject_Area_Id                SERIAL NOT NULL,
      Subject_Area_Effective_Date    DATE NOT NULL,
      Status_Code                    CHARACTER NULL,
      Subject_Area_Description        CHARACTER NULL
);


ALTER TABLE Subject_Area
     ADD  ( PRIMARY KEY (Subject_Area_Id,
            Subject_Area_Effective_Date) ) ;


CREATE TABLE Subject_Area_Table_Map (
      Target_Table_Effective_Date    DATE NOT NULL,
      Target_Table_Type              CHARACTER NOT NULL,
      Target_Table_Name              CHARACTER NOT NULL,
      Subject_Area_Effective_Date    DATE NOT NULL,
      Subject_Area_Id                INTEGER NOT NULL
);


ALTER TABLE Subject_Area_Table_Map
     ADD  ( PRIMARY KEY (Target_Table_Effective_Date,
            Target_Table_Type, Target_Table_Name,
            Subject_Area_Effective_Date, Subject_Area_Id) ) ;


ALTER TABLE ETL_Process_Source_Map
     ADD  ( FOREIGN KEY (Process_Id, Process_Effective_Date)
            REFERENCES ETL_Process ) ;


ALTER TABLE ETL_Process_Source_Map
     ADD  ( FOREIGN KEY (Source_Id, Source_Effective_Date)
            REFERENCES Source ) ;


ALTER TABLE ETL_Process_Statistics
     ADD  ( FOREIGN KEY (Target_Table_Name,
            Target_Table_Type,
            Target_Table_Effective_Date)
            REFERENCES Target_Table ) ;
```

```
ALTER TABLE ETL_Process_Statistics
    ADD  ( FOREIGN KEY (Process_Id, Process_Effective_Date)
          REFERENCES ETL_Process ) ;


ALTER TABLE Table_Column_Map
    ADD  ( FOREIGN KEY (Target_Column_Name,
          Target_Column_Effective_Date)
          REFERENCES Target_Column ) ;


ALTER TABLE Table_Column_Map
    ADD  ( FOREIGN KEY (Target_Table_Name,
          Target_Table_Type,
          Target_Table_Effective_Date)
          REFERENCES Target_Table ) ;


ALTER TABLE Query_Table_Column_Hits
    ADD  ( FOREIGN KEY (Query_Id)
          REFERENCES Query_Statistics ) ;


ALTER TABLE Query_Table_Column_Hits
    ADD  ( FOREIGN KEY (Target_Column_Effective_Date,
          Target_Column_Name, Target_Table_Effective_Date,
          Target_Table_Type, Target_Table_Name)
          REFERENCES Table_Column_Map ) ;


ALTER TABLE Source_Domain
    ADD  ( PRIMARY KEY (Source_Effective_Date, Source_Id,
          Source_Column_Effective_Date, Source_Column_Name)
) ;


CREATE TABLE Source_To_Target_Column_Map (
    Mapping_Semantic_Resolution   CHARACTER NULL,
    Source_Effective_Date         DATE NOT NULL,
    Source_Id                     INTEGER NOT NULL,
    Source_Column_Effective_Date  DATE NOT NULL,
    Source_Column_Name            CHARACTER NOT NULL,
    Target_Column_Effective_Date  DATE NOT NULL,
    Target_Column_Name            CHARACTER NOT NULL,
    Target_Table_Effective_Date   DATE NOT NULL,
    Target_Table_Type             CHARACTER NOT NULL,
    Target_Table_Name             CHARACTER NOT NULL
);


ALTER TABLE Source_To_Target_Column_Map
    ADD  ( PRIMARY KEY (Source_Effective_Date, Source_Id,
          Source_Column_Effective_Date, Source_Column_Name,
          Target_Column_Effective_Date, Target_Column_Name,
          Target_Table_Effective_Date, Target_Table_Type,
          Target_Table_Name) ) ;
```

```
CREATE TABLE Target_Domain (
     Target_Domain_Value            CHARACTER NOT NULL,
     Target_Domain_Effective_Date   DATE NOT NULL,
     Target_Domain_Description       CHARACTER NULL,
     Status_Code                     CHARACTER NULL,
     Business_Rules                  CHARACTER NULL,
     Target_Column_Effective_Date    DATE NOT NULL,
     Target_Column_Name              CHARACTER NOT NULL
);


ALTER TABLE Target_Domain
     ADD  ( PRIMARY KEY (Target_Column_Effective_Date,
          Target_Column_Name) ) ;

CREATE TABLE Source_To_Target_Domain_Map (
     Mapping_Semantic_Resolution    CHARACTER NULL,
     Source_Column_Effective_Date   DATE NOT NULL,
     Source_Column_Name             CHARACTER NOT NULL,
     Source_Effective_Date          DATE NOT NULL,
     Source_Id                      INTEGER NOT NULL,
     Source_Domain_Effective_Date   DATE NOT NULL,
     Source_Domain_Value            CHARACTER NOT NULL,
     Target_Column_Effective_Date   DATE NOT NULL,
     Target_Column_Name             CHARACTER NOT NULL,
     Target_Domain_Effective_Date   DATE NOT NULL,
     Target_Domain_Value            CHARACTER NOT NULL
);


ALTER TABLE Source_To_Target_Domain_Map
     ADD  ( PRIMARY KEY (Source_Column_Effective_Date,
          Source_Column_Name, Source_Effective_Date,
          Source_Id,
          Target_Column_Effective_Date, Target_Column_Name)
) ;

CREATE TABLE Subject_Area (
     Subject_Area_Id                SERIAL NOT NULL,
     Subject_Area_Effective_Date    DATE NOT NULL,
     Status_Code                    CHARACTER NULL,
     Subject_Area_Description        CHARACTER NULL
);


ALTER TABLE Subject_Area
     ADD  ( PRIMARY KEY (Subject_Area_Id,
          Subject_Area_Effective_Date) ) ;

CREATE TABLE Subject_Area_Table_Map (
     Target_Table_Effective_Date    DATE NOT NULL,
     Target_Table_Type              CHARACTER NOT NULL,
     Target_Table_Name              CHARACTER NOT NULL,
```

```
        Subject_Area_Effective_Date    DATE NOT NULL,
        Subject_Area_Id                INTEGER NOT NULL
);

ALTER TABLE Subject_Area_Table_Map
     ADD  ( PRIMARY KEY (Target_Table_Effective_Date,
            Target_Table_Type, Target_Table_Name,
            Subject_Area_Effective_Date, Subject_Area_Id) ) ;

ALTER TABLE ETL_Process_Source_Map
     ADD  ( FOREIGN KEY (Process_Id, Process_Effective_Date)
            REFERENCES ETL_Process ) ;

ALTER TABLE ETL_Process_Source_Map
     ADD  ( FOREIGN KEY (Source_Id, Source_Effective_Date)
            REFERENCES Source ) ;

ALTER TABLE ETL_Process_Statistics
     ADD  ( FOREIGN KEY (Target_Table_Name,
            Target_Table_Type,
            Target_Table_Effective_Date)
            REFERENCES Target_Table ) ;

ALTER TABLE ETL_Process_Statistics
     ADD  ( FOREIGN KEY (Process_Id, Process_Effective_Date)
            REFERENCES ETL_Process ) ;

ALTER TABLE Table_Column_Map
     ADD  ( FOREIGN KEY (Target_Column_Name,
            Target_Column_Effective_Date)
            REFERENCES Target_Column ) ;

ALTER TABLE Table_Column_Map
     ADD  ( FOREIGN KEY (Target_Table_Name,
            Target_Table_Type,
            Target_Table_Effective_Date)
            REFERENCES Target_Table ) ;

ALTER TABLE Query_Table_Column_Hits
     ADD  ( FOREIGN KEY (Query_Id)
            REFERENCES Query_Statistics ) ;

ALTER TABLE Query_Table_Column_Hits
     ADD  ( FOREIGN KEY (Target_Column_Effective_Date,
            Target_Column_Name, Target_Table_Effective_Date,
            Target_Table_Type, Target_Table_Name)
            REFERENCES Table_Column_Map ) ;
```

Glossary

24x7 operation   Refers to an application that is operational 24 hours a day, seven days a week.

3270 terminals   Character-based display terminals that are directly connected to a host computer, usually a mainframe. These terminals have no internal computing capability; the host accomplishes all processing. Also known as *dummy* terminals.

access   Operation of reading or writing data on a storage device.

access method   Technique used to access data from physical storage device.

access time   Interval between the instant a computer instruction initiates a request for data and the instant the data satisfying the request is delivered.

activeX   A Microsoft standard for computer application components.

ad hoc processing   Query or analysis that is nonrecurring, or random.

address   Identification (e.g., number, name, etc.) for a physical storage location where data is stored.

agent technology   Event-driven software that is structurally invisible to the business user and is always active.

aggregate   Act of summarizing one or more data sources or dimensions to create a new dimension.

aggregation Usually a sum, count, or average of underlying detail transactions or data from one or more tables. Aggregations tend to be calculated along logical business dimensions (e.g., sales by product by region).

algorithm Set of statements organized to solve a specific problem in a number of processing steps.

alias Alternative label used to refer to a data element.

alphanumeric Physical data that is represented by numbers and/or letters and/or punctuation.

ANSI Acronym for American National Standards Institute.

API Acronym for application programming interface; reference built into computer applications to facilitate communication among applications.

application Group of algorithms and data linked together to support specific computer processing.

archival database Collection of data organized to support a specific application.

artificial intelligence (AI) Ability of a computer program to mimic human intelligence.

ASCII Acronym for american standard for computer information interchange; format for data storage and transmission, commonly referred to as *text* format.

ATM Acronym for asynchronous transfer mode; packet-based, switched point-to-point data transmission protocol capable of transmitting data, voice, video, and audio simultaneously at very high speeds.

atomic level data Lowest (i.e., most detailed) level of data stored in a data warehouse.

attribute Property that can assume values for physical database tables or entities; a table typically has multiple attributes.

audit trail Data that traces system activity to a physical database or application.

availability (1) Amount of time a system is functioning and is accessible to its users, or (2) a measurement of computer system reliability. The amount of time a system is accessible to its users is divided by the amount of time that it is not accessible to its users.

backbone Part of a communications network that usually links nodes or LANs in a diverse arrangement of communications facilities that support multiple users, either inside a building, across a city, or between countries. The backbone provides a central support system and is generally one of the most permanent parts of a communications network.

backup (1) Table or file that that stores a copy of the database tables used for an application, or (2) process of copying a file or files to another storage device (e.g., disk or tape) to ensure that the data can be restored if the primary copy is accidentally or intentionally destroyed or damaged.

bandwidth   Transmission capacity of a communication channel or the amount of data that a particular device or type of cable can carry (i.e., a measurement of its throughput).

batch   Computer application that runs in a sequential series of processing steps and is not user-interactive.

binary element   Base element of data that either exists as two values or states true or false, or one or zero.

binary search   Technique for searching through physical data that is sorted sequentially. This search partitions the data into two equal parts.

bit   One unit of binary information. A bit represents a one or a zero.

bitmap indexing   Efficient method of data indexing in which nearly all operations on database records can be performed on the indices without resorting to looking at the actual data underneath. The number of database reads is significantly reduced by performing operations primarily on indices.

block   Basic unit of physical data storage. A block usually contains one or more records or the space to store one or more records.

blocking   Combining two or more physical records so that they are physically collocated, enabling the records to be accessed by a single machine instruction.

bottom-up   Data warehousing strategy that espouses building incremental data marts to test products, methodologies, and designs first, then using these data marts to justify the construction of an enterprise data warehouse.

browsers   "Thin-client" applications used to navigate and access the World Wide Web. Generally end users' tools of choice for accessing and navigating data warehouses to extract decision support information and meta data.

b-Tree   Binary storage structure and access method that maintains order in a database by continually dividing possible choices into two equal parts and reestablishing pointers to the respective sets, while prohibiting more than two levels of difference to exist concurrently.

bus   Hardware connection that allows data to flow from one component to another in a computer system (e.g., from a CPU to a printer).

business case (or business driver)   Business problem, situation, or opportunity that justifies the pursuit of a technology project.

business process reengineering (BPR)   Process for analyzing and redesigning business processes and associated application systems.

business rules   Logic applied to calculate or otherwise derive a business-related value.

byte   Unit of data storage; a byte is eight bits of data.

call   To invoke the execution of a program or process.

cardinality   Number of database table rows that correspond to the rows in another table (relationship).

CASE   See computer aided software engineering.

catalog   Directory of all files available to a computer.

central processing unit (CPU)   Processor that contains the sequencing and processing facilities for instruction execution, interruption action, timing functions, initial program loading, and other machine-related functions.

CGI   See common gateway interface.

change data capture   Process of identifying and/or segmenting the incremental data generated from an OLTP system over a given period of time.

checkpoint   Identified location in a database where the transactions against the database are frozen or made inactive.

checkpoint/restart   Means of restarting a program or process at some point other than the beginning. Checkpoints may be set at different intervals throughout application programs or processes. When a failure or interruption occurs in a process, these checkpoints allow the process to be restarted without rerunning all processes before the checkpoint.

child   Unit of data existing in a 1:n relationship with another unit of data called a parent; the parent must exist before the child can exist, but a parent can exist even when no child exists. Parent/child structures are common methods for representing a hierarchy.

CIO   Acronym for Chief Information Officer; individual in charge of all information processing functions within an organization.

CISC   See complex instruction set computer.

client/server system   Software application in which application processing is jointly performed by components that are physically separate (i.e., the client and the server). For example, a client computer may communicate over a network to exchange data with a server computer that stores a database.

clustering   Act of requiring physical database tables to reside adjacent to one another on a storage media. Such physical location provides significant performance gains when accessing a large number of rows in a sequential pre-fetch.

clusters   Grouping of interconnected SMP machines that partition the work among them.

COBOL   Acronym for Common Business Oriented Language; high-level, third-generation programming language that is used primarily for business applications.

collision   Event that occurs when two or more data records are assigned to the same physical location.

column   Vertical table where values are selected from the same domain. A row is composed of one or more columns.

commit   Condition raised by the programmer signaling to the DBMS that all update activity performed by the program should be executed against a database. Prior to the commit, all update activity can be rolled back or cancelled with no adverse effects on the contents of the database.

common gateway interface (CGI)   Industry-standard specification for communication between a Web server and a database server.

communication network   Collection of transmission facilities, network processors, and so on, that provide for data movement among terminals and information processors.

complex instruction set computer (CISC)   Central processing unit designed to support the direct execution of very complex operations in one (or very few) processor cycles.

computer aided software engineering (CASE)   Computer application that automates the process of designing databases, developing applications, and implementing software.

concatenate   To link two strings of characters, generally to use them as a single value.

conceptual schema   Consistent collection of data structures that express the data needs of an organization. This schema is a comprehensive, base level, logical description of the environment in which an organization exists, free of physical structure and application system considerations.

concurrent operations   Activities executed simultaneously or during the same time interval.

CPU   See central processing unit.

current value data   Data that is accurate at the moment of execution.

cursor   (1) Indicator that designates a user's current position on a computer screen, or (2) System facility that allows a program or process to go from one record to the next after the program or process has retrieved a set of records.

cylinder Storage area of DASD that can be read without mechanical movement.

DASD See direct access storage device.

data Recording of facts or instructions on a storage medium for communication, retrieval, processing, or presentation.

data aggregate Collection of data items.

data cleansing Correcting errors or omissions in data extracted from a source system, usually before attempting to load it into a data warehouse. Also known as *scrubbing*.

data cube Proprietary data structure used to store data for an OLAP end-user data access and analysis tool.

data definition Specification of data entities, including their attributes and relationships, in a coherent database structure to create a schema.

data definition language (DDL) Language used to define a database and its schema to the DBMS.

data dictionary Cross-reference of definitions and specifications for data categories and their relationships.

data element An attribute (i.e., field) of an entity (i.e., table).

data integrity Condition that exists so long as there is no accidental or intentional destruction, alteration, or loss of data.

data manipulation language (DML) Programming language supported by a DBMS and used to access a database schema.

data marts Set of data designed and constructed for optimal end-user decision support access. Data marts can either be sourced from a data warehouse (i.e., dependent data marts) or from legacy systems (i.e., independent data marts).

data mining Process of examining large sets of detail data to determine relationships, trends, and projections.

data model Physical database model that stores the meta data, including the business functions and rules that govern data in the associated information systems. A meta model is created at a higher level of abstraction than the thing being modeled.

data modeling Activity of representing data and its relationships in diagrammatic form.

data propagation/replication Process of transmitting a copy of the data inside tables in a database to another, remotely connected database. This process often involves keeping the two databases synchronized for data changes.

data record Identifiable set of data values (or fields) treated as a unit.

data refresh Process of continuously updating a data warehouse's contents from its data sources.

data structure   A logical relationship among data elements that is designed to support specific data manipulation functions.

data visualization   Process of displaying data in a graphical form (i.e., pie charts, scatter charts, bar graphs, etc.) to facilitate analysis.

data warehouse   An enterprise-wide collection of data that is subject oriented, integrated, nonvolatile, and time variant; organized for end user access and use.

database   Collection of interrelated data stored together with controlled redundancy according to a schema to serve one or more applications.

database administrator (DBA)   Individual responsible for the design, development, operation, safeguarding, maintenance, and use of a database.

database key   Unique value that exists for each record in a database table. The value is often indexed, although it can be randomized or hashed.

database management system (DBMS)   Computer software application used to store and manage data.

decision support system (DSS)   Computer application that contains data sets used to help business users with strategic planning and related business decisions.

decryption   Transformation of data from an unrecognizable form (i.e., encrypted) to a recognizable form. Process that takes an encrypted record and restores it to its original form.

delimiter   Flag, symbol, or convention used to mark the boundaries of a record, field, or other unit of storage.

delta   Difference between two values.

denormalization   Technique of placing normalized data in a physical location that optimizes the performance of a computer system.

derived data   Data that results from calculations or processing applied by the data warehouse to incoming source data.

dimension tables   Tables used in a star schema database design to store descriptive, hierarchical, and metric information about an aspect of the business that is used for analysis (e.g., time, product, or customer).

direct access storage device (DASD)   Mainframe disk drives that store information.

directory   A table that specifies the relationships between items of data. The directory may be a table or index that provides the data addresses.

disaster recovery   Policies and plans for restoring a computer system following a system failure.

distributed database   A database controlled by a DBMS in which the data storage devices are geographically dispersed or not attached to the same computer processor.

domain   Set of allowable values from which actual values are derived for an attribute of a data element.

download   Act of moving of data from one data storage device to another.

drill-down   Act of exposing progressively more detail by making selections of items in a report or query.

DSS   See decision support system.

dynamic SQL   SQL statements that are prepared and executed within a program during its execution.

dynamic storage allocation   Technique in which the storage areas assigned to computer programs or processes are determined during execution.

EDI   Acronym for Electronic Data Interchange; standard for electronically exchanging information among computer systems. Commonly used to pass order, billing, and shipping information between corporations.

EIS   See executive information system.

encoding   Abbreviation of a physical value (e.g., M = male, F = female).

encryption   Transformation of data from a recognizable form to a form that is unrecognizable without the algorithm used for the encryption. Commonly used to safeguard data in a database or during transmission.

enterprise architecture   High-level, enterprise-wide data warehouse framework that describes the subject areas, sources, business dimensions, metrics, business rules, and semantics of an organization. Also identifies shared sources, dimensions, metrics, and semantics in an iterative data mart or iterative subject area development methodology.

entity relationship diagram (ERD)   Data model or schema in a database that describes the attributes (fields) of entities (tables) and the relationships that exist among them.

ETL   Acronym for extraction, transformation, and load. ETL tools are software applications that assist in the task of gathering data from various sources and integrating the data for storage in a database structure (typically a data warehouse or data mart).

event   Signal that an activity of significance has occurred.

executive information system (EIS)   Information system designed for top-level corporate executives; typically provides trend and drill-down analysis capabilities.

extent   Physical unit of disk storage attached to a data set after the initial allocation of data has been made.

fact table   Table used in a database star schema to store detail transaction level data.

fat client   Workstation that manages both the informational processing and the graphical user interface in a client/server architecture.

FDDI Acronym for Fiber Distributed Data Interface; an international standard for light wave network physical topology devices using fiber optic connections for high-speed data transmission.

field See attribute.

file Set of related records treated and stored together under a single file/table name.

file transfer protocol Commonly used to transfer data files across TCP/IP networks, including the Internet and intranets.

firewall A computer, router, or other device that insulates an internal computer network from Internet access. The firewall allows only specifically qualified traffic to pass into and out of the internal network.

first normal form (1NF) A table that satisfies the properties of a relation is said to be in first normal form. A relation cannot have a composite key (multiple attributes) or more than one value (atomic).

flag Indicator or character that signals the occurrence of some condition.

flat file Collection of records that are related to one another or that are not stored on a database table.

foreign key Unique identifier used to connect a table in a relational database to another external or *foreign* table. An attribute that is not a primary key in a relational system, but whose values are the values of the primary key of another relation.

format Arrangement or layout of data on a storage device.

fragmentation Condition in which storage areas on a hard disk are too small and too scattered to be used productively.

frequency of update Time period between updates of data sets in a data mart or data warehouse (e.g., daily, weekly, monthly, etc.).

FTP See file transfer protocol.

granularity Refers to the level of detail in a data warehouse. The higher the granularity, the more detailed the data (i.e., the higher the level of abstraction).

GUI Acronym for Graphical User Interface; computer system interface that uses visual elements, including icons and graphical controls, to facilitate interaction with end users.

hash To convert the value of the key of a record into a location on disk.

header record Record containing identification information for a group of records that follow.

heuristic Type of analysis in which the next step is determined by the results of the current step of analysis.

hierarchical model Data schema that uses a tree structure to relate data elements or groups of data elements. Each parent node in the structure represents a group of data elements.

history table   Table used to capture changing relationships in a decision support system. Commonly used to capture slowly changing elements of a dimension table.

hit   Occurrence of data that satisfies a defined search criteria.

host   Processor receiving and processing a transaction.

HTML   Acronym for Hyper Text Markup Language; text tagging protocol that provides uniform display of fonts, tables, and other WWW page elements on most browser applications.

HTTP   Acronym for Hyper Text Transfer Protocol; standard for transmitting and exchanging HTML pages.

image copy   Process that physically copies a database to another storage device.

indexing   Technique for improving database performance by improving the access method for finding and retrieving database records.

information   Data that human beings assimilate and evaluate to solve problems or make decisions.

integration   Process of combining data from multiple, nonintegrated OLTP systems to populate a data warehouse or data mart.

integrity   Property of a database that ensures that the data contained in the database is as accurate and consistent as possible.

interactive   Type of processing in which the end users interact with the data as it is being processed.

Internet   Worldwide system of interconnected computer networks. The Internet is built on a series of low-level protocols (HTTP, HTML, FTP) and provides easy and powerful exchange of information.

intranet   An organization's internal system of connected networks built on Internet-standard protocols and usually connected to the Internet via a firewall.

ISDN   Acronym for Integrated Services Digital Network; a non-leased digital phone line. ISDN is a digital standard that allows data transmission of up to 128Kbps over standard copper twisted-pair wiring and is the most common means for delivering high-speed data services to remote locations.

JAD   See joint application development.

Java   Powerful, cross-platform development language for building computer applications developed by Sun Microsystems as a subset of the C language. Java is commonly used for WWW, applet, and thin-client application development.

JCL   Acronym for Job Control Language; mainframe programming language used to control the execution of applications.

join Operation that takes two relations and produces one new relation by concatenating the rows and matching the corresponding columns when a stated condition occurs between the two.

joint application development (JAD) Development technique in which end users and system developers work together to define the system requirements for an application.

justify To adjust the value representation in a character field to the right or to the left.

key Data item or combination of data items used to identify or locate a record instance.

label Set of symbols used to identify or describe a file, item, record, or message.

LAN See local area network.

latency Time taken by a DASD device to position the read arm over the data storage device.

legacy systems Sources of historical data (e.g., existing OLTP systems) for a data warehouse.

linked list Group of records where each record contains a pointer to the next record in the group.

local area network (LAN) Short-distance data communications network used to link computers and peripheral devices; usually limited to communication within a building or campus.

log Journal of activity.

mainframe Large-capacity computer that provides high levels of processing power, security, and stability.

managed query environment Informational processing capability in which the access and meta data tools hide the complexity of the data structures with a "semantic layer" of business terms and rules.

massively parallel processor (MPP) Interconnected group of processors with processing functions divided among the individual processors.

Mbps (megabits per second) 1,000 kilobits per second. Usually used to express network bandwidth or throughput rates.

meta data All physical data and knowledge possessed by an organization, including that retained in software and other media and possessed by employees. Includes information about the physical data, technical and business processes, rules/constraints of the data, and structures of the data used by an organization.

meta data repository Physical database tables used to store meta data.

meta language Language used to specify other languages.

methodology Procedural documentation of the steps required for a successful design, implementation, and maintenance of a data warehouse or data mart.

middleware Layer that exists between the application and the underlying complexities of a network, the host operating system, and any resource servers (e.g., database servers). Middleware makes vastly different platforms appear the same to an application by placing an API between the application and the resource that the application needs.

migration Process by which data is moved to or from one data storage device to another.

MIPS Acronym for Millions of Instructions per Second; measurement of computing power. Refers to the number of instructions executed by a CPU within one second.

mission-critical system Software applications that are considered essential to the continued operation of an enterprise. If these systems experience failure, the very viability of the enterprise is jeopardized.

MOLAP See multidimensional online analytical processing.

MPP See massively parallel processor.

multidimensional aggregation tables Aggregation that contains metrics calculated along multiple business dimensions, such as sales by product by customer across regions.

multidimensional online analytical processing (MOLAP) OLAP analysis provided by a system relying on dedicated, precalculated data sets.

network System of interconnected computing resources (computers, servers, printers, etc.).

network bandwidth Measurement of the transmission speed of the interconnection medium of a network. Usually expressed in Mbps (e.g., 10 Mbps).

network computer "Thin-client" computer that relies on server resident computation, resources, data, and applications to provide computing services to users.

normalized Type of database design that disperses data into tables that contain only unique and pertinent attributes of the subject of the table.

null Data item or record for which no value currently exists.

numeric Data representation using only numbers and a decimal point.

OLAP Acronym for Online Analytical Processing; computer application that allows multidimensional manipulation, display, and visualization of data for reporting purposes.

OLTP Acronym for Online Transaction Processing; computer application that automates one or more business processes, such as order entry.

OODB   Acronym for Object Oriented Data Base; database that allows the storage and retrieval of multiple data types, such as text, video, audio, and tabular data.

operational data   Data used to support an organization's daily processing.

operational data store (ODS)   Set of integrated data; does not incorporate history or summarization for tactical decision support.

optimizer   Element of database systems that seeks to optimize the use of the database resources and speed the retrieval of data by controlling the order of processing and the use of internal resources.

padding   Technique used to fill a field, record, or blank with default data (e.g., zeros).

page   Basic unit of data on DASD or memory.

parallel query execution   Method for improving database performance that splits the database query into components and permits all components to be simultaneously executed in parallel through concurrent processes.

parameter   Data value that is sent to a program or process.

parent   Unit of data in a 1:n relationship with another unit of data (i.e., child) where the parent can exist independently.

parsing   Algorithm that translates a program or process into meaningful machine instructions.

partition   Division of data into multiple physical units. Partitioning is used to divide a single table from a source into two or more tables inside a data warehouse, typically using time as a basis for the division (e.g., year-by-year partitions).

PERL   Acronym for Practical Extraction and Report Language; an interpreted programming language common in the UNIX environment.

pointer   Physical address of a data record or other groupings of data that are contained in another record. Enables a program to access the former record when it has retrieved the latter record.

primary key   Portion of the first block of each record in an indexed data set that can be used to find the record in the data set.

process   Any operation or combination of operations on data.

program   Sequence of instructions that tell the computer what processing to do.

protocol   Set of semantic and syntactic rules that determines the behavior of functions in achieving communication.

query   Clearly specified formal request posed by a user to retrieve information from a data warehouse.

RAID   See redundant array of inexpensive disks.

RAM Acronym for Random Access Memory; electronic computer component that stores data in a very fast read/write environment. Operating systems and applications are loaded into memory from disk, where the processor sequentially executes them.

RDBMS See relational data base management system.

record Set of data that is treated as a unit.

recovery The act of restoring a database or files to an earlier state or condition.

reduced instruction set computer (RISC) Processor designed to execute a very limited set of instructions at very high speed.

redundancy Storing more than one occurrence of data.

redundant array of inexpensive disks (RAID) DASD that uses a series of interconnected disk drives to provide storage. RAID 1 and RAID 5 are the two most common RAID implementations in data warehousing and data marts. RAID 1 is a mirroring standard, where data is written to two identical disk arrays, providing full backup of information. RAID 5 involves at least one parity disk drive, which facilitates the re-creation of data if a primary data storage disk fails. RAID 1 is fast but expensive; RAID 5 requires fewer drives, but is much slower.

referential integrity Feature of some database systems that ensures that any record stored in the database is supported by accurate primary and foreign keys.

regression analysis Statistical operations that help to predict the value of the dependent variable from the values of one or more independent variables.

relational data base management system (RDBMS) Data storage system based on the relational model, which uses tables, columns, and views to organize and store data in a series of joined tables.

relational online analytical processing (ROLAP) Computer application that provides OLAP functionality from data stored in a relational database.

repeating groups Collection of data that can occur several times within a given record occurrence.

replication server Dedicated computer system that executes a replication application.

RISC See reduced instruction set computer.

ROLAP See relational online analytical processing.

roll-up Act of creating higher levels of summarization or aggregation for reports and queries.

rollout Act of distributing the same data warehouse solution to a larger audience than the one initially served by the first implementation. Rollout involves concerns of standardization and scaling the DSS to many additional users.

scalability   Capability of a hardware/software system to expand to accommodate future requirements.

schema   Diagrammatic representation of the data storage aspects of a database system.

second normal form (2NF)   A relation that is in first normal form (1NF) and every nonkey attribute is dependent on each key of the relation. The goal of second normal form is to ensure that all information in one relation is only about one thing.

semantic layer (SL)   GUI abstraction layer placed between the user and the technical structure of a database.

sequential file   File in which records are ordered according to values of one or more key fields.

serial file   Sequential file in which the records are physically adjacent to one another.

slice and dice   Analyzing data along many dimensions and across many subsets, including analyzing a data warehouse from the perspective of fact tables and related dimensions.

SMP   See symmetrical multi processing.

snowflake schema   Extension of the star schema database design in which each of the points of the star radiates out into additional points. The dimension tables in a snowflake schema are more normalized than they are in a conventional star schema, which improves query performance and minimizes disk storage by joining smaller, normalized tables rather than large denormalized ones. Such normalization also increases the flexibility of applications and lowers the granularity of the dimensions.

spiral development methodology   Iterative software development methodology that delivers software functionality in incremental stages, identifying improvements by deploying the software with tight controls but ever-increasing functionality.

SQL   Acronym for Structured Query Language; computer programming language used to communicate with database systems.

staging area   Collection of data extracted from OLTP systems and provided for population into DSS systems.

star schema   Modeling technique that uses a single table (i.e., the fact table) in the middle of the schema to connect to a number of other tables (i.e., the dimension tables) encircling it. This schema is optimized for end user business query and reporting access.

subject area   Set of data organized to reflect a specific area of business, such as expenses, finance, or sales.

symmetrical multi processing (SMP)   Computer system design that uses multiple processors sharing memory and DASD resources, thereby dividing the workload among multiple processors on one CPU.

syndicated data sources   Commercially available databases that contain representative data for specific vertical markets; typically available as one-time database samples or as subscription services. This information is useful for market assessment and simulation of proposed business strategies.

system of record   OLTP system that has been identified as the sole and/or primary source for a target data warehouse or data mart field.

T1/DS1   Dedicated, leased digital transmission facility capable of speeds of 1.544 Mbps.

T3/DS3   Dedicated, leased digital transmission facility capable of speeds of 45 Mbps.

table   Array of data in which each item can be unambiguously identified by means of a key.

TCP/IP   See transmission control protocol/internet protocol.

thick client   Workstation that manages the informational processing and graphical user interface in a client/server architecture.

thin client   Workstation that principally manages the GUI in a client/server architecture while a server handles the informational processing.

third normal form (3NF)   A relation that is in second normal form (2NF) and every nonkey attribute is nontransitively dependent on each candidate key.

time stamping   Technique of tagging each record with a value that represents the time that the data was accessed, processed, or stored.

time variant data   Data whose accuracy is relevant to some moment in time.

top-down   Data warehousing technique in which an enterprise data warehouse is constructed first, then all dependent data marts are sourced off of it.

topology   Refers to the organization of physical devices and connections in a computer or network system.

transformation engine   Computer application that transforms data dynamically via a direct connection to the source system and a direct load of the target system.

transmission control protocol/Internet protocol (TCP/IP)   Networking protocol that supports communication across interconnected networks, between computers with diverse hardware architectures, and various operating systems. Generally regarded as the industry standard for PC and Internet connections.

trend analysis   Process of looking at homogeneous data over a duration of time.

UNIX   Multiuser, multitasking operating system commonly used to run complex data processing or communications systems. Also offers the ability to move programs from one kind of computer to another with little or no modification.

update   To add, change, or delete data values.

URL   Acronym for Uniform Resource Locator; Address for a resource on the WWW. All public Web sites have URLs (e.g., http://www.ewsolutions.com). The first part of the URL (before the colon) specifies the access method. The part after the color is interpreted according to the access method (e.g., two slashes indicate a machine name), and the part after the period indicates the type of organization that owns the site (e.g., COM indicates a commercial site).

verification mode   Data analysis technique in which the contents of a data warehouse are used to verify the accuracy of an existing hypothesis

VLDB   Acronym for Very Large Data Base; database containing a very large amount of data.

WAN   Acronym for Wide Area Network; network of computers that is usually privately owned and covers a wide geographic area; may interconnect LANs.

waterfall development methodology   Development methodology that mandates that every step of the process be fully completed before moving on to the subsequent step. This methodology is not appropriate for developing data warehouses or data marts due to the inherently slow development process.

www   Acronym for world wide web; huge body of information available through the Internet. Although Web and Internet are often used synonymously, Web actually refers to the software and related conventions that store information on the Internet.

What's on the CD-ROM?

This CD-ROM contains electronic files with information that can help you plan and build a meta data repository. These include:

Project Plan.doc. This is a Microsoft Word 6.0 document that has the detailed meta data project plan, as discussed in Chapter 6.

Tool Checklist.xls. This is a Microsoft Excel 5.0 spreadsheet that has the detailed vendor interview and weighted tool evaluation checklist, as discussed in Chapter 4.

ER_Examp.doc. This is a Microsoft Word 6.0 document that has the DDL (data definition language) for the physical meta model used in Figure 9.3.

GenDDL.doc. This is a Microsoft Word 6.0 document that has the DDL (data definition language) for the physical meta model used in Figure 9.11.

Object.doc. This is a Microsoft Word 6.0 document that has the DDL (data definition language) for the physical meta model used in Figure 9.6.

Meta.doc. This is a Microsoft Word 6.0 document that has the DDL (data definition language) for the physical table keys used in Figure 9.11.

Making a Backup Copy

For the procedures to follow when making copies of a disk, please refer to the documentation that came with your operating system.

Running the Software

The following is a standard Windows installation for a CD-ROM product:

1. Start Windows on your computer.

2. Place the CD-ROM into your CD-ROM drive.

3. From Program Manager, Select files from **X:** (where X is the correct letter of your CD-ROM drive) and open.

4. Follow the screen prompts to complete the installation.

User Assistance and Information

The software accompanying this book is being provided as is without warranty or support of any kind. Should you require basic installation assistance, or if your media is defective, please call our product support number at (212) 850-6194 weekdays between 9 A.M. and 4 P.M. Eastern Standard Time. Or, we can be reached via e-mail at: **wprtusw@wiley.com.**

To place additional orders or to request information about other Wiley products, please call (800) 879-4539.

Index